THE UNITED STATES OF EXCESS

THE UNITED STATES OF EXCESS

Gluttony and the Dark Side of American Exceptionalism

ROBERT PAARLBERG

OXFORD
UNIVERSITY PRESS

OXFORD
UNIVERSITY PRESS

Oxford University Press is a department of the University of Oxford.
It furthers the University's objective of excellence in research, scholarship,
and education by publishing worldwide.

Oxford   New York
Auckland   Cape Town   Dar es Salaam   Hong Kong   Karachi
Kuala Lumpur   Madrid   Melbourne   Mexico City   Nairobi
New Delhi   Shanghai   Taipei   Toronto

With offices in
Argentina   Austria   Brazil   Chile   Czech Republic   France   Greece
Guatemala   Hungary   Italy   Japan   Poland   Portugal   Singapore
South Korea   Switzerland   Thailand   Turkey   Ukraine   Vietnam

Oxford is a registered trade mark of Oxford University Press
in the UK and certain other countries.

Published in the United States of America by
Oxford University Press
198 Madison Avenue, New York, NY 10016

© Oxford University Press 2015

Library of Congress Cataloging-in-Publication Data
Paarlberg, Robert L.
 The United States of excess : gluttony and the dark side of American exceptionalism /
Robert Paarlberg.
   p.   cm.
Includes bibliographical references and index.
ISBN 978–0–19–992262–8 (hardcover : alk. paper)   1. Food consumption—United States.
2. Energy consumption—United States. 3. Energy policy—United States. 4. Obesity—
United States. 5. Medical policy—United States. 6. United States—Social policy. 7. United
States—Economic policy. 8. United States—Politics and government. I. Title.
 HD9006.P273 2015
 339.4'70973—dc23
                       2014030691

9 8 7 6 5 4 3 2 1

Printed in the United States of America on acid-free paper

Contents

Preface

I am ordinarily suspicious of those who single out America for having fundamental flaws. In my own work, I freely criticize my country's policy failings, but denigrating the nation itself is something I try to avoid. America's reflexive critics too often have suspect motives or credentials. Some are Europeans, jealous of America's wealth and influence, and resentful that their own historical moment has passed. Others are smug bicoastals who have never visited what they dismiss as "flyover country." Still others are shallow utopians for whom all of reality is a disappointment.

My own motive for writing this book about America's excess food and fuel consumption is more explanatory than judgmental, yet a sad judgment does emerge in the end. America's inability to contain its overconsumption of food and fuel is not simply a policy failing; it is deeply rooted in the nation's distinct material circumstances, its unique political institutions, and also its singular national culture. America's overconsumption is overdetermined by national flaws that are in fact quite fundamental.

For those wishing to change America's fundamentals, this book has little to offer. George Bernard Shaw (1856–1950) once wrote, "You see things; and you say 'Why?' But I dream things that never were; and I say 'Why not?'" Shaw's words have often been lifted out of context (for example, by both John and Robert Kennedy) to suggest elevated visions of future possibility. Yet in the original, in Shaw's play *Back to Methuselah,* these were words spoken to Eve by the Serpent, so dreams are for serpents as much as for saints. Dreaming about things that never were I will leave to others. In this book I stick to the prior task of explaining why things are as they are.

As a teacher and scholar of international relations, I have focused over my career on everything from American foreign policy to global food and agricultural policy—everything from guns to butter. In my work on food, it has been frustrating to watch America flip so quickly from a nation where a significant share of the population was still underfed, to one in which more than one-third are now clinically obese. In my work on foreign policy, I have also watched with frustration, as my country has repeatedly refused to accept strong commitments to mitigate climate change. Why is the United States unable to discipline its own consumption of food calories and fossil fuels? I suspected there might be parallel explanations for these two examples of American excess, and in this book I find such parallels.

My first proposed titled for this book was "Eating While Driving," a vivid image of America's food and fuel excess, but this is not a book about lax personal behavior. My search is for the deeper foundations of excess, and these I have found in the nation's original material endowments, its distinct demography, its unique political institutions, and its durable national culture, none of which can quickly be altered. Together they trap the nation in a posture of excess that defies easy correction. Because mitigation is mostly blocked, the most likely policy response to these crises will be to pursue a second-best option of adaptation. Unable to eliminate the excess, the nation will seek distinctively American ways to live with obesity and climate change. This non-optimal approach will work better for some than for others.

My training in political science remains the foundation for this project, yet I draw on other resources as well, including diverse and valued relationships with academic colleagues from other disciplines, my own brief firsthand experiences inside the federal government, in both the executive and legislative branch, my contributions to several (mostly unsuccessful) national political campaigns, and my continuing work to the present day for think tanks and international organizations as a policy consultant, plus a great deal of international travel. Seeing firsthand how other countries operate is often the best way to appreciate what makes America different.

What emerges here is a confirmation of America's exceptionalism, yet not the kind we should want to celebrate. Two decades ago, my esteemed graduate school professor, Seymour Martin Lipset, correctly labeled American exceptionalism a "double-edged sword." The distressing part of America's exceptional overconsumption of both fuel and food comes from seeing so much inequity in the damage. America's excessive CO_2 emissions do not impose an impossible burden on the United States, where self-protective adaptations to climate change will be relatively affordable for a long time. The greatest damage will be felt by poor countries in Africa and Asia that lack such options. When it comes to the increased prevalence of obesity in America, here as well the damage will be selective. Obesity now threatens both rich and poor Americans, but the poor are far less able to avoid the condition, and they find it more difficult to treat the adverse health consequences.

But now I am getting ahead of the story. It is essential in this preface, before I begin, to express thanks to those who have helped me with this project. I have been fortunate to enjoy direct assistance from a number of trusted friends who kindly set aside time to read selected chapters from an early draft, including Tom Burke, Beth DeSombre, Michael Jacobson, Jack Kyte, David Lindauer, and Nora Ng, John Odell, and Lawrence Sullivan. Any errors that might remain in the final draft are of course my own responsibility. A friend and editor with another publisher, Michael Fisher, also took a supportive interest in the project. Wellesley College provided me with yet another luxurious sabbatical leave from teaching, which I needed to complete the manuscript.

Steve Bloomfield, William Clark, Calestous Juma, and Karl Kaiser at Harvard University have helped by involving me in numerous scholarly conversations about these topics. Without knowing it, my students at Wellesley and Harvard have also helped me shape the argument, with their patient listening and sharp questioning. My former teachers at Harvard, particularly Stanley Hoffmann, Samuel Huntington, Seymour Martin Lipset, and Joseph Nye have remained an intellectual inspiration. Angela Chnapko, my valuable editor at Oxford University Press, was willing to listen and offer advice when I first presented the idea, and then she gave me both time and freedom to execute the project to my satisfaction.

Finally, I must emphatically thank my wife Marianne Perlak, with whom I share, over coffee and breakfast every morning, the reading of several newspapers. This is always my first and most enjoyable seminar of the day. Marianne's wide-ranging interests, her nose for sloppy thinking (I am glad that she also read my draft manuscript), her strong moral compass, and her consistent love and support have energized and sustained me throughout.

THE UNITED STATES OF EXCESS

The Origins of Excess

Excessive food consumption has given the United States the highest obesity prevalence in the industrial world. At the same time, excessive consumption of fossil fuel makes America a global leader, by an equally wide margin, in per capita carbon dioxide (CO_2) emissions. Other rich countries today are also prone to overconsume food and fuel, but why is America's excess so extreme? Vaclav Smil, a distinguished Canadian geographer, has pointed out the "inescapable" parallels between these two dimensions of America's excess, yet they have never been examined side by side (Smil 2011). In this book, I correct that omission.

Excess consumption on a society-wide basis first became possible during the second half of the twentieth century, thanks to a revolutionary decline in the cost of all consumable goods relative to income. Throughout most of human history, the use of food and fuel had been disciplined out of necessity because of high costs, so self-control did not have to be exercised. Then, during the second half of the twentieth century, personal incomes grew throughout the industrial world while the cost of securing both food and fuel dropped sharply, so overconsumption became a widespread social option. Our long-standing human struggle to obtain enough food and fuel was suddenly replaced by an unfamiliar new challenge: to avoid consuming too much.

In preindustrial societies today, the traditional struggle to secure enough food and fuel remains as challenging as before. In the African countryside today, one out of three adults is chronically undernourished. Purchasing enough food remains difficult because incomes are typically less than two dollars a day, and producing food is difficult because the prevailing agricultural techniques are primitive and unimproved. Fields are still cleared by hand, crops are still planted by hand, and weed control remains a time-consuming chore throughout the growing season. Then comes the labor of harvesting, winnowing, pounding, and drying the grain, followed by a daily trek on foot to fetch wood and water, and finally cooking the grain over a hand-built fire.

In traditional settings of this kind, the sustained overconsumption of either food or fuel is for most people a physical impossibility, and intentional waste is essentially unknown. Some grain is lost in the field to insect damage, and some is spoiled by rain or eaten by rodents in storage, but at the consumption stage almost nothing goes to waste. According to the World Bank, only 5 percent of food loss takes place at the consumption stage in sub-Saharan Africa, and the non-essential burning of scarce firewood is almost unheard of.

In today's rich countries, by contrast, food and fuel are no longer scarce relative to income, so both are routinely wasted or consumed to excess. Fuel ceased being scarce when modern societies learned how to access the carbon and hydrocarbon energy supplies stored below ground in the form of coal, oil, and natural gas. These "fossil" supplies of fuel are the remains of plant and animal matter that incompletely decomposed over a period of 500 million years before humans. Once people began to access these fossil fuels and leverage them to power an industrial revolution, techniques for recovering still more fuel, and for growing more food, underwent spectacular improvement. Personal incomes increased across the board, so excess consumption of energy and food eventually became affordable for nearly all.

The history of illumination is one way to show the magnitude of this change. Two centuries ago, when wood fires, oil lamps, or flames from wax candles were all we had for lighting, very little illumination of any kind took place. After dark, it was mostly dark. Opportunities to provide light expanded dramatically when gaslights from fossil fuel appeared, and then when the burning of coal to generate electricity was paired with the invention of incandescent light bulbs. Over the following decades, illumination costs fell dramatically. In Britain between 1800 and 2000, the cost of lighting services dropped to only one three-thousandth of the original level. Because per capita GDP increased 15-fold over this same period, lighting services became ridiculously affordable, and on a per capita basis the use of lighting increased 6,500 times (Fouquet and Pearson 2006). The current switch from incandescent bulbs to LED lighting will drop the energy costs of illumination still more. In most of today's high-income fossil fuel–burning world, human actions to illuminate dark spaces are straying into careless excess. Unoccupied buildings and vacant parking lots remain lit throughout the night, and light pollution makes it impossible now for two-thirds of Americans to see the Milky Way from their own backyard (NPS 2014).

Technology improvement and income growth have also led to careless excess in food consumption. Data on American military recruits going back to the Civil War show steadily increasing ratios of weight to height (Flegal et al. 2010). The trend has been relentless, and at present 27 percent of all potential recruits are too fat for military service (Mission: Readiness 2010). Income growth and revolutionary gains in agricultural productivity have brought us to this state. Nitrogen fertilizers, hybrid seeds, modern irrigation systems, and GPS auto-steered tractors have cut the cost of food production sharply. The real wholesale price of a bushel of grain in the United States fell by more than 50 percent over the course of the twentieth century, even as income increased 400 percent. This made the consumption of too many food calories an easily affordable option for nearly all, and all too many exercised the option.

When consumption increases, pure waste increases as well. The wasteful use of both food and energy are now hallmarks of American life. In terms of energy, of the 95.1 quadrillion BTUs of raw energy (known as "quads") that flowed into the American economy in 2012, only 37.0 quads were constructively used as "energy services," while the other 58.1 quads were technically wasted (LLNL 2013). Food waste is almost as bad. According to the Department of Agriculture, America wasted about 133 billion pounds of food in 2010, which was 31 percent of the nation's total food supply. Two-thirds of this waste took place at the individual or household level, where many consumers now think nothing of discarding uneaten food, including food they purchased but never even bothered to prepare (Cain 2014). In an absurd way, most Americans today would actually be healthier if they ate less and threw away a bit more.

Waste, in fact, is not the real issue. More serious are the physical harms we impose on ourselves by consuming too much. Excessive consumption of fossil fuel is now destabilizing the Earth's climate. A National Climate Assessment in the United States in 2014 found that a number of events linked to higher greenhouse gas concentrations were already imposing costs such as increased heat and drought in the Southwest, more punishing rains and coastal flooding in the East, and shrinking glaciers in Alaska (USGC Research Program 2014). In 2014, the Intergovernmental Panel on Climate Change (IPCC) warned that a continued increase in atmospheric concentrations of greenhouse gases such as CO_2 would lead to "severe and widespread impacts on unique and threatened systems, substantial species extinction, [and] large risks to global and regional food security. . . ." A tipping point might eventually be reached, resulting in "abrupt and irreversible change" (IPCC 2014).

In parallel fashion, the excessive consumption of food has destabilized energy balances within the human body, bringing on a "metabolic syndrome" consisting of increased blood pressure, high blood sugar levels, excess body fat around the waist, and abnormal cholesterol levels. These factors increase personal risks of heart disease, stroke, and diabetes (Mayo Clinic 2013). America's Centers for Disease Control and Prevention (CDC) report that when an individual becomes obese (clinically defined as a body mass index greater than 30) risks also increase for cancers, liver and gallbladder disease, sleep apnea and respiratory problems, osteoarthritis, and gynecological problems including infertility for women (CDC 2012a).

Because food and fuel no longer ration themselves, unprecedented self-disciplines must now be constructed, at both the social and individual level. This is extremely difficult with both food and fuel, yet for completely different reasons. For climate change, disciplines are difficult to enforce because the payoffs will not be noticed immediately by those making the consumption sacrifice. Climate change is driven by an accumulated stock of greenhouse gases in the atmosphere, not by small changes in annual emissions flows. Even if annual flows are cut sharply, the accumulated stock changes very little at first, so current trends in temperature increase can remain essentially unaltered for decades (IPCC 2014, p. 10). Also, when the payoffs do finally come, they will take the form of bad things that did not happen, which are always hard to notice, measure, and document. In addition, the payoff will only come if all of the largest industrial countries agree to share in the sacrifice, a global cooperation problem that has yet to be solved.

For food consumption, constructing self-imposed disciplines will be hard for entirely different reasons. At an individual level, the health benefits derived from more disciplined eating can be noticed and measured almost immediately, and they can be secured without global cooperation. By reducing calorie intake by 500–1,000 calories per day while maintaining a constant level of physical activity, an individual will immediately begin to lose about 1 to 2 pounds of body weight every week, and even a modest weight loss of 5–10 percent of total body weight usually brings measurable improvements in blood pressure, blood cholesterol, and blood sugars (CDC 2011). Individuals can experience these gains even if their friends and neighbors are continuing to overconsume. Obesity studies that once suggested a contagion factor, where simply being around heavy people changed our view of what weight was acceptable, have now been challenged as statistically unsound (Kolata 2011).

Healthy disciplines on food consumption are nonetheless difficult to maintain, because our species has an evolved predisposition to eat whenever food is available, and then rest to conserve energy for the next food hunt or food search. In our evolutionary history it helped to have a strong taste for food, and for the nutritional components of food such as fats, carbohydrates, and salts, since this motivated us to make the strenuous efforts originally needed to secure the nourishment our bodies required (Tepper and Keller 2011). Our evolved attraction to the taste of food, and to the physical comfort of rest, make us poorly adapted to current conditions, where food is continuously available and vigorous physical activity no longer a necessity. Under modern industrial and postindustrial circumstances, as explained by Daniel Lieberman, people eat too much, exercise too little, and increasingly suffer from chronic noninfectious diseases such as cardiovascular illness, type 2 diabetes, osteoporosis, breast cancer, and colon cancer (Lieberman 2013).

Our species has not lost its "discipline" over food consumption—because we never really had (or needed) that discipline. Most who become seriously overweight today would rather not be in that state, because the condition carries high economic and social costs, in addition to medical risks. Many are actually working hard to avoid the weight gain, expending time and money on diets and personal exercise routines. Trapped in a continuous battle to suppress their evolved instincts to eat and rest, large numbers are losing the battle. Life expectancies continue to increase in wealthy societies, thanks to more frequent and more sophisticated medical interventions, but an epidemiologic transition has taken place, with lower death rates now coexisting alongside much higher rates of chronic disease.

What Makes America Exceptional

These basics about the new risks of living with abundance are widely known. Less well understood is why the United States has become such an egregious outlier among today's wealthy countries, both in obesity prevalence and the overconsumption of fossil fuels. America is the king of excess in both categories. Per capita CO_2 emissions in the United States are roughly twice the average for the rest of the wealthy world (defined here as the 34 member countries of the Organisation for Economic Co-operation and Development, or OECD). Compared to the European Union (EU) countries, America's per capita emissions are more than twice as high. In the case of food consumption, 34 percent of American adults are now obese, roughly twice the European average and more than six times the average for Japan. Self-damaging excess has been on the rise nearly everywhere, but why does America remain in a category by itself?

In the chapters that follow, explanations for America's outlier status are sought—and found—in three closely connected domains. First, we consider the nation's unique material and demographic endowment. The United States is resource abundant and sparsely populated compared to other rich countries, and it is also unusually multiracial, with both factors making a difference. Second is America's unique political system, with its multiple veto points that block strong government actions to correct the overconsumption of fuel and food. Third is America's unique culture. Americans are distinct from the citizens of other rich countries due to their mistrust of government authority, the value they place on individual versus social responsibility, their readiness to embrace religion, and also their unusual optimism about what science and technology can provide. These national values provide positive payoffs in many settings, but not for moderating food and fuel consumption.

America is not just an outlier in obesity prevalence and per capita greenhouse gas emissions; it is also an outlier in the weakness of its policy response to these difficulties. The same forces that generate the excess have blocked a timely or adequate correction to that excess. In fact, America's overconsumption of fuel and food is now so overdetermined that effective mitigating actions will probably remain blocked even as the damage continues to increase. In place of effective mitigation, the American response to its own excess will likely become a scrambling form of adaptation. Obesity will bring increasing health risks, but rather than diet or exercise, most Americans will opt for more medical treatments plus physical accommodation and social acceptance for those who become overweight. This will help us remain alive and productive, but at a growing economic cost. In the case of climate change, America will again prefer adaptation over mitigation, leading to a wider danger. The United States will be wealthy enough to protect most of its own citizens in the near future from the damaging consequences of climate change, but if America opts for adaptation rather than mitigation, the international effort to secure adequate global cutbacks in CO_2 emissions will fall short. Vulnerable developing countries that lack their own self-protection options will then pay the biggest price. The excess that traps America will thus have consequences beyond our shore.

CHAPTER 1

America the Exception

Americans who take pride in their "exceptionalism" are not always aware that exceptional excess is part of the package. Even compared to other wealthy countries, the United States stands out as a gluttonous overconsumer. When burning fossil fuels, Americans emit more than twice as much carbon dioxide (CO_2) per capita compared to the average for the 27 nations of the European Union. Obesity prevalence in America is double the industrial world average (OECD 2012). Not only is America exceptional in its overconsumption of fuel and food; it is also exceptional in the weakness of its national policy response to these two problems. We examine in this chapter the timing, trajectory, and dimensions of these distinctly American patterns of overconsumption, plus America's exceptionally weak policy response.

Regarding fuel consumption, we focus here on the burning of fossil fuels, a process that releases CO_2 into the Earth's atmosphere, thereby increasing the atmospheric concentrations of this heat-trapping gas, leading to an acceleration of climate change. America has long been the world's leading burner of fossil fuels on a per capita basis. Thanks to slower economic growth, technology change, fuel switching, and industrial outsourcing (particularly to Asia), per capita CO_2 emissions have recently been falling in most wealthy countries, but the United States remains far ahead of Europe, as shown in Figure 1.1.

Two OECD (Organisation for Economic Co-operation and Development) countries do have higher per capita CO_2 emissions than the United States, but both are anomalies. One is Australia, which narrowly surpassed the United States in per capita emissions during the 2009 recession. Per capita numbers for Australia are high because this is the least densely settled country in the world, and disproportionately dependent on coal. The other exceptional case is Luxembourg, a tiny urban principality known for selling low-cost transport fuel to cross-border travelers.

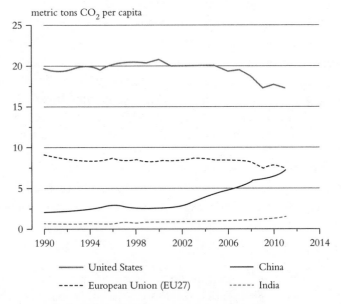

FIGURE 1.1. CO_2 Emissions per Capita in the United States, the European Union, China, and India, 1990–2011 **Source:** PBL Netherlands Environmental Assessment Agency, "Trends in Global CO2 Emissions; 2012 Report," Report 18–07–2012, http://edgar.jrc.ec.europa.eu/CO2REPORT2012.pdf

Regarding food calories, overconsumption at the individual level is conventionally measured in terms of body mass index (BMI), a ratio of body weight to body height, with weight measured in kilograms and height in meters squared. Individuals with a BMI of 25 or higher are considered overweight, and those with a BMI of 30 or above are considered obese. At the society level, obesity prevalence among the adult population is the reference point used most frequently for comparisons. Figure 1.2 shows trends in obesity prevalence in 10 different OECD countries, and once again America is a significant outlier, especially compared to continental Europe and East Asia, and with few signs of convergence.

Mexico, which is now also an OECD country, has recently achieved an obesity prevalence approaching that of the United States. In fact, according to one 2013 report from the United Nations Food and Agriculture Organization (FAO), Mexico

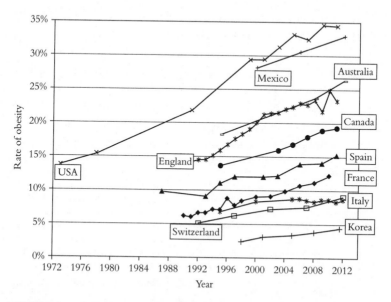

FIGURE 1.2. Trends in National Obesity Prevalence **Source:** OECD, Obesity Update 2014, http://www.oecd.org/els/health-systems/Obesity-Update-2014.pdf

actually surpassed the United States in obesity prevalence. At the other extreme among OECD countries is Japan, with just a 4 percent obesity rate in 2009 (OECD 2012).

The future trajectory of obesity in America is uncertain. A computer model at Duke University in 2012 projected that 42 percent of Americans would be obese by 2030, including 11 percent who would be severely obese, with a BMI over 40 (Finkelstein 2012). This is worrisome, because while moderate obesity increases healthcare costs by 20 to 30 percent compared to a healthy weight, severe obesity more than doubles those costs (Norton 2012). Since this projection was made, however, actual measures of obesity prevalence in America have begun to level off. In 2013, only six states saw obesity continuing to increase. Yet in no state did obesity decline, and 20 states had obesity rates above 30 percent, which was remarkable considering that in 1980 not a single state had an obesity rate above 15 percent (RWJF 2014; RWJF 2013a).

Within any population, some will be genetically more prone to obesity than others. Roughly 25 to 40 percent of BMI is thought to be inheritable (Anderson and Butcher 2006). When obesity prevalence increases across an entire national population, those genetically prone to add weight will typically gain more than the rest, leading to a significantly wider range of outcomes within the population. Because the overall genetic composition of national populations change very little in the short run, however, the trend increases shown in Figure 1.2 derive from factors well beyond genetics.

Consumption versus Consumerism

Excess consumption of food and fuel differs from "consumerism," which is conventionally understood as the purchase of material goods for acquisition or display, or merely shopping for recreation. Food and fuel differ because these goods actually are consumed, rather than being acquired for display. The nineteenth-century American economist Thorstein Veblen unfortunately confused this issue by branding material goods acquisition "conspicuous consumption," in his landmark book *Theory of the Leisure Class* (1899). This conflating of acquisition with consumption persists to the present day. For example, Amitai Etzioni, director of the Institute for Communitarian Policy Studies at George Washington University, defines consumerism in a Veblen-like way, as "the obsession with material possessions" (Etzioni 2012). Extending the confusion, there is now an academic subdiscipline called consumer culture theory (CCT), but it as well deals with "acquisition behaviors" rather than actual consumption (Arnould and Thompson 2005, p. 871). Eating food and burning fuel are not acquisition behaviors.

Nonetheless, excessive energy use and excessive eating came to America in much the same way as excessive material acquisition, and at roughly the same time. Early in the twentieth century, personal spending doubled, and in some cases tripled, for things like clothing, housing, and transportation (Cabe 2001). The cause was industrialization and broadly based income growth. This onset of rapid material gain was welcomed by most as the "American Dream," yet from the start some warned that it would become a competitive trap. Harvard economist James Duesenberry demonstrated in 1949 that a simultaneous effort by everyone to "keep up with the Joneses" would become socially exhausting and would leave no one more advantaged in the end (Duesenberry 1949). In 1998, Juliet Schor confirmed this fear, showing that decades of competitive material display had driven Americans to work too many hours and take on too much debt (Schor 1998). In 1999, Robert H. Frank wrote a book titled *Luxury Fever* that itemized the costs of excess consumption in terms of reduced leisure time, increased debt, and even bankruptcy (Frank 1999).

Consumerism of this kind can also be damaging in terms of social equity and environmental sustainability. In 2003, Lizabeth Cohen depicted postwar America as a "Consumers'

Republic" energized by material acquisition yet lacking in class, race, or gender equity (Cohen 2003). According to historian Gary Cross, "[s]uccessful and lucky Americans were locked in a seemingly endless upward spiral of emulation, and the less fortunate were frustrated when they could not follow" (Cross 2000). James Gustave Speth saw consumerism threatening the natural environment and bravely called for a social campaign instructing us all to "own less" (Speth 2012).

Asking Americans to consume less should be easier than asking them to "own less," because excess consumption of food and fuel is both harmful and less critical to social status. When we over-consume energy by failing to insulate our attic, or by driving to work solo rather than carpooling, we seldom impress others, and when we consume too much food and gain excessive weight our social standing usually goes down rather than up. In preindustrial societies it is still socially advantageous to be plump (because thinness is associated with poverty), but in wealthy postindustrial societies, where even the poorest can become plump, the pursuit of status now requires restrained eating, to stay thin.

Excess food and fuel consumption do differ from each other in important ways. Food consumption is more individualized. Food today is industrially produced and marketed by large corporations, but the calories themselves enter the body through independent and largely voluntary individual actions. With fuel, consumption will likewise be controlled by single individuals or individual households at times, but a great deal of energy use also takes place at a social scale, as when municipal power plants burn coal to generate electricity for a region-wide grid, one that serves not just individual households but also large commercial, municipal, and industrial users.

When Did America Become the Consumption Outlier?

America became a clear consumption outlier among other rich countries during the first half of the twentieth century, when it alone escaped serious material damage from both the First and Second World Wars. Britain went into the First World War in 1914 with a per capita gross domestic product (GDP) virtually equal to that of the United States, but by 1950, five years after the Second World War, Britain's per capita GDP had slipped to only 72 percent of the US level. Per capita GDP in Germany fell over the same time period from 79 percent of the US level to only 43 percent (Broadberry and Klein 2011). By the end of the Second World War in 1945, per capita GDP in the United States was roughly twice as high as in Western Europe overall (Maddison 2006).

The United States also emerged from the Second World War primed to increase personal spending on consumption. Americans had postponed marriage and children during both the Great Depression and the war, so a baby boom began immediately after the war ended. To house, feed, clothe, and transport this new generation of Americans, the nation went on a prolonged personal acquisition and consumption binge, at a time when Europe and Japan were still struggling to clear the rubble and rebuild.

In postwar Europe and Japan, food and fuel consumption were constrained by actual physical shortages. It took Marshall Plan assistance from the United States to finance the imports of food, energy, and raw materials that Europe needed to rebuild. Success then came quickly, and from 1948 to 1969 Europe actually experienced average economic growth rates higher than those of the United States—but this was from a lower starting point, so Europe never caught up. Once growth rates on both sides of the Atlantic became more equal after 1969, Europe found it was still locked into a permanent disadvantage in absolute terms (Winship 2013). As of 2008, even prior to Europe's most recent economic slowdown, per capita GDP (PPP) in the United States averaged $46,588, compared to only $31,182 for the European Union. Even the poorest state in America—Mississippi—had a GDP per capita in 2008 greater than the EU average (Political Calculations 2010).

This enduring transatlantic income gap helps to explain a significant part of America's early outlier status in material goods acquisitions. Americans always got things first, and got more. In 1960 America had 41 personal automobiles for every 100 citizens, while Great Britain had only 14, and Germany only 7 (Dargay et al. 2007). Despite stagnating wages for middle- and low-income Americans since the 1970s, household purchasing power has continued to increase thanks to more women entering the workforce, plus the easy availability of consumer credit, and also thanks to growing transfer payments through programs such as Social Security and Medicare. Between 1960 and 2009 overall, spending on personal consumption in America, discounted for inflation, grew at an average annual rate of 2.2 percent on a per capita basis (McCully 2011).

The consumption of services and the acquisition of material goods both consistently increase with income, but food and fuel consumption are different. Income growth initially pushes up an individual's consumption of food and fuel energy, but added growth eventually starts pushing it down. This "Kuznets Curve" effect weakens the importance of America's overall income advantage in explaining recent transatlantic gaps in per capita food and fuel consumption.

For fossil fuel consumption, America's early postwar economic boom did drive up per capita CO_2 emissions sharply, from 15.7 metric tons in 1950 to 20.8 million tons in 1970, but per capita emissions then leveled off and declined slightly, as seen in Table 1.1. This decline took place in America even though economic activity and consumer spending both continued to increase. In the 1970s, an interlude of much higher energy prices motivated investments in energy-efficient appliances and buildings, plus fuel-efficient vehicles, bringing down per capita emissions by the 1980s. A second energy price spike in 2007–2008 led to a similar dip in per capita emissions—this time an even steeper drop, due to a severe economic recession plus a market-driven switch in power generation from dirty coal to cleaner shale gas.

TABLE 1.1. United States per Capita CO_2 Emissions from Fossil Energy Sources, 1950–2010 (metric tons of CO_2)

1950	15.7
1955	16.1
1960	16.1
1965	17.8
1970	20.8
1975	20.6
1980	21.0
1985	19.3
1990	20.2
1995	20.3
2000	20.8
2005	20.3
2010	18.1

Source: U.S. Energy Information Agency, Annual Energy Review, September 27, 2012. http://www.eia.gov/totalenergy/data/annual/showtext.cfm?t=ptb1101

Larger processes have also been at work in this recent decline in America's per capita CO_2 emissions, particularly the outsourcing of more industrial goods production to developing countries such as China. America's appetite for energy-intensive consumer goods is not decreasing, but a larger share of that appetite is now being satisfied through imports. America has nonetheless remained the outlier in per capita emissions among wealthy countries, as seen in Figure 1.1, because these other countries had also been cutting per capita emissions—and from a much lower starting point—by also incorporating better technologies and outsourcing industrial production.

Turning to food calories, here as well per capita consumption will initially increase with income gains, but then eventually begin a decline. Yet obesity can actually continue to increase, because the calories we burn through physical activity also tend to go down as our income goes up, offsetting some of the consumption decline benefit. With industrial development and suburbanization, physical activity tends to go down. In 1950, 30 percent of all Americans still worked in high-activity occupations, but as people continued shifting out of farming and manual labor, this number eventually fell to just 22 percent by 2000. The percentage of Americans working in sedentary jobs had meantime increased from 23 percent to 41 percent (Brownson et al. 2005). This shift to sedentary employment translated into an average energy-burning reduction of about 120 to 140 calories a day (Parker-Pope 2011).

Outside the workplace, activity levels also tend to fall as income goes up. Between 1960 and 2000 in America, the percent of trips to work that took place in automobiles, versus walking or public transportation, increased from 67 percent to 88 percent. Automobile use increased in Europe as well, but not by as much. In the United Kingdom in 2006, autos were used for only 65 percent of trips outside the home, and for Germany in 2002 only 60 percent (Bassett et al. 2008). Between 1969 and 2001, the percent of US schoolchildren who walked or rode their bikes to school declined from 40 percent to only 13 percent (McDonald 2007). Personally scheduled exercise has not compensated for these sedentary work and transport habits. Between 1988 and 2006, the percent of Americans saying they exercised three times a week fell from 57 percent for men, and 49 percent for women, down to 43 percent for both sexes (Rabin 2009).

Physical activity levels were consistently falling in America after the Second World War, but per capita calorie intake levels did not level off and decline until the first decade of the twenty-first century. Measuring per capita food calorie intake for large populations is difficult, but one crude approach is to track the total quantity of food available in the marketplace and then subtract estimates for spoilage and other waste. Using this method, the US Department of Agriculture (USDA) has calculated that per capita consumption of food calories in America increased through the 1990s, then finally began a decline after 2005, as shown in Table 1.2.

Survey methods confirm that calorie intake in America is now in decline. Data from the National Health and Nutrition Examination Survey (NHANES) show that food calorie intake per capita in 2010 had declined about 5 percent from a peak level of 2,328 in 2005–2006. Part of this recent decline was attributed to the aging of the baby boom generation, but even on an age-adjusted basis there was still at least a 3.4 percent decline (Todd 2014). The economic recession that followed the 2008 financial crisis may have played a role as well, since total food spending in the United States fell during that recession by about 5 percent.

TABLE 1.2. Average Daily per Capita Calories from Food Available in the United States, Adjusted for Spoilage and Other Waste, 1970–2010

1970	2,076
1975	2,048
1980	2,112
1985	2,270
1990	2,313
1995	2,418
2000	2,600
2005	2,601
2010	2,568

Source: http://www.ers.usda.gov/data-products/food-availability-%28per-capita%29-data-system/.aspx#.Ud7IKuuE660

At America's advanced stage of economic development, higher levels of personal income begin to predict less obesity, not more. The greatest obesity prevalence in America today is among low-income citizens, not high-income citizens. Among Americans who earn more than $50,000 a year, the obesity rate is only 25.4 percent, compared to 31 percent for those who earn less than $25,000 a year (RWJF 2013b). America's continuing edge in income and purchasing power compared to Europe and Japan therefore ceases to be a good explanation for the nation's higher obesity prevalence.

Summarizing, America's overconsumption of fossil fuel reached a per capita peak in the 1970s, while overconsumption of food calories did not peak until the early years of the twenty-first century. In each case, per capita consumption was tracking along a curve that first brought increases linked to gains in postwar purchasing power, eventually followed by declines even as purchasing power continued to increase. Despite the declines, America remained dramatically more extreme than either Europe or Japan as a per capita consumer of fossil fuel and of excess food calories.

Policy Responses: America Again the Outlier

The modest declines currently seen in calorie consumption and per capita CO_2 emissions in the United States are gratifying, but government policies are not the explanation for these declines. America remains distinctly obese and distinctly excessive in fossil fuel consumption, compared to other rich countries, in part because its national policy response to both kinds of excess has been unusually weak. We might hope that the nation with the biggest overconsumption problem would be working hardest to correct the problem, but America is doing less than any other rich country, not more. An outlier as an overconsumer, the United States is also an outlier as an under-responder.

America's Weak Policy Response to Climate Change

The US government has failed so far to implement any strong actions to control CO_2 emissions. As the British sociologist Anthony Giddens pointed out in 2011, ". . . [T]he US, the country with the greatest responsibility to develop a far-reaching climate change policy, has done nothing at all on a national level" (Giddens 2011, p. 89). The United States has yet to adopt either a national carbon tax or a cap on carbon emissions. Energy use overall in the United States is taxed at the lowest rate in the industrial world (OECD 2013).

Some actions have been taken at the state level, with partial cap-and-trade schemes in place in California since 2006, and also in the Northeast region through a 2003 Regional Greenhouse Gas Initiative that now includes Connecticut, Delaware, Maine, Massachusetts, Maryland, New Hampshire, New York, Rhode Island, and Vermont. Effective action at the state level is difficult, however, because of a wish not to compromise competitiveness by imposing high electricity prices, and also because the states with the strongest fossil fuel interests—especially coal states—opt not to act at all.

Governments beyond the United States have acted more boldly to reduce the burning of fossil fuels. In 2013, the World Bank reported that more than 40 national governments around the world had either put in place a carbon-pricing scheme or were planning one for the years ahead (World Bank 2013). Since 2005, the European Union has had in place an emissions trading system (ETS) that sets an overall cap on carbon emissions for about half of Europe's industries, and some individual European governments have gone much further. By 2013, carbon taxes were in place in Denmark, Finland, Norway, and Ireland. In 2012, Japan imposed a tax per ton on emitted CO_2, with revenues to be used for efforts to mitigate greenhouse gas emissions. Germany has gone the furthest. In 1999, under a social democratic/environmentalist ("Red-Green") governing coalition, Germany passed an "eco-tax" to encourage energy savings. This was one reason that the nation's total greenhouse gas emissions fell by roughly 20 percent between 1990 and 2004 (Weidner and Eberlein 2009).

America's strongest measures at the federal level have until recently been limited to the use of non-coercive subsidies or tax breaks to promote purely voluntary deployments of non-fossil solar and wind power. This strategy so far has replaced only a small amount of power generation from fossil fuel sources such as coal or natural gas. Most of America's recent decline in total CO_2 emissions reflects a switch from dirty coal in power generation to cleaner natural gas, a switch driven not by federal policy but instead a production boom in natural gas linked to hydraulic fracturing ("fracking"). For example, CO_2 emissions in the United States declined by 3.8 percent in 2012, but growth in renewable energy output was not the reason, since the Energy Information Agency confirmed that power generation from renewables was also declining in 2012 (EIA 2013).

Stronger federal measures to reduce CO_2 emissions have consistently been rejected by Congress. In 1993, Congress rejected President Bill Clinton's proposal for a BTU tax. Clinton then negotiated a new international agreement on future emissions reductions among rich countries, the Kyoto Protocol, but even before this treaty was complete Congress had also rejected this approach, by a vote of 95–0 in the Senate. Republican President George W. Bush, Clinton's successor, sought no strong measures at all to reduce emissions; in 2007 he did sign a measure to improve fuel efficiency for cars, but as a means to pursue energy independence, not to slow climate change. Independent efforts by Democrats to enact climate-motivated measures failed in Congress both in 2003 and in 2007 (Giddens 2011).

Elected in 2008 to deliver "change," Democratic President Barack Obama once again failed, as had Clinton, to secure legislation from Congress to reduce greenhouse gas emissions. A modest cap-and-trade measure passed the House of Representatives by a narrow margin in 2009, but it then failed in the Senate, making it impossible for Obama to play a strong role in a December 2009 Copenhagen summit on climate change. National governments at that summit failed to agree on any firm or immediate actions to replace the soon-to-expire Kyoto Protocol. The November 2010 midterm elections then gave Republicans control of the House, forcing Obama to retreat on climate change. He did not mention the issue in his 2011 State of the Union message and ignored it during his 2012 re-election campaign.

Upon winning a second term, President Obama finally returned to climate change, pledging now to take strong action by executive fiat, whether Congress approved or not, saying ". . . if Congress won't act soon to protect future generations, I will" (Obama 2013). This was dramatic language, but an uncertain promise coming from a lame duck president who had no mandate on the issue, and who enjoyed dwindling popular support. In June 2014, Obama's Environmental Protection Agency (EPA) announced new rules to reduce CO_2 emissions from power plants, but an immediate pushback came from coal state congressmen and governors. Coal interests, angered by the president's go-it-alone tactic, knew they could mount a credible challenge either in Congress or the federal courts, and if that failed they could always go slow in rule-writing at the state level, hoping that Obama's successor would take a more lenient approach after 2016.

Is America's Weak Climate Response Truly Exceptional?

Regarding fossil fuel consumption, we must ask if the weakness of America's action is genuinely exceptional. If the goal is to prevent disruptive climate change, the United States may be doing less than other rich countries, but nobody has been doing enough. While 40 different countries have now adopted carbon-pricing policies, these countries together account for only 20 percent of global carbon emissions, and in most cases their schemes cover just some industries. As a result, only 7.7 percent of total emissions around the world have actually been priced (World Bank 2013). After his harsh criticism of the United States, Anthony Giddens went on to admit that "[n]ot a single country in the world is yet on track to reduce its emissions to a level compatible with limiting global warming to a 2 °C increase" (Giddens 2011, p. 92). Perhaps strong policies in this area are too much to ask.

Germany seems the exception at first, but fully half of Germany's greenhouse gas reductions between 1990 and 2004 came from the closure of emission-intensive coal-fired plants in East Germany following national reunification, a unique and one-time-only opportunity. Germany also saw emissions declines during this period because it was experiencing a low per capita rate of economic growth, less than 1.5 percent a year, hardly a sustainable posture (Weidner and Eberlein 2009). Moreover, Germany's progress was not replicated elsewhere in Europe. In Austria, Finland, Greece, Ireland, Italy, Portugal, and Spain, greenhouse gas emissions actually increased between 1990 and 2007. More recently, Europe has seen significant annual greenhouse gas emissions reductions, but again due more to slow economic growth than strong policy action. The European Union's ETS virtually ceased functioning in 2013 because of Europe's recession; carbon prices fell to just a fraction of what would have been required to force more conversions from coal to gas (Plumer 2013).

If the goal is to prevent disruptive climate change, even Germany's performance is insufficient. The Intergovernmental Panel on Climate Change (IPCC) calculates that to avoid a probability of severe climate outcomes it will be necessary to limit any further warming to no more than 2 °C (3.5 °F) relative to pre-industrial levels. This in turn requires that atmospheric concentrations of greenhouse gases peak at no more than 450 parts per million (ppm) of CO_2 equivalent, a seemingly unreachable goal. Figure 1.3 shows atmospheric concentrations of

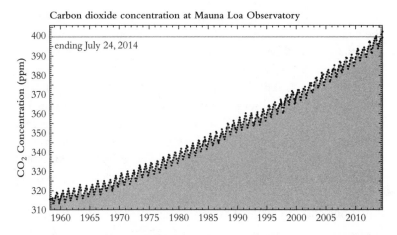

FIGURE 1.3. Atmospheric Concentrations of CO_2 **Source:** Scripps Institute of Oceanography https://scripps.ucsd.edu/programs/keelingcurve/

CO_2 alone on a steady rise, and already passing 400 ppm in the spring of 2013.

Concentrations of CO_2 and other greenhouse gases are already so high that preventing significant climate disruption will require cuts in annual emissions far greater than the German standard. In order to avoid accumulated concentrations above the disruptive 450 ppm level by 2050, according to the IPCC, annual emissions from today's industrial countries as a group will have to decline by 2050 to a level *80–95 percent below the 1990 level* (IPCC 2007). Realistically, can any democratic government ask its citizens to accept the higher energy costs that would accompany such cuts? Optimists insist that the economic sacrifice would actually be quite small. In 2007 the IPCC estimated, from a review of studies available at that time, that the global GDP reduction needed to achieve a goal of atmospheric CO_2 equivalent stabilized at 445–535 ppm by 2050 would be a fairly modest 5.5 percent. This could be absorbed through annual GDP growth rate reductions that would be nearly imperceptible, at one-eighth of 1 percentage point (IPCC 2007, Table SPM.7).

The year-by-year sacrifice might be nearly imperceptible, but the year-by-year benefit would also be nearly imperceptible. The benefits will also be uncertain in magnitude, since the IPCC is unable to say exactly how much of the recent warming has been human-induced. The IPCC's 2007 assessment concluded only that "most" of the observed increase in global average temperatures since the mid-twentieth century was very likely due to a human-caused increase in greenhouse gas concentrations (IPCC 2007). Reading this conclusion carefully, skeptical citizens could conclude that up to 49 percent of the current warming trend has not been human-induced and might continue even after costly emissions cuts are made. The more recent IPCC assessment adds little clarity here, finding it only "extremely likely" that human influence had been the "dominant cause" of observed warming since the mid-twentieth century (IPCC 2013).

Strong mitigation policies may also be too much to expect so long as the largest emitter—China—shows little interest in making any sacrifice of its own. Per capita GDP in China is still only one-quarter the OECD average, so Beijing sees no justice in sacrificing its own growth prospects to help solve a problem originally created by North Americans and Europeans. Because of China's size and heavy dependence on coal, it has already passed the United States as the biggest emitter of CO_2 despite its low income, and by 2050 it may be emitting as much CO_2 from fuel combustion as all of today's OECD nations combined (Carraro and Massetti 2012). Until 2014, China had only pledged a reduction in the "carbon intensity" of its economy per unit of GDP, a goal that did not threaten GDP growth and delivered benefits primarily to China itself, in the form of cleaner air and increased economic productivity (Calvin et al. 2012). In November 2014, China did pledge that its total emissions would peak by 2030, but without saying how high that peak would be.

Other non-OECD countries are likely to follow China's example, prioritizing continued economic growth ahead of emissions reductions. If they behave this way, according to OECD calculations, their combined energy-related emissions by 2040 will be twice as high as the emissions from today's rich countries, as shown in Figure 1.4.

Because countries like China, India, Brazil, and Indonesia are unlikely to mitigate in the near future, the OECD currently expects annual global greenhouse gas emissions to be 50 percent higher in 2050 compared to today (OECD 2011). Since holding warming to less than 2 °C will require something like an 80 percent reduction in annual emissions by 2050, not a 50 percent increase, it seems that the battle to prevent disruptive climate change has already been lost. In fact, the OECD is now projecting that average global temperatures will increase by 3 to 6 °C by 2100, well past the 2° danger point. Amid this discouraging reality, perhaps governments should be excused for investing less in mitigation while devoting more resources to climate change adaptation instead. We will return to this emerging political temptation in later chapters.

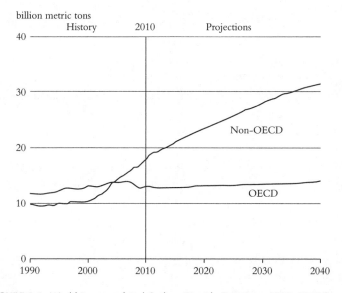

FIGURE 1.4. World Energy-related Carbon Dioxide Emissions, 1990–2040 **Source:** US Energy Information Administration, International Energy Outlook 2013. http://www.eia.gov/forecasts/ieo/emissions.cfm

Weak Policy Response to Obesity

Despite the highest obesity rate among rich countries, America is again the nation with the weakest policy response. Here there can be no excuses such as uncertain or invisible benefits, or high dollar costs. Among obese individuals, weight loss generates quick and highly visible health payoffs, particularly reduced blood pressure (IQWiG 2006). The cost of treating obesity-linked ailments in the United States has been estimated at $147 billion annually, so reducing obesity will bring not costs but society-wide economic payoffs (CDC 2012). Obesity mitigation also speeds rather than slows economic growth, by increasing worker productivity and decreasing absenteeism. Finally, there is no requirement for multiple nations to act at the same time.

On the other hand, finding public policies that can mitigate obesity is not a simple task under today's circumstances, which are dominated by sedentary living and food abundance. It is not an option, for example, to reimpose the social conditions that prevailed in America before obesity became a problem. In the early 1970s, obesity prevalence in America was still below 15 percent, but this was made possible by higher physical labor requirements both at work and at home, less consumer purchasing power, more expensive food, more cigarette smoking, no microwave ovens, no personal computers, and less freedom for women to work outside the home. If reviving these conditions is the only way to restore a low prevalence of obesity, we are better not to try.

Without turning back the clock, governments nonetheless can take effective actions. They can tax problem behaviors such as excess drinking of caloric soda, restrict food advertising to children, modify public school meal and exercise routines, re-engineer food assistance programs to the poor, require calorie counts on restaurant menus, require more disclosure and health ratings on packaged foods, subsidize nutrition education through health insurance programs, and spend more on public recreation, bicycle, and sidewalk infrastructures. One OECD study in 2010, titled *Fit Not Fat*, drew an upbeat conclusion about the cost and efficacy of such options. It calculated that by using the policy measures available, governments in wealthy countries could reduce the prevalence of obesity and avoid hundreds of thousands of deaths from chronic diseases every year, at negligible public costs ranging from just $12 to $32 per capita (OECD 2010a).

Encouraged by such calculations, a number of governments both in Europe and Asia are now taking significant measures against obesity. The government of Hungary in 2011 introduced a tax on selected manufactured foods with high sugar, salt, or caffeine content, including carbonated sugary drinks, with the revenues going to help cover healthcare costs. Two years later the World Health Organization said that this tax appeared to be changing consumption behavior (Guthrie, Luhnow, and de Cordoba 2013). Finland introduced a tax on confectionery products in 2011, set at 0.75 euro per kilogram, and an existing excise tax on soft drinks was raised from 4.5 cents to 7.5 cents per liter. Norway now taxes both sugar and chocolate. At one point Denmark went further, imposing a tax on foods containing more than 2.3 percent saturated fats (including meat, cheese, better, edible oils, margarine, spreads, and snacks), which obliged consumers in 2011 to pay 16 kroner (euro 2.15) per kilogram of saturated fat—equivalent to a 30 percent tax on a pack of butter. Denmark had earlier increased its excise taxes on chocolate, ice cream, sugary drinks, and confectionery by 25 percent. In 2012 France imposed a 0.072 euro per liter excise tax, paid by manufacturers and importers, on drinks with added sugars and on drinks with artificial sweeteners, and a number of other European countries were considering taxes on unhealthy foods and drinks, including Belgium, Ireland, Romania, Israel, and the United Kingdom (OECD 2012).

Europe's experience with these "fat taxes" has not always been an easy one. The Danish tax on foods containing saturated fat had to be rescinded after one year, when farmers complained that it was driving too many cheese-buying Danes across the border to make purchases in Germany or Sweden (Strom 2012). Also, the taxes were being imposed partly to raise revenue to help cover Europe's sovereign debt crisis, so they were generally set at levels designed to maximize revenue collection rather than force down consumption. In Mexico, however, the Congress in 2013 approved both a significant soda tax (8 cents per liter) and an 8 percent sales tax on high-calorie foods, including potato chips, sweets, and cereal. Mexico, the biggest per capita consumer of Coca-Cola products in the world, was understandably worried about its death rate from diabetes, which was eight times the OECD average (Guthrie, Luhnow, and deCordoba 2013). It was a minor irony that the campaign for Mexico's soda tax was partly funded by a $10 million grant from a private foundation controlled by New York Mayor Michael R. Bloomberg, whose own efforts to impose tighter regulations on sugary drink sales back home had failed (Malkin 2013).

European governments have also used their regulatory powers to restrict damaging food advertising to children. The United Kingdom moved toward ad restrictions in 2003, under pressure from health and child advocacy organizations. Regulations were jointly formulated by the government's Food Standards Agency (FSA), its Advertising Standards Authority (ASA), and Ofcom, an independent regulator for television, radio, telecom, and wireless communications. The regulations that came into effect in 2007 restricted both the content and the timing of advertisements for foods high in fat, salt, or sugar (known as HFSS). On television, ads for HFSS foods and drinks could not appear around programs commissioned for or likely to appeal to children up to 16 years of age, and no HFSS ads could appear on dedicated children's channels (ASA 2012). Between 2005 and 2009, this policy reduced the exposure of children to HFSS advertising by 37 percent (OECD 2010, p. 214) In addition to the United Kingdom, governments in Greece, Denmark, and

Belgium also restrict food advertising to children. In Sweden and Norway, and also Quebec in Canada, advertising to children under the age of 12 is simply not legal.

In industrial Asia, despite far lower rates of obesity, some governments have taken even more extreme measures. In 2008, Japan's Ministry of Health passed a so-called metabo law that obliges employers once a year to measure the waist size of all employees between ages 40 and 74. Firms were told to cut the number of overweight workers (for men, those with a waist size above 33.5 inches) by 10 percent in the first four years, and by 25 percent by 2015. Employers who failed to meet this test could be required to pay nearly 10 percent more into the national health insurance program. There are obvious risks with this approach, such as unjust discrimination against those with a genetic predisposition to being heavy, so it is fortunate that the requirements have not been rigidly enforced (Yujoongjae 2013). Still more extreme were the measures taken by non-democratic Singapore, where the Ministry of Education in 1992 introduced a Trim and Fit (TAF) Program in the nation's schools, emphasizing healthy food and regular physical activity. This program was credited with reducing the percentage of overweight students from 11.7 percent in 1992, down to 9.5 percent by 2006 (Soon et al. 2008). Unfortunately, TAF relied in part on segregating overweight students at lunch and recess in ways that increased teasing and emotional stress. By 2002, TAF had led to a sixfold increase in eating disorders such as anorexia nervosa and bulimia, and had to be scaled back (AP 2007).

America goes to the other extreme of doing too little. Despite facing a far larger obesity crisis than either Europe or Asia, the federal government has so far limited its response to education and public exhortation, calls for voluntary cooperation from industry, and modest adjustments to menu options in public schools. None of the legislative or regulatory measures most strongly favored by anti-obesity advocates in America has yet been taken. America stops short of taxing soda and junk foods, and it has not placed any restrictions on food advertisements for children. At the state and municipal level, stronger measures have occasionally been taken, but only with spotty success.

Roughly 50 percent of all television ads directed at children in the United States are for food, and one 1994 analysis of Saturday morning television programming found that 50 percent of all foods advertised fell into the category of fats, oils, or sweets (Kotz and Story 1994). As early as 1978, the Federal Trade Commission (FTC) took provisional steps to restrict such ads on television, but Congress in 1980 passed a "Federal Trade Commission Improvements Act" that withdrew authority from the FTC to impose industry-wide regulations on ads (Gantner 2007). As a result, the US government retreated to suggesting voluntary guidelines. Then in 2012, the Obama administration had to drop even this voluntary approach when Congress voted, by a wide margin, to require a cost/benefit analysis of such guidelines before they could be promulgated, including a calculation of the number of food-industry and marketing-related jobs that might be lost.

In addition to blocking restrictions on food ads to children, Congress has also rejected taxes on caloric soda. In 2009, when anti-obesity advocates proposed a small tax on the sale of sweetened soft drinks to help pay for national healthcare reform, the American Beverage Association (ABA), which represents the beverage industry, spent $18.9 million in a lobbying effort to help turn this idea aside. Soda taxes have been blocked at the state and local level as well. In 2010, after the state legislature in Washington actually imposed a small tax on soft drinks to help balance the state budget during the economic recession, the ABA spent $16.5 million on a ballot initiative that overturned the tax. In 2012, voters in two midsized California towns rejected soda taxes after the ABA spent several million dollars to block these measures, using both advertisements and paid canvassers. Finally late in 2014, voters in the California city of Berkeley did approve a penny-per-ounce soda tax, but voters in San Francisco did not.

America's most significant federal anti-obesity law so far has been the 2010 Healthy, Hunger-Free Kids Act, a measure that operates through the National School Lunch Program. This law expanded the number of low-income children eligible for meal subsidies, on the condition that schools serve increased portions of fruits, vegetables, and whole grains, while limiting sodium, fat, and calories. The law was initially blunted when the frozen pizza industry secured language from Congress in 2011 qualifying their product as a vegetable, if served with tomato sauce, and when potato farmers managed to block curbs on how often french fries could be served. In 2012 the measure was weakened further when USDA agreed to drop the daily limits on meats and grains and relax requirements on whole grains. In 2014, under pressure from food industries and the School Nutrition Association, the House Appropriations Committee even voted 31 to 18 to allow schools to waive the standards for a year.

A second federal initiative has operated through a supplemental feeding program for Women, Infants, and Children, known as the WIC program. In 2009, the government began reducing WIC funding for fruit juices, cheese, and eggs, while increasing the value of vouchers given for fruits and vegetables (Jalonick 2014). Following this change, measurable benefits did seem to emerge. Between 2008 and 2011, according to a study from the Centers for Disease Control (CDC), 19 states and territories in America saw a small but significant drop in obesity rates among low-income preschoolers, many from within WIC's pool of beneficiaries (Rosenberg 2013). As a continuing symptom of policy weakness, however, the federal government did not place any nutrition restrictions at all on its vastly larger $80 billion food stamp (SNAP) program. SNAP benefits can still be used by low-income Americans to purchase candy and caloric soda. In the 2014 farm bill, Congress passed a small $20 million annual "nutrition incentives" program to subsidize fresh fruit and vegetable sales to SNAP recipients through local farmers' markets, but this was a token measure that left more than 99 percent of SNAP spending still not targeted in any way toward healthy eating.

Since 2009, the umbrella for federal anti-obesity programs has been First Lady Michelle Obama's "Let's Move" campaign, but again with a somewhat narrow focus on children. In addition to school lunch menu reform, this program seeks to remove junk food ads from schools, provide healthier snacks at child-care centers, and persuade food companies to voluntarily cut calories from their products (Hagstrom 2014). The impact from such measures is modest thus far. A 2014 CDC study revealed that between 2003–2004 and 2011–2012, obesity rates among American children ages 6–11 did decline, from 18.8 percent down to 17.7 percent, but obesity rates among teens continued to increase (McKay 2014). Controlling the food environment in public schools can only gain so much, since children typically get less than one-third of their total food consumption in school (in fact only about 10 percent, if weekends and summers are taken into account). For example, removing soda machines from schools can do very little because adolescents in America purchase only 5 percent of their soft drinks in school (Wang et al. 2012). Some school breakfast programs even risk over-feeding the children who arrive in the morning having already had a meal at home (Saul 2012).

Michelle Obama's campaign has also sought to persuade grocers like Walmart, Walgreens, and Supervalu, through voluntary agreement, to restrict sales of unhealthy foods and to locate more stores in low-income neighborhoods, pursuant to a belief that families in such "food desert" neighborhoods lack access to fresh fruits and vegetables. Private companies have responded. Walmart announced that, by 2015, it would remove all transfats from its stores and would reduce salt and added sugars by 25 percent and 10 percent, respectively. Similarly, a team of grocery industry groups, healthcare organizations, and banks committed $200 million to eliminating "food deserts" in California. The value of this response is questionable, however, given the growing evidence that exposure to new supermarkets has no significant impact on daily fruit and vegetable intake, let alone on obesity. A 2011 study published in the *Archives of Internal Medicine*, based on 15 years of data on 5,000 people in five cities, found no connection between access to grocery stores and more healthful diets (Boone-Heinonen et al. 2011). A four-year study in 2013 of 650 residents near new supermarkets further revealed that only half used the new market for any food shopping at all, and there was no significant effect on diet (Cummins et al. 2013). A 2014 study at Tufts University found that poor and obesity-prone Americans actually enjoyed a closer average proximity to supermarkets than Americans who were not poor (Wilde et al. 2014).

Policy actions have also been taken at the state and local level in America. Even before the federal government acted in 2010, from 500 to 600 school districts across the country had policies in place limiting the amount of fat, transfat, sodium, and sugar in food sold or served at school. The state of California banned the sale of soft drinks in public schools, and since 2007 has specified that snacks sold during the school day must contain no more than 35 percent sugar by weight and derive no more than 35 percent of their calories from fat. In 2012, researchers determined that these measures had helped to reduce high school student food intake in California by 158 calories a day, compared to other states. Where state and local authorities take strong actions, they do get measurable results. Massachusetts began requiring weight and height measurement of students in public schools in 2009, and the average prevalence of obese and overweight students declined from 34.3 percent to 30.6 percent in 2013. Thanks in part to vigorous responses at the municipal level in New York City and Philadelphia, the number of obese schoolchildren declined by 5 percent between 2007 and 2011, and in Los Angeles by 3 percent (Tavernise 2012).

Even at the local level, however, when strong measures are attempted outside of the public schools they encounter resistance or deliver disappointing results. Beginning in 2008 in the City of New York, restaurant chains were obliged to post calorie counts for the dishes they serve, but one New York University study found that total calories purchased did not change as a result; health-conscious customers paid attention, but they had never been the overeaters. The new 2010 federal Affordable Care Act (ACA) nonetheless established a uniform national law to require calorie labeling in restaurants (Bollinger et al. 2010). Also in 2010, New York City sought permission from the USDA to eliminate caloric soda from eligibility for local purchase under the SNAP program, but this request was refused. In 2012, New York Mayor Michael Bloomberg tried blocking sales of soda and other high-calorie drinks in containers larger than 16 ounces, but this measure was thrown out by a state judge early in 2013, one day before it was set to take effect.

Moving Toward an Explanation

America thus emerges as exceptional among wealthy countries, both in its tendency to overconsume fossil fuels and food calories and also in the weakness of its public policy efforts to correct these tendencies. Other wealthy countries are doing much more in both cases, even though their national overconsumption patterns are less extreme.

How can we explain these distinctly American patterns of excess? In the chapters that follow, explanations will be sought from three different sources:

- America's unusual material and demographic circumstances.
- America's unusual political institutions.
- America's unusual culture.

We will see that all three of these factors contribute, leaving the outcome substantially overdetermined. Trapped by its own most fundamental characteristics, the United States often fails to fight consumption excess, and when it does try to fight, it loses. This dynamic of failed prevention is now pushing the nation toward a second-best pathway of adaptation to excess, a pathway that will bring less than optimal outcomes both at home and abroad.

CHAPTER 2

America's Unusual Material Endowments

America's material circumstances—including its geography, geology, and demography—are one place to start when explaining the nation's distinct overconsumption of both fuel and food. Americans consume more fuel and food in part because these goods have always cost less than for consumers in Europe or Japan. America's vast reserves of oil, gas, and coal help to explain the lower consumer cost of fuel, at least indirectly. America's more sparse settlement patterns also play a role in explaining high fuel consumption. In contrast, basic material endowments do much less to explain America's lower food costs, despite highly favorable climate, land, and water resources for farming. Demography is a surprisingly important factor, due to America's significant population of disadvantaged minority groups, and the higher rates of obesity among those groups.

The conclusions drawn in this chapter are only the first part of the story. The rest of the explanation for America's tendency to overconsume food and fuel comes in the two chapters that follow, on the nation's distinct political institutions and on its unusual culture.

America's Unusually Large Fossil Fuel Endowments

Compared to the other wealthy nations of Europe and Asia, the United States has always been exceptionally well endowed with oil, gas, and coal. The modern petroleum age was born in the United States, where the world's first commercially successful well was drilled in Titusville, Pennsylvania, in 1859. During the formative decades of the nation's industrial development and well into the twentieth century, America was both the world's largest producer and largest exporter of petroleum. America eventually switched to being a net importer of oil in 1946, but to the present day it remains a fossil fuel giant among Western industrial powers.

The United States is currently the third largest producer of oil in the world, after Saudi Arabia and Russia. For each of the three key fossil fuels—oil, gas, and coal—both America's production and its proven reserves swamp those of the European Union. As shown in Table 2.1, proven oil reserves in the United States are currently more than twice as great as in all of the EU countries combined, proven gas reserves are also more than twice as great, and proven reserves of coal more than three times as great. Note that these differentials in proven reserves are matched by equally large differentials in current production.

America is also less densely populated than Europe or Japan, so its resource endowment lead is even greater in per capita terms. The total population of the EU-27 in 2012 was 503 million, compared to 316 million for the United States, so if the figures in Table 2.1 were expressed in per capita terms, America's advantage would grow by another 60 percent.

International fuel shipments from surplus countries to deficit countries could theoretically offset these endowment differences and eliminate consumer price differences country by country, net of transport costs. International trade has indeed helped equalize fossil fuel prices in Europe and Japan compared to the United States, but differences in tax policy have countered the

TABLE 2.1. United States and European Union: 2011 Production and Proven Reserves of Fossil Fuels

		Oil	Gas	Coal
Production	US	7.8 mil bbl/dy	651 bil cub. m	557 mil tonnes*
	EU	3.9 mil bbl/dy	359 bil cub. m	196 mil tonnes*
Proven Reserves**	US	30.9 bil bbl	8.5 tril cub. m	237 bil tonnes
	EU	14.1 bil bbl	4.1 tril cub.m	78 bil tonnes

*oil equivalent
**Proven reserves are taken to be those quantities that geological and engineering information indicate, with reasonable certainty, can be recovered in the future from known reservoirs under existing economic and operating conditions.

Source: BP Statistical Review of World Energy, June 2012, bp.com/statisticalreview

equalization effect. Europe and Japan tax fossil fuel consumption far more heavily than the United States, driving up prices for consumers. According to OECD calculations, combined federal and state tax rates on petroleum consumption in the United States, as of January 2012, were only 0.1 euro per liter, while in Poland tax rates were four times as high, in Japan five times as high, in France six times as high, and in Italy, Norway, and the Netherlands more than seven times as high (OECD 2012a, Figure 1.1). In an interesting way, different resource endowments have been one source of these different tax levels. Because America's domestic fossil fuel industries are so much larger than those in Europe, they exercise greater influence over public policy and are thus better able to resist heavy taxation.

The Link Between Resource Endowment and Low Taxes on Energy Consumption

All advanced industrial countries tax energy use, including fossil fuel energy, but the US government taxes this activity far less.

In 2013 the OECD published a study titled "Taxing Energy Use," a systematic comparative analysis of the structure and level of taxes on energy in all OECD countries. Separate calculations were made for the effective tax rate on total energy used and specifically on carbon emissions. Based on statutory rates in effect on April 1, 2012, the range of taxes on total energy went from an extreme low of euro 0.2 per gigajoule (GJ) in Mexico to a high of euro 6.58 per GJ in Luxembourg. The United States taxed energy at a level nearly as low as Mexico, at euro 0.3 per GJ, or less than 20 percent of the weighted OECD average of euro 1.77 per GJ. Considering tax rates on the CO_2 content of energy, the lowest rate was again in Mexico, at euro 2.8 per ton, while the highest rate was in Switzerland at euro 107.2 per ton. Once again the United States rate, at euro 4.8 per ton, was nearly as low as Mexico and less than one-quarter the weighted OECD average of euro 21.1 per ton (OECD 2013a). Table 2.2 compares tax rates in the United States with those in a sampling of other OECD countries.

TABLE 2.2. All Taxes on All Fuels, as of July 1, 2012

	All Fuels (euro per GJ)	All Fuels (euro per metric ton of CO_2)
Denmark	6.3	81.7
United Kingdom	4.6	73.2
France	2.5	61.1
Germany	4.0	58.3
Japan	2.6	37.4
Australia	1.6	19.6
Canada	0.4	7.1
United States	0.3	4.8
Mexico	0.2	2.8

Source: OECD (2013a), *Taxing Energy Use*, OECD Publishing. Annex B, p. 248

The OECD countries with the highest overall effective tax rates on the CO_2 content of energy have been the countries of northern Europe, many of which have explicit taxes on carbon, including Denmark, Iceland, Ireland, Norway, Sweden, and Switzerland. The non-European OECD countries have lower energy tax rates, with the United States (and Mexico) at the very bottom. Fossil fuels in the United States typically face no consumption taxes at all, except within the transport sector. According to one 2010 inventory, the United States was one of only four industrial countries out of 31 not to impose electricity taxes on industry, and one of only nine not to tax household electricity consumption (Finnish Energy Industries 2010). America is also one of only three out of 31 not to tax heavy fuel oil for business, one of only 10 not to tax natural gas for business, and one of only four not to tax coal for business. The United States does tax light fuel oil for household use, but at a trivial rate less than one-twentieth the rate in Sweden. The United States even has 36 separate tax prohibition or exemption policies for petroleum at the federal and state level (OECD 2013a). America does tax diesel and gasoline for transport, but at rates dramatically lower than the rest of the industrial world. In 2008, average gasoline taxes in the United States were 13 cents per liter, versus 32 cents in Canada, 59 cents in Japan, and an average of $1.19 per liter in Western Europe (Sterner 2011).

These higher tax rates on auto fuel make it far more expensive to drive in Europe and Japan, reducing auto use. In the United States in January 2011, federal and state taxes contributed only 13 percent to the final consumer price of regular gasoline, compared to more than 60 percent of the final price in Europe. This goes a long way to explain why average per capita consumption of gasoline in America is more than four times higher than in the United Kingdom (Sterner 2011). Economists calculate that every 10 percent increase in the cost of gasoline reduces consumption by 7–8 percent (Graham and Glaister 2002). America's much lower gasoline prices have shaped everything from its distinct residential patterns (more spread out), to the different composition of its auto fleet (many more gas guzzlers), to the frequency of unnecessary driving (extremely high), and also its passenger rail options (slow, inferior, and few).

As noted, America's unusually low energy taxes are in part an indirect result of the nation's exceptionally large fossil fuel endowment. The large endowment means a large domestic industry that is more capable of lobbying to limit both its own tax burdens and those of its customers. Energy taxes are an exceptionally convenient revenue source for governments, so in countries without large domestic industries positioned to object, energy taxes tend to be extremely high. In these other countries, ordinary consumers cannot block high energy taxes by themselves because the revenue value to the state is concentrated and highly direct, while the costs to consumers are less direct and dispersed, making coordinated political action difficult (Victor 2009).

Industrial countries without large domestic fossil fuel industries also tax energy more because they tend to be substantial importers, meaning some of the resulting reduction in demand can be pushed onto foreign companies. In 2010 the EU-27 countries imported 85 percent of their petroleum and 62 percent of their natural gas (Eurostat 2012). Japan imports 99 percent of its petroleum and 96 percent of its natural gas. In such regions and countries, it is much easier for governments to impose heavy consumption taxes on fuels because the reduced demand caused by the tax takes income away from foreign producers, who do not vote, more than from domestic producers.

In America, even in 2005 when import dependence reached its peak, only 60 percent of oil consumption was being satisfied from abroad, and since that time US oil output has increased by 50 percent, thanks to exploitation of shale formations in Texas and North Dakota, reducing imports. Natural gas production has also increased, thanks to the development of hydraulic fracturing. By 2013 the United States had overtaken Russia as the world's number one producer of oil and gas combined, further reducing the need for imports. In its 2013 projection, in fact, the US Energy Information Administration expected that the United States would become a net exporter of natural gas by 2020, and America might even resume exporting oil if an antiquated 1975 legislative ban on exports could be removed (EIA 2013). America's smaller energy import requirements compared to Europe and Japan have diminished its political inclination to drive up consumer prices for fossil fuels through high energy taxes.

Industrial Policies That Influence Fuel Prices

Final consumer energy costs in America have also been influenced by government policies designed to manage domestic production, yet these policies have had smaller and less consistent impacts. Motivated by such diverse concerns as domestic price stability, regional equity, and national security, these policies have at times actually increased prices.

Fossil fuel production in the United States has certainly been subsidized. A 2012 OECD inventory of producer support policies in the United States listed 15 such measures at the federal level, and additional measures were found in 10 different states (OECD 2012a). In 2011, the Center for American Progress alleged that American oil companies alone got nine different subsidies, together worth about $7 billion a year. Leading the list were four tax breaks: a domestic manufacturing tax deduction, a percentage depletion allowance, a foreign tax credit, and a write-off option for intangible drilling costs (CAP 2010). Not all of these tax breaks were specific to petroleum, however, with other manufacturing sectors also enjoying last-in-first-out (LIFO) accounting rules, foreign tax credits, and section 199 deductions (Matthews 2013). When it comes to corporate tax breaks in America, oil is hardly alone.

Government production subsidies are definitely lucrative for America's oil companies, yet their contribution to America's low consumer energy prices, and hence to high consumption, is actually quite small. This is because not all the tax breaks lead to more oil production; many reward companies for exploration and production actions they would be taking anyway. Also, when added production does result, it is sold into an integrated global market, so any resulting fall in prices becomes available to foreigners as well as to Americans. Eliminating tax subsidies for fossil fuels might be a good idea, but it would have only a small impact on America's greenhouse gas emissions. By one calculation, subsidy elimination would bring a reduction in US oil production of only 26,000 barrels a day, a miniscule fraction of the 7.8 million barrels produced (Aldy 2013). Another study found that an elimination of all the energy-related subsidies that increased CO_2 emissions in America in 2005–2009 would have reduced emissions by only 1 percent (Allaire and Brown 2012).

Government interventions to support the domestic fossil fuel industries sometimes actually raise the final price that Americans pay for energy. Regarding coal, for example, price-boosting trade restrictions go all the way back to 1789, when a tariff was placed on the sale of British coal arriving in American ports as ship ballast (J. Johnson 2011). Also, high-cost domestic production regions such as Appalachia have at times been protected from low-cost competitors through price-fixing schemes such as the Guffey Coal Acts of the 1930s. For petroleum after the Second World War, when domestic oil producers were threatened by a drop in international prices due to rapidly increasing production in the Middle East, they lobbied Congress for import protection, and President Dwight Eisenhower did impose restraints on imports in 1959, purportedly on national security grounds. This pleased the domestic industry because it prevented domestic prices from falling still more, yet it also pleased allied countries in Europe and Japan because it reduced America's demand for Middle Eastern supplies and lowered import prices for them (Kapstein 1990).

These oil import restrictions and a continuing drop in international prices soon triggered formation of the Organization of Petroleum Exporting Countries (OPEC), determined to raise prices through production restraints, and the resulting producer actions plus inflationary global macroeconomic circumstances eventually drove oil prices so high that President Richard Nixon intervened in 1971 to impose price controls on the domestic market. Washington was now intervening to block a further increase in domestic prices, not a further decline. Nixon also launched a program, which he likened to the Manhattan Project, to promote domestic oil production, a so-called Project Independence.

To the present day, politicians friendly to the domestic oil industry argue that America needs to pursue energy independence by opening up new options for domestic exploration, and by drilling offshore and in protected areas, claiming that this can also help in holding down consumer prices. Politicians less friendly to the fossil fuel industry also want low consumer prices and energy independence, but their preferred path is to use taxpayer money to subsidize energy production from wind, solar, and biofuels. So long as both the political right and the political left in America embrace the goal of low fuel prices, little progress will be made in reducing overconsumption of fossil fuels. Increasing fossil fuel consumer prices in America would require a consumption tax or a set of regulations more nearly resembling what we see in Europe, yet America's large domestic coal, gas, and oil industries have consistently blocked such an outcome. This industry influence is sustained by the unusual size of America's domestic fossil fuel reserves, so fundamental resource endowments must be counted as a major contributor to this outcome.

Low Population Density

Geography and demography are also important sources of high fossil fuel consumption in America. The United States is distinct among wealthy industrial countries for having a low population density per square kilometer of land. Population density in America has increased over the past half century, as shown in Table 2.3, yet it remains dramatically lower than in Europe or Japan. Other things being equal, such dispersed populations consume more fossil fuel per capita, both for residential heating and cooling, and for transport. Working in combination with America's lower energy prices, these factors account for another significant chunk of the nation's excessive fuel consumption.

Population densities vary not only over time but also by location. Overall density may increase, but in a mature stage of industrial development, local densities in rural areas are likely to decrease, due to continued labor migrations out of agriculture. Eventually, urban densities may also decrease, once suburban sprawl begins, as it did in the United States after the Second World War. Differences in per capita land endowment do not by themselves determine how urbanized a nation will become. For example, compared to the United Kingdom, the US population is only one-seventh as dense, yet it is actually more urbanized (82 percent versus 80 percent). In poor agricultural societies, meanwhile, even the most densely populated countries may scarcely be urbanized at all. Bangladesh has a national population density five times greater than the United Kingdom, yet it is only 28 percent urbanized.

The United States is now comparably urbanized alongside Europe and Japan, but Americans have never filled urban or rural

TABLE 2.3. Population Density, 1960 and 2012 (persons per km²)

	1960	2012
United States	19.4	32.8
EU-27	94.0	117.0
Japan	245	335

Source: Eurostat, Population and Population Density, 1960 and 2012.png

spaces as densely. Heavily populated cities had become a notable European reality hundreds of years ago. Originally, these cities were laid out in tightly contained areas, and typically crammed behind walls for physical security. By contrast, America has no cities that could be considered "old" by European standards, and none so dense. Most American cities in the South and West have been built to their current size quite recently, when the emergence of private automobiles, cheap gasoline, and open space was combining to make sprawl an option.

Cities in Europe also began to sprawl from the mid-1960s onward, once higher income made private autos more widely affordable. As a result, from the mid-1960s to 2000, central cities in Europe actually lost 3 million people while suburban areas gained 27 million (Cox 2009). Both Europe and the United States sprawled, but there was less space for Europeans to sprawl into, so even European suburbs today are far more dense than American suburbs. European suburbs average 6,600 persons per square mile, compared to 2,700 for the United States (Cox 2009). These persistent differences in population density combine with already mentioned differences in fuel cost to generate significant differences in both auto driving and dwelling size.

Miles of Auto Travel

Annual auto vehicle miles of travel (VMT) per person in America are 35 percent higher than in France, 44 percent higher than in Germany and the United Kingdom, and 141 percent higher than in Japan (DOT 2011). Higher income and lower fuel prices explain part of this greater auto-mobility, but America's lower population density is critical as well, as can be seen from differences state by state. VMT per capita is more than twice as high in sparsely settled Colorado (18,281 miles per year) than in densely populated Massachusetts (8,565 miles per year). City-to-city comparisons of fuel use per capita in transport also confirm the importance of lower population density. Figure 2.1 shows the much higher transport-related energy consumption levels, in gigajoules per capita per year, for a number of large American cities compared to cities in Australia, Europe, and Asia.

In sparsely populated countries like the United States, road space and parking space are also more abundant, so both auto use and ownership go up, and average auto size goes up as well (Zhao and Kockelman 2002). In 2002, there were 812 vehicles

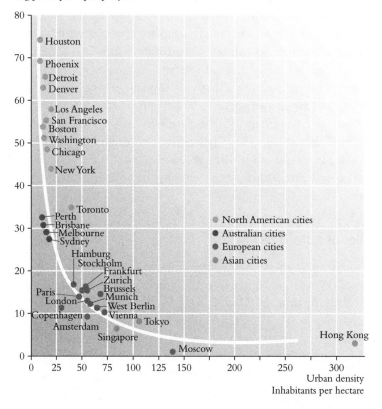

FIGURE 2.1. Urban Density and Transport-related Energy Consumption **Source:** Year: 2009 From collection: Kick the Habit: A UN Guide to Climate Neutrality, UNEP/GRID-Arendal

for every 1,000 people in the United States, compared to 586 in Germany, 576 in France, 515 in Great Britain, and 599 in Japan. American households in less densely populated areas purchase more minivans, pickups, and SUVs than those living in high-density areas, even after factors such as income, household size, and fuel prices have been taken into account. In a telling link to the nation's obesity crisis, larger vehicles are also more favored in America because the people driving those cars have themselves become larger (LaReau 2011).

Size of Dwellings

Because Americans enjoy more physical space, they also tend to live in larger homes, including detached single-family homes that require more energy for heating and cooling. This difference is important in the OECD world, where the household sector is responsible for 15–25 percent of primary energy use (Dzioubinski and Chipman 1999). Data from the UN Center for Human Settlements and the World Bank in 2007 show that average housing space in the United States was 721 square feet per capita at that time, almost twice the 377 square foot average for the United Kingdom, France, Germany, and Japan (BBC 2009). Higher income levels in America explain some of the difference but not all. The 12 percent of America's population officially classified as poor still had an average of 439 square feet of housing per capita, which was higher than the European and Japanese average (Rector 2007). In 1973, the average size of a *newly built* single-family house in America was 1,660 square feet. By 2010 that had increased to 2,392 square feet (US Census Bureau 2012). By 2013, it actually reached 2,647 square feet.

The US income tax code favors housing investments through mortgage interest deductions for owners, but this policy is not uniquely American. In one study of 14 other rich countries in Europe, all but three also provided mortgage interest deductions. Moreover, most towns in America levy significant taxes on residential property, so the interest deduction is partly offset by higher tax burdens at the local level (Chaney and Emrath 2006). Some might see America's preference for large detached homes as a unique cultural trait, handed down from the original agricultural settlers who grew up with social expectations of greater space and household privacy. Australia, another settler country, is second only to the United States in the average floor space of newly built homes. Yet in both America and Australia it was an abundant area of largely unoccupied land that drove the settlement process in the first place.

The larger average size of American homes is in any case a significant contributor to the nation's larger emissions of CO_2 per capita. When household energy consumption is compared to other high income countries with similar climates, American homes use much more. Per capita household energy consumption in North America overall is approximately 50 percent higher than in Europe overall (Dzioubinski and Chipman 1999). Japan is a rich country with roughly the same heating and cooling degree-days as the United States average, yet household energy consumption in the United States is more than twice as high as in Japan, and consumption specifically for space heating is five times as high. America's combination of larger home size and lower energy prices, both traceable indirectly to the nation's distinct physical endowments, have helped drive such differences (Zhang 2004).

Is America Less Threatened by Climate Change Than Other Rich Countries?

America's distinct geography, geology, and demography influence the nation's CO_2 emissions in one other way. The United States is physically less vulnerable to climate warming and destabilization than most other countries, so it has less motivation to reduce greenhouse gas emissions. A 2011 study from the Center for Global Development comparing 233 states confirmed that the 20 states most vulnerable to extreme weather impacts from climate change were all developing countries, not rich countries, and even compared to a number of other rich countries, America is less vulnerable. Comparing populations vulnerable to sea-level rise in low-elevation coastal zones (LECZ), Europe has roughly twice the number of exposed individuals as North America, largely reflecting differences in population density (Wheeler 2011). Regarding agriculture, in the short run America might actually make net gains from climate change. Higher temperatures will permit earlier planting and longer growing seasons, in some cases allowing two crops per season. In addition, thanks to a carbon fertilization effect on crops and higher rainfall, the IPCC has projected that in the first several decades of the twenty-first century, climate change may increase America's rain-fed aggregate crop yields by 5–20 percent (EPA 2013). We shall return to this question of America's lower relative vulnerability to climate change in a later chapter, when explaining why the United States is more likely in the years ahead to prefer self-protective adaptation policies that accept something close to the current rate of climate change, compared to uncertain mitigation policies designed slow or halt the warming.

Resource Endowments and Obesity?

Turning to obesity, America's basic resource endowments are playing only a small and diminishing role on the calorie consumption side of the equation, but they do play a role on the calorie expenditure side. Too little physical activity contributes a substantial share to obesity in the United States, and Americans are less active than Europeans in part because of their distinct settlement patterns, which emerged in response to low population densities and extremely low energy prices.

In one study of 17 wealthy countries in 2006, Americans walked, biked, or used public transportation (which typically requires some walking) only 12 percent of the time when taking trips outside the home. Sparsely populated Australia and Canada were only a little better, with just 14 percent and 19 percent of trips, respectively, employing these more active methods. By contrast, active transport methods were used 35 percent of the time in the United Kingdom, 39 percent of the time in Denmark, 40 percent of the time in Germany, 47 percent of the time in Spain, and 52 percent of the time in the Netherlands (Bassett et al. 2008). Every year, Europeans walk almost three times as far as residents of the United States: 382 kilometers per person versus 140 kilometers. Estimating calories burned, metabolic energy requirements linked to active transportation are equal to the oxidation of five to nine pounds of fat per person per year in Europe, versus only two pounds in the United States (Bassett et al. 2008).

These differences in active transport habits across countries cannot be attributed entirely to settlement density or even to differences in energy costs, since other factors such as the availability of sidewalks, bike lanes, and public transport also make a difference. In many European cities, traffic regulation and enforcement strongly favor pedestrians or cyclists over motorists. The different land-use mix in urban areas is another factor, since walking trips will be more frequent in neighborhoods where residential, commercial, and civic buildings are interspersed— for example, in Europe's older cities. Yet it was a lower settlement density in America that originally induced the provision of fewer public transport services, fewer bike lanes, and fewer sidewalks, and the younger age of America's cities tended to induce a lower land-use mix, so the nation's distinct geographic and demographic circumstances once again come into play.

Moving from physical exercise to calorie intake differences, material endowments become less important. America's superior farmland resources help a bit to explain why its people consume too much food, but only to a small and diminishing extent. As with energy consumption, food consumption initially became excessive in America because of low retail prices relative to rapidly rising income, yet in most respects food commodities are unlike fossil fuel resources. Food is not simply recovered from nature; agricultural commodities must be grown or raised anew every year by farmers, and the final food product may be heavily processed and packaged by food manufacturers. Final retail prices to consumers depend less on the natural resource base and more on the production systems that farmers and food companies have developed to make use of that resource base. Final prices to consumers also depend on sales tax policies, and on government interventions in the market intended to boost the income of farmers. Food tends to be less expensive in America compared to Europe because of more productive farm and food company technologies, plus lower taxes and lower price-boosting subsidies, not just because of superior farm resource endowments.

Among the 20 wealthiest OECD countries, it is the United States that offers consumers the lowest average prices for food and non-alcoholic beverages, and this has contributed directly to America's higher per capita consumption. As seen in Table 2.4, average consumer food prices in the European Union overall have been 30 percent higher than in the United States, and in Japan 94 percent higher.

These higher prices in Europe or Japan cannot be explained through quality differences. We can demonstrate this by comparing prices for one common food product that is served both in America and Europe with no quality variation at all—the McDonald's Big Mac hamburger. Compared to the United States, Big Macs in the United Kingdom and Japan cost 16 percent more, 18 percent more in Germany and Italy, 36 percent more in France, 42 percent more in Sweden, and 61 percent more in Denmark. The only European countries where Big Macs cost less than in the United States are Ireland, at 98 percent of the US price, and relatively poor Greece, at 91 percent of the US price (Alston et al. 2008). Because of higher costs for ingredients, higher labor costs, higher energy costs, and higher costs

TABLE 2.4. Comparative 2008 Price Levels for Final Expenditures on Food and Non-Alcoholic Beverages at PPP (OECD average = 100)

Japan	161
Norway	161
Denmark	142
Switzerland	137
Ireland	136
Iceland	125
Finland	119
Belgium	118
Austria	118
Luxembourg	118
Germany	115
Sweden	114
France	113
Canada	111
Australia	110
EU Average	108
Italy	108
New Zealand	107
United Kingdom	105
Netherlands	99
United States	83

Source: OECD data, ECP_7.6_EN.xls, Table 1.1

of nearly every other kind, foods of identical quality are more expensive for consumers in Europe than in the United States.

Average retail food prices do have noticeable impacts on per capita calorie intake. One review of 160 different studies revealed that estimated price elasticities for foods and nonalcoholic beverages in the United States ranged from −0.27 to −0.81, meaning that a 10 percent increase in price would trigger a reduction in consumption of about 3–8 percent, which is significant over time for body weight outcomes (Andreyeva, Long, and Brownell 2010). In 2010, Americans consumed an estimated 2,614 food calories per person per day, according to the Department of Agriculture (USDA 2013a). A 3–8 percent reduction in this total intake would mean a daily cutback of roughly 78–209 food calories. Models of weight loss suggest that a permanent consumption reduction of 100 food calories per day causes a 4.7–7.7 pound decrease over one year for an average individual, and eventually a steady-state 12.8 pound decrease in weight (Alston et al. 2013). Food price differences by themselves can therefore have significant impacts on body weight.

Japan is at the opposite end of the spectrum from America, in terms of food prices, food calorie consumption, and also obesity prevalence. One study in 1999 found that the overall price of food in Tokyo was 49 percent higher compared to New York City (Ministry of General Affairs 1999). Another comparison in 2006 found that a loaf of white bread, a carton of eggs, a pint of Haagen-Dazs ice cream, and five kilograms of medium-quality rice cost more than twice as much at a supermarket in Tokyo compared to a supermarket in St. Paul, Minnesota (Senauer and Gemma 2006). This is one reason average per capita food energy intake in Japan is currently below 1,900 calories a day, compared to more than 2,500 in the United States, and why obesity prevalence in Japan was just 4 percent in 2009, compared to more than 30 percent in the United States (Smil and Kobayashi 2012).

The De-Materialization of Farming

Natural resource endowments were at one time important in explaining food price differences between the United States and Europe. On its expanding western frontier throughout the nineteenth century, America had essentially unlimited options for bringing more land into production for crops and cattle. But this frontier was eventually closed, and since early in the twentieth century land area has been replaced by technology enhancement as the key to keeping American farm commodity prices low. Since 1950, nearly all of America's continuing gains in commodity production have come from improved biological and chemical technologies (Gardner 2002). Due to technology improvements in the late twentieth century, natural resources such as land, energy, and water became far less important to farm productivity gains, a process known as the "dematerialization" of farming (Ausubel, Wernick, and Waggoner 2012). European farmers shared in these gains. For example, between 1990 and 2004, total food production in the OECD area increased in volume by 5 percent, yet the area of land taken up by agriculture declined by 4 percent, water use on irrigated lands declined by 9 percent, and greenhouse gas emissions fell by 3 percent (OECD 2008).

Because America has led in technology improvements, requirements for material resources have fallen more quickly in American farming than in Europe. Between 1980 and 2011, corn production in America doubled, but land, energy, and irrigation water use per bushel of corn declined by 30 percent, 43 percent, and 53 percent, respectively (Field to Market 2012). America's lead in the uptake of modern farm technology is also reflected in a widening gap in total factor productivity (TFP) growth. Between 1970 and 2006, the annual rate of growth in total factor productivity in American agriculture increased from 1.49 percent to 1.91 percent. In Europe, TFP is lower and growing more slowly (Fischer, Byerlee, and Edmeades 2009).

Thanks to steady gains in productivity—not an increased use of natural resources—real farm commodity prices in America fell at an average rate of 1.6–2.5 percent every year between 1950 and 2005 (Alston, Okrent, and Parks 2013). These lower commodity prices, plus higher productivity in the food manufacturing and retailing sectors, made excessive food consumption increasingly affordable. According to one calculation, the falling price of food in the United States over the two decades between 1976 and 1994 was responsible for up to 40 percent of the nation's increase in BMI during that period (Lakdawalla and Philipson 2002). Contrary to popular thinking, healthy as well as unhealthy foods were becoming less expensive. Between 1980 and 2006, inflation-adjusted prices for unhealthy obesity-inducing foods, such as chocolate chip cookies, cola, ice cream, and potato chips, fell by an average of 0.5–1.7 percent each year, while the in-season and quality adjusted price of healthy foods, such as applies, bananas, lettuce, and dry beans, fell at an almost identical 0.8–1.6 annual rate (Kuchler and Stewart 2008).

Resource endowments were not the key to this science-driven story, except in one indirect way. Some of America's best agricultural science has traditionally come from the nation's land grant university system, created by Congress in 1862 under the Morrill Act. This visionary law granted federally controlled land to the states, for them to sell, with the proceeds to be used to endow "land grant" colleges tasked with improving agricultural science and education. It was America's generous endowment of land that funded this early and successful public commitment to science-based farm productivity growth, so in this sense the original resource endowment made a lasting difference.

The De-commodification of Food

Differences in farm commodity prices between countries are, in any case, of diminishing importance in explaining retail food price differences. Costs linked to the storage, transport, processing, packaging, and advertising of food commodities are now responsible for 85 percent of the final price paid by consumers (USDA 2013b). This diminished contribution of commodity costs to the final retail price of food reduces even more the importance of America's farm resource endowment in explaining the nation's lower food prices relative to Europe or Japan. International trade also weakens the importance of basic farm resource endowments. Countries with poor resources for farming have the option of importing food from the world market. It is of interest that neither Europe nor Japan has made full use of this option, preferring instead to place restrictions on farm commodity imports. In 1980, when the nominal rate of protection for farm commodities in the United States was 0 percent, it was 38 percent for the European Community, and 85 percent for Japan (Anderson and Hayami 1986). More recently in 2001, the average applied tariff rate for agricultural and food products in the United States was 2.4 percent, compared to 13.9 percent in the European Union and the European Free Trade Association (EFTA) countries, and 29.4 percent in Japan (CBO 2005). By 2009–2011, nominal protection rates in Europe had dropped to just 5 percent, due to a sharp spike in international commodity prices (Matthews 2012).

Note that the domestic impact of farm subsidies in the OECD world is to boost rather than lower commodity prices, a fact often missed in popular narratives. It is not farm subsidies that make food cheap in the United States. If farm support policies in America could somehow be removed, the nation's low food prices (which were made possible by science and technology gains) would be lower still. One study by three economists published in the journal *Food Policy* in 2008 found that if all national farm subsidy policies in America were eliminated, the price to consumers of soybeans, rice, sugar, fruits and vegetables, beef, pork, and milk would all decline (Alston, Sumner, and Vosti 2008). A later study published in the journal *Health Economics* calculated that if all farm subsidies in America were removed, the domestic price of sugar and dairy products would go down, enough to induce a small increase in per capita calorie intake for a typical adult, leading to further weight gain (Rickard, Okrent, and Alston 2012).

The policies in Europe and Japan that boost commodity prices more than in the United States are in one indirect sense linked to relative resource endowments. Economic models show that 60–70 percent of all variation in the nominal protection that governments offer to domestic farmers is explained by a comparative disadvantage those farmers come to experience relative to the industry and service sectors, during the industrial transformation (Anderson and Hayami 1986). As nations with poor farming resources begin to industrialize, they start providing price protection to their increasingly disadvantaged farmers, usually by imposing import restrictions at the border. These border restrictions can grow to be extremely high in countries with poor agricultural resource endowments, such as mountainous Japan, or Europe's Nordic and Alpine countries. At the other extreme are some industrializing nations that still possess underutilized land and water resources for farming or ranching, such as the United States, Canada, Australia, or New Zealand. In these nations the government supports given to prop up crop prices never grow very large. Resource endowments thus help determine how protectionist a nation's commodity policies will become, but this is far more important to commodity producers than to final food consumers, since the commodity component of final food retail prices is now so small.

Consumer Subsidy Policies

Farm subsidies do not make food cheap in America, but some consumer subsidies do have that effect. In 2012, the US government spent $114 billion to make food less expensive for low-income Americans, through programs such as the Supplemental Nutrition Assistance Program (SNAP, previously called the "food stamp" program), through school lunch programs, and through a food assistance program for women, infants, and children, known as WIC (USDA 2013c). Because of such programs, according to the OECD, the cost to consumers of purchasing food commodities in America was reduced overall by about 13 percent in 2011 (although these commodity costs are now just 15 percent of final retail food prices). In Europe, by contrast, the balance between farmer support and consumer support increased consumer spending on food commodities by 2 percent, and in Japan by a remarkable 43 percent (OECD 2012b).

These food subsidies for low-income Americans make only a small contribution to higher obesity rates (Fan 2010; Baum 2012). A research review done in 2008 by the USDA found that participation in SNAP did not increase the probability of obesity for men, or for the elderly, or for children. SNAP participation did increase the probability of women becoming obese, but only by 2 to 5 percentage points (Ver Ploeg and Ralston 2008). Other studies claim to find that SNAP participation even reduces obesity (Schmeiser 2012). The logic here is that SNAP gives recipients the equivalent of a cash benefit, part of which can be used to replace unhealthy food choices with more expensive but more healthful purchases (Gundersen 2013).

Food Tax Policies

In the end, as with fossil fuels, tax policy differences emerge as the most direct factor keeping American food prices low compared to Europe. Food consumption has not generally been taxed in the United States, but it has been in most of Europe, under a value added tax (VAT) system. The VAT in Europe operates much like a sales tax. It taxes consumer goods relative to the value each production step adds to the price of a product, generating higher retail prices for the final consumer. Within the European Union, VAT taxes at the member state level must comply with an EU VAT law, which requires states to have a minimum standard VAT rate of 15 percent, plus one or two reduced rates not to fall below 5 percent, except as separately negotiated. The actual VAT rates that are applied to food production in the EU range from zero in the United Kingdom, to 5.5 percent in France, 7 percent in Germany, and 25 percent in Sweden and Denmark (EU 2013). In the United States by contrast, retail food sales are completely untaxed at the federal level, and 37 of the 50 states either have no sales taxes at all, or sales taxes that exempt food entirely. Five do impose sales taxes on food, but they allow either rebates or credits to compensate poor households. Among the remaining handful that do tax food sales, the average rate applied is only 2 percent (FTA 2014).

America's Greater Ethnic and Racial Diversity

One final material circumstance that makes America unusual relative to other rich countries is the larger share of its population that are racial minorities, some with rates of obesity high enough to pull up the national average. Too much can be made of this issue, since obesity in America has been increasing across all categories of citizens, not just racial minorities. Between 2008 and 2013, for example, the prevalence of obesity increased among Whites as well as among Blacks and Hispanics, among men as well as women, among Easterners and Westerners as well as among Southerners and Midwesterners, and also among high, medium, and low-income groups (Sharpe 2013). Yet America's distinct multiracial character and its differing rates of obesity across racial categories are factors we cannot ignore.

Unusual racial diversity has always set America apart. While visiting America in 1831, Alexis de Tocqueville wrote at length about the "three races" in America: red, white, and black. Tocqueville also described in vivid terms the cruel and callous way in which White Americans treated the other two groups. This racial mix seen by Tocqueville resulted from a large importation of African slaves, plus the presence of an indigenous native population not yet crowded out or killed off. Subsequent historical events added to the mix. Not long after Tocqueville's visit, the United States waged a brief war of conquest against Mexico, incorporating lands populated by Mestizo people of mixed Iberian-Amerindian heritage. The 1849 gold rush then brought migrants from China into California. In the twentieth century, other non-European people began coming to America from East Asia, South and Southeast Asia, the Middle East, and also in large numbers from Mexico, Latin America, and the Caribbean. The cumulative result has been a degree of racial diversity that sets America apart, dramatically, from other rich countries.

America's 2010 census revealed that individuals not classified as White (i.e., European) had grown to constitute 36.6 percent of the total population (Nhan 2012). In Japan, the share of the population not Japanese is only about 1.5 percent. Data from the European Social Survey in 2007 revealed that among 26 different European countries, only 4 percent of all survey respondents identified themselves as "belonging to an ethnic minority group." The ethnic minority percentage in the United Kingdom was 3 percent, in France 4 percent, and in Germany 5 percent. In Italy, only 1 percent of residents identified as being an ethnic minority (Oudhof 2007). Interpreting such percentages is of course difficult because of divergent understandings and definitions of ethnicity, country by country, plus a reluctance in some countries to self-identify as a minority. An increasing number of Europeans are also now of mixed-race parentage, making them more difficult to classify. One study in the United Kingdom found that the mixed-race population even outnumbered those formally defined as minorities (Nandi and Platt 2011). Nonetheless, Europe remains dramatically less multi-racial than the United States. Visitors to cities like London can be fooled when they see a population there that is now 40 percent non-White; in England and Wales overall in 2011, the unmixed "White" population was still 86 percent of the total (Gye 2012).

The high proportion of non-European minorities in America is important because a disproportionate share of the nation's obese population can be found among these groups. Among

White Americans over the age of 18, the obesity rate is 26.2 percent, while for Hispanic/Latinos it is 31.8 percent, and for African Americans it is 39.1 percent. If non-White minority populations are excluded from the national calculation, rates of adult obesity in the United States thus scarcely differ from those seen in the rest of the Anglo-Protestant world. In Great Britain, according to the OECD, the percent of adults who are obese is 26.1 percent, essentially identical to the White rate in America. In New Zealand the rate is actually higher, at 27.8 percent. In Australia the rate is just a bit lower at 24.6 percent (OECD 2013b).

A few much smaller racial minority groups in America are even more prone to be obese. The Office of Minority Health of the US Department of Health and Human Services reported in 2010 that American Indians, including Alaskan Natives, were 70 percent more likely to be obese than Whites. For Native Hawaiians and Pacific Islanders, the tendencies toward obesity are even greater (HHS 2012).

There is no single explanation for much higher obesity rates among some minority racial groups in America. Persistent discrimination against these groups by White Americans is clearly one part of the explanation, because it constrains opportunities among non-Whites to secure adequate housing, schooling, employment, and healthcare. This leads to poor health outcomes across the board, with obesity emerging now as just one of those many poor health outcomes.

In order to make this argument, we do not have to describe Americans as more likely than Europeans to discriminate against non-Whites. What makes America different is the much larger population of non-Whites in the population positioned to face racial discrimination and to suffer poor health outcomes as a result. We will return to this issue in a later chapter. For now, what matters is that America's distinct demography—as a nation with a much larger population of racial minority citizens facing discriminatory treatment—is one contributing factor to its higher rate of obesity overall.

Conclusion: Resources, Geography, and Demography
Only a Starting Point

We have seen in this chapter that America's distinct tendency to overconsume both fossil fuel and food is partly a result of the nation's distinct geographic, geologic, and demographic endowment. America's vast fossil fuel resources relative to its population size have played a role in keeping the price of coal, oil, and natural gas low in America, mostly by supporting a large domestic fossil fuel industry capable of blocking significant taxes on consumption. Combined with low fuel prices, America's large land endowment relative to population size also makes Americans more prone to rely on automobile transport and to live in large, energy-demanding single-family homes.

Regarding obesity, the nation's automobile dependence contributes to a lower level of physical activity compared to other wealthy societies. Retail food prices are also lower than in other rich countries, boosting calorie intake, yet agricultural resource endowments are a poor explanation for these lower prices. The more important factors include lower taxes on food consumption, lower trade restrictions on food imports, and much lower food production costs linked less to material resources and more to technical and managerial innovation. One demographic circumstance that matters is America's larger population of disadvantaged racial minorities, for whom obesity risks are one of many unfortunate health consequences linked to racial discrimination.

America's unusual material and demographic circumstances can thus be a starting point when explaining America's distinct overconsumption of both fuel and food. In the next chapter we show that America's equally unusual political institutions do their part as well.

CHAPTER 3

America's Unusual Political Institutions

America's material and demographic endowments provide a start for explaining the nation's unique tendency to overconsume fossil fuels and food calories, but the nation's highly unusual political institutions are the second part of the story. The political institutions of the United States are distinctly generous in the options they give both to self-interested lobby groups and ordinary citizens who want to block government action. Proposed government actions to constrain fossil fuel use or discipline food calorie consumption have been blocked accordingly.

Ratified in 1789, the US Constitution is hailed as the oldest still in use, but its preindustrial origins are in some ways a drawback. The Constitution fails to deliver the capacity for centralized state action that most societies have found essential to good government in the modern age. The original circumstances of the document explain its weakness. America's colonists lived an ocean away from the centralized state authorities that dominated in England, so in the 1770s they were able to throw off that authority once French forces no longer presented a threat on the western frontier. Political power then fell into the hands of a loose alliance of 13 separate states. The inadequacy of this arrangement led quickly to a new Constitution, but weakness at the center persisted, creating space for an outright war between the states in 1861–1865.

America's federal Union survived this Civil War, but a strong central state never emerged in the following decades, despite rapid industrial development and urbanization, because the nation's constitutional arrangements had already been consolidated around a fragmented system of weak federal executive powers, part-time state legislatures, decentralized political parties, and an independent judicial branch that invited continuous legal challenges in front of locally selected judges (Kagan 2001). This American past differs dramatically from historical experience in most of Europe and in Japan, where centralized states have long been a constant.

Most Americans have been happy with state weakness. In fact, two years after the Constitution was ratified, 10 amendments were added that weakened the power of the federal government still more. Under this "Bill of Rights," it was explicitly guaranteed that the new federal government could not establish a religion, could not abridge speech or press freedom, could not restrict peaceable assembly, could not infringe the right to keep and bear arms, could not quarter soldiers in homes in peacetime, could not search or seize personal effects without a warrant based on probable cause, could not hold a suspected criminal without a Grand Jury indictment, could not convict a criminal suspect without a public jury trial, and could not impose excessive bail. The tenth of these amendments then said, "The powers not delegated to the United States by the Constitution, nor prohibited by it to the States, are reserved to the States respectively, or to the people."

America's original constitutional design has been modified numerous times since the eighteenth century, yet to the present day it contains power-limiting elements that set the United States apart from every other advanced industrial state. In 2002, political scientist Robert Dahl compiled a list of 22 countries that had been democratic and stable since at least 1950, including 15 European countries plus Japan, Australia, New Zealand, Canada, Costa Rica, Israel, and the United States. He then made a list of what he considered to be the seven most important features of America's constitutional-political design: a strong power divide between the federal government and the separate states, strongly bicameral legislatures, significantly unequal representation in the upper house of those legislatures (e.g., residents of the most heavily populated states are seriously under-represented in the US Senate), a strong judicial review of national legislation, plurality elections in single member districts, a strong two-party system, and a single popularly elected chief executive with important constitutional powers. Surveying the other 21 countries, he found only seven that shared even a single one of these American political system traits. Of these, Germany and Australia shared four of the seven traits, Canada and Switzerland shared three, and Britain, New Zealand, and Costa Rica shared one. The other 14 countries on the list, including Austria, Belgium, Denmark, Finland, France, Iceland, Ireland, Israel, Italy, Japan, Luxembourg, Netherlands, Norway, and Sweden, shared exactly zero of these seven most important American political system traits (Dahl 2002).

Five of Dahl's seven traits (all but the electoral rules, and party structures) contribute directly to the unique weakness of America's federal government vis à vis society. Federalism does this by explicitly limiting the power of Washington, D.C. over the states. Bicameral legislatures do this by making the passage of law more difficult (since both houses must agree before a law can be enacted). Unequal upper house representation does this by creating divergent constituencies, thus increasing the likelihood of disagreement between the two houses, and hence paralysis. Judicial review does this by empowering the Supreme Court on its separate authority to strike down acts by the other branches and levels of government. A separately elected chief executive, with veto powers over legislation and significant appointment powers, does this by dividing the executive from both legislative and judicial authority. As a consequence, America's federal government finds it difficult in peacetime to impose any costs at all on domestic society. Each separate branch must concur in such an action, including the House and Senate separately within the legislative branch. In some cases, each relevant committee within each house has an effective veto power, and in the Senate even individual members can emerge as potential veto points, by invoking an informal procedure known as a "hold" (Kroger 2010). Motivated organizations in America can block or severely weaken government action by either offering money or making threats to key actors at these veto points. Compared to democratic systems in the rest of the advanced industrial world, America's system makes strong governmental action uniquely difficult if organized groups decide to object (Steinmo 2010).

Even when government actions are taken in America, they remain subject to challenge and reversal, due to a distinct "adversarial legalism" within the American system (Kagan 2001). These multiple options for blockage or reversal explain why so many lobbyists are sent to the nation's capital in the first place, as opportunities for blockage trigger the proliferation of would-be blockers (Immergut 1990). According to the Center for Responsive Politics, in 2012 some 12,411 individual registered lobbyists were at work in the nation's capital, more than 20 for each individual member of Congress. Nationwide, the count of registered lobbyists is more than three times as high. The government in Washington did expand its peacetime role beginning in the 1960s, but groups in society were able to push back against things they did not like. Court challenges to governing agencies became business-as-usual in Washington, along with legal actions against individual government officials. Between 1960 and 1980, the number of federal court appellate cases involving constitutional issues increased sevenfold in

America, and between 1970 and the late 1980s, federal indict-
ments of public officials increased from less than 100 per year to
nearly 1,000 per year (Kagan 2001).

Does a central government this weak have any hope of
intervening to constrain excessive domestic food and fuel
consumption? Under full national mobilization in wartime,
governmental powers can expand to make this possible. For
example, when America entered the First World War in 1917,
President Woodrow Wilson was able to strong-arm Congress into passing a Food and Fuel Control Bill that granted
him the power to fix prices and exert other controls over the
production and distribution of consumer goods. As a means
to free up food supplies for shipment to Allied countries in
Europe, Wilson called upon Americans to go "meatless" at
least one meal each day and one day each week. Americans
complied, and in the first year of the war the United States
cut its consumption enough to double its normal food shipments to Europe. To conserve coal and oil for industrial and
military use, the government ordered non-war-related facto-
ries to shut down for days at a time. Americans were asked to
endure "heatless" Mondays and "gasless" Sundays, and "light-
less" nights were required twice a week, even on Broadway
(Berg 2013). The Second World War brought a return to strict
federal rationing of both food and fuel consumption. America's governmental institutions are fully capable of constraining consumption, but only under emergency circumstances in
support of national security objectives.

Without the emergency powers granted in wartime, political
institutions in America have been too weak to impose discipline. This institutional weakness is one reason that America has
the lowest tax rates on energy and food consumption in the industrial world, as described in the previous chapter, and it helps
to explain why recent efforts to constrain fuel and food consumption through governmental action have nearly all failed.
Basic material and demographic circumstances in America open

the path for consumption excess, but America's unusually weak central governing institutions help keep the path open.

Vetoing Higher Energy Prices

America's governmental system is shot through with potential veto points, and groups opposed to fossil fuel taxes have used them to good effect. The history of this blockage is important to recall, in part because it confirms the veto point explanation, yet also because it demonstrates that fossil fuel industries were not the only vetoing agents. Strong government actions to reduce the consumption of fossil fuels encounter resistance from a broad spectrum of the American population, suggesting that something more than corporate self-interest has been at work.

On two separate occasions in Congress, environmental advocates made strong efforts to enact constraints on America's excessive consumption of fossil fuels. In 1993 these advocates pushed for an across-the-board tax on energy consumption, a so-called Btu tax. This effort was successful in the House but then failed in the Senate. Environmental advocates came back to Congress in 2009, this time with a proposed "cap-and-trade" law that would drive a reduction in America's consumption of fossil fuels in a more disguised manner, without any visible tax. As with the Btu tax, this legislative effort first succeeded narrowly in the House but then failed in the Senate. Blocked in Congress, President Barack Obama launched a final attempt in 2014 to restrict "carbon pollution" from power plants, by stretching his authority under existing law. This action triggered political and legal challenges from coal state interests, and its final success may not be known for several years.

The two legislative efforts to secure significant emissions reduction actions through Congress, in 1993 and 2009, were initiated under circumstances that seemed promising at the time. In each case the environmental community had adequate support from a newly elected Democratic president who enjoyed a "honeymoon" of high approval ratings and wide popularity, and in each case the president's fellow partisans enjoyed majority control in both houses of Congress. In 1993, Democrats held a 258–176 margin in the House and a 57–43 margin in the Senate. In 2009, Democrats enjoyed a comparable 256–178 margin in the House and a 57–41 margin in the Senate. The failure of these majorities to control the legislative outcome illustrates the use of "veto points" in America's system by minority opposition groups. The fossil fuel industry lobbied hard against both the Btu tax in 1993 and cap-and-trade in 2009, and got the result it wanted. Yet a closer look reveals opposition from a broader array of groups, including organized labor as well as business, and Democrats as well as Republicans. A broad range of ordinary citizens in America, driven by cultural values as well economic self-interest, contributed to the legislative failure.

1993

In January 1993, when President Bill Clinton asked Congress for a tax on the heat content of energy (a Btu tax), his primary goal was to raise revenue as part of a five-year $500 billion budget deficit reduction plan; greenhouse gas reductions were never more than a secondary motive. Clinton was looking for a large new stream of federal revenue, and he knew it would have to come either from a general tax on consumption across the board (for example, a national VAT) or from a specific tax on the consumption of energy. Vice President Al Gore, who as a senator had called for a carbon tax in his 1992 bestselling book, *Earth in the Balance*, strongly backed the energy tax approach on climate change grounds.

It was Clinton's awareness of several potential veto points in Congress that led him to propose not a narrow carbon tax but instead a broader Btu tax on the heat content of all energy. Looming as one veto point was Chair of the Senate Committee on Appropriations, Senator Robert Byrd from the coal-rich state of West Virginia. Clinton needed Byrd's cooperation to secure his larger deficit reduction plan, so the president decided that a coal-punishing carbon tax should be taken off the table from the start (Erlandson 1994). In its place, Clinton put forward a proposed Btu tax that would treat coal like natural gas, despite coal's higher carbon emissions per unit of energy. At the same time, Clinton proposed a steeper Btu tax burden on petroleum, superficially for "national security" reasons (to reduce dependence on foreign oil) but more clearly as an indirect way to tax gasoline consumption. The indirection was necessary because during the 1992 campaign Clinton had conspicuously rejected raising revenue through a direct federal gasoline tax increase, a proposal then being made by third-party candidate Ross Perot. Clinton had pandered for middle-class votes by calling the Perot's tax proposal "back-breaking."

Clinton's own 1993 Btu tax proposal was far from backbreaking. It translated into the equivalent of a 5 percent increase in the price of gasoline at that time, plus a 3 percent increase in residential electricity prices, and an 8 percent increase in the price of home heating oil (Oil & Gas Journal 1993). The tax would be collected at the point of production, rather than as a visible add-on to the final wholesale or retail price, in a further effort to minimize consumer resistance.

As modest as this proposal was, the fossil fuel industry objected immediately. Charles DiBona, president of the American Petroleum Institute (API), called the proposed energy tax "a thinly disguised gasoline tax" that would be a job killer on a mammoth scale, jeopardizing the post-recession economic recovery then underway (Oil & Gas Journal 1993, p. 4). Republicans in the House of Representatives firmly opposed the tax, but Democrats used their majority to get the measure through the Ways and Means Committee in May 1993, on a straight partyline vote. The committee statement reporting on the measure invoked global warming concerns, and later in May the entire House approved the tax as part of the president's larger budget proposal, but with a thin victory margin of only six votes (Milne 2008).

Clinton's measure faced more formidable veto points in the Senate, where jurisdiction over tax matters falls to the Finance Committee. Democrats would hold a two-vote majority on this committee only if they could keep the support of two oil-state Democrats, David Boren of Oklahoma and John Breaux of Louisiana. When Boren and Breaux signaled that they would not support a Btu tax, the proposal died, effectively vetoed by Democrats (Hilzenrath and Pianin 1993). In the end, a much weaker stand-alone increase in gasoline taxes, only half as great as the implicit increase contained in the Btu tax, was passed by both the House and Senate in August, yet once again by only the narrowest of margins (Erlandson 1994).

Superficially, Clinton's Btu tax proposal had been blocked by coal and oil interests exploiting veto points within key congressional committees. President Clinton's Treasury Secretary, Lloyd Bentsen, blamed the defeat on energy companies, which had waged a public campaign against the idea by hiring lobbyists to discredit the tax as unfair and economically disastrous for energy-producing states (Hosler 1993). The American Petroleum Institute alone had pledged $5 million to help defeat the tax (Erlandson 1994). Yet this lobby effort against the tax was backed by more than just the nation's energy industries, and it drew broad strength from public opinion, not just a few institutional veto points.

Because there was underlying citizen resistance to the tax, industry lobbyists found it easy to mobilize an effective show of public disapproval. Protest rallies against the Btu tax were staged in North Dakota, Oklahoma, Louisiana, and Montana, through an organization named Citizens for a Sound Economy, which purported to have 250,000 individual members. This libertarian action organization had been created in 1984 by oil billionaire David Koch (Mayer 2010). Utility companies also fought the tax, sending mailers to all of their customers warning it would bring higher prices. Outside the energy sector, the National Association of Manufacturers (NAM) formed an American Energy Alliance to defeat the tax, claiming more than 1,000 members around the country—supposedly the largest coalition of business interests ever to oppose a single legislative proposal up to that point (Erlandson 1994). This public mobilization strategy was successful not because of anything distinctive about America's governmental institutions; the key factors were the unusual size and wealth of America's energy sector, as discussed in the previous chapter, plus a reflexive hostility among many middle-class Americans toward any government measure constraining their economic freedom.

In February 1993, even before industry launched its campaign against the Btu tax, a Yankelovich survey asked Americans what kinds of taxes they could accept to reduce the federal budget deficit. While 75 percent approved new taxes on tobacco and alcohol, only 23 percent favored taxes on energy (Kempton, Boster, and Hartley 1995). The fossil fuel industry was therefore able to wage a successful campaign against the Btu tax in 1993 because roughly three-quarters of all Americans were opposed to the tax even before the battle began. In this case, energy interests defeated environmental interests not simply because they had more veto points to exploit; they also were able mount an appeal to deeper cultural values. They accurately described the proposed tax as a burden on the middle class and regressive on the poor, both of which became deal-breaking concerns among progressive Democrats. Representative David Obey, a liberal Democrat from the non-energy state of Wisconsin, rejected the Btu tax and broke with Clinton on the issue because it went against the president's own 1992 campaign pledge to reduce tax burdens on the middle class (Erlandson 1994).

Asking Americans to pay higher energy prices to repair a federal budget deficit had proved difficult, but when President Clinton and Vice President Gore subsequently shifted to a more explicit focus on climate change, congressional resistance actually grew stronger. The Clinton administration, with Gore in the lead, hoped this resistance might be lessened by negotiating an international agreement among all industrial countries to reduce CO_2 emissions at the same time. This hope was dashed in the summer of 1997, when the US Senate demanded that poor as well as rich countries join such an agreement. The Senate passed a nonbinding resolution, sponsored by Democrat Robert Byrd and Republican Chuck Hagel, expressing the sense of the Senate that developing as well as developed countries would have to accept mandated limits on emissions under any new treaty. This Byrd–Hagel resolution passed the Senate by a unanimous vote of 95 to zero.

The trigger for Byrd–Hagel had been a controversial decision by Clinton in 1995 to exclude developing countries from anticipated treaty obligations, a so-called differentiated responsibilities approach. This decision had been made necessary by the refusal of India, China, and other non-OECD countries to accept any mandated limits. Since the Senate knew of this refusal, passing Byrd–Hagel was an implicit warning to Clinton not to go forward at all. The 95–0 margin gave the resolution emphatic significance, since it is the Senate that must ratify treaties, by a two-thirds favorable vote. Vice President Gore flew to Japan at the last minute in 1997 to lead the US negotiating effort, but the developing countries still refused to accept emissions constraints, so Gore had to sign a Kyoto Protocol he knew the Senate would never ratify (Hovi, Sprinz, and Bang 2010). Opting not to prolong the failure, President Clinton never submitted the treaty for Senate ratification. The constitutional requirement for a two-thirds Senate vote to ratify a treaty does represent a unique veto point within America's political system, yet in this case the requirement was largely immaterial, because the Senate had already gone on record as unanimously opposed to any Kyoto-like treaty that lacked parallel CO_2 limitation promises from big developing countries like China.

A German Comparison

To judge the distinctiveness of America's policy institutions in the context of climate change policy in 1993, it helps to take a parallel look at what was happening in Germany. While Clinton and Gore were failing to set in place a stronger policy in the United States, political leaders in Germany were succeeding with little difficulty. As early as June 1990, the federal cabinet in Germany had adopted an ambitious 25 percent CO_2 emissions reduction goal for the year 2005, compared to 1987 levels (Weidner and Eberlein 2009). To help meet this goal, Germany in 1991 adopted an Electricity Feed Act that compelled utilities to purchase electricity generated from renewable sources at a subsidized rate, plus a Waste Avoidance and Waste Management Act, plus an Ordinance on Heat Insulation that mandated insulation standards for new buildings (Hatch 1995). In 1995, Germany's federal ministries for the environment (BMU) and for economics (BMWi) then entered into negotiations with private industry associations and soon reached informal agreements that pledged a 20 percent reduction in specific CO_2 emissions from a 1990 base year. Eventually, nearly 80 percent of Germany's total industrial energy consumption was covered by these agreements, with an independent third party institute monitoring and assisting in evaluating compliance (Hatch 2007). All of these measures were taken by a relatively conservative, industry-friendly CDU/FDP federal government, headed by Chancellor Helmut Kohl.

When a new SPD/Green (Red-Green) coalition government came to power following elections in 1998, even stronger actions on climate change emerged. In an agreement that formed the governing coalition, the parties affirmed a 25 percent reduction target for CO_2 emissions, and pursuant to this target a comprehensive National Climate Protection Programme was launched in 2000, adding no fewer than 64 measures to promote renewable energy and impose CO_2 reduction targets in seven different sectors of the economy (Weidner and Eberlein 2009).

The new government also put into effect an "eco-tax" in 1999, to increase gradually the price of gasoline, heating oil, natural gas, and electricity. In 2000 it then introduced a Renewable Energy Sources Act (EEG), to encourage the expansion of wind power in particular. Thanks to all of these measures—plus a fortunate shutting down of dirty industries in East Germany after the Berlin Wall fell in 1989—Germany by 2005 had reduced its CO_2 emissions by 16 percent from the 1990 level. Over that same time period, emissions in the United States had risen 16 percent (Weidner and Eberlein 2009). For present purposes, we must ask if Germany had a greater ability to act on climate change compared to the United States because of differences in that nation's governmental institutions.

German political institutions, by themselves, should be relatively easy for special interest groups to block; it was Germany's lack of any significant oil and gas production industry that allowed these strong measures to go forward. Germany does have coal, and for this reason the consumption of coal was specifically exempted from the eco-tax. In addition, Germany's politically influential auto transport sector was given a reduced tax rate (Hatch 2007). Germany's electoral rules (proportional representation) result in a multi-party rather than a two-party system, making necessary at times the negotiation of coalition agreements among parties to form a government. This gives potential veto power to minor parties, yet it also opens a path for positive influence if one of those parties, like Germany's Green Party, is a strong advocate for restrictions on fossil fuels. Between 1998 and 2005 the German environment ministry was under Green Party control. Party discipline is also much stronger in Germany, in part because there is no separate election of a chief executive, so it is the elected members of the majority party in the *Bundestag* who choose the chancellor from among their own ranks, and who become locked together with that individual, sharing a common political fate at election time. The upper chamber, the

Bundesrat, can nonetheless emerge as a significant veto point, as it gives separate representation to the nation's independent state governments.

Material interests and political institutions matter, but we must also consider important cultural differences between Germany and the United States. Politics in Germany is conventionally understood to be "corporatist," featuring close collaboration between the state and functionally organized interest groups in society (Katzenstein 1985). In Germany, both labor and industrial associations tend to be hierarchical and disciplined—a bit like German political parties—and comfortable negotiating consensual agreements with the national government. In the case of climate change, it was negotiations between the government and more than a dozen industry associations that led first to voluntary emissions reduction targets, and then to the policy actions needed to reach those targets. The process was strongly informed by the participation of German scientists, who originally brought the government along with a 1987 parliamentary study commission—composed of experts and parliamentarians sitting side by side—to consider "Preventive Measures to Protect the Earth's Atmosphere."

A follow-on parliamentary committee was set up for the 1990–1994 period, and the federal government adopted all of the central recommendations of both committees (Weidner and Eberlein 2009). All the while, within the cabinet, an Inter-Ministerial Group remained in continuous operation to smooth over inevitable disagreements between the environment and economy ministries. As a result, a high degree of political consensus emerged among German parties in the 1990s regarding the need for a strong climate change mitigation policy. This consensus was on full display in the spring of 2002, when both houses of the German parliament ratified the Kyoto Protocol without a single dissenting vote (Weidner and Eberlein 2009). Recall that the US Senate had also voted unanimously, but for rejection rather than ratification.

If German-like institutions to facilitate state-society collaboration were miraculously introduced into the United States, would the result be comparably strong actions to reduce CO_2? Given the differences in America's fossil fuel resource endowment, plus a much stronger cultural aversion to government authority and to paying taxes, the answer is almost certainly no. Culturally, Germans are easier to govern than Americans. Obedient and orderly Germans even continued paying taxes in 1945 after Allied bombs had destroyed the Treasury in Berlin, including all of its tax records (Speer 1981). Such cultural differences between Americans and Europeans will be considered in the next chapter.

2009

A new opportunity to strengthen America's climate change policies appeared in 2009, following the election of another Democratic president who once again came into office with significant majorities in both the House and Senate. President Barack Obama and most Democrats wanted to strengthen climate change policy, but they knew better this time than to propose an explicit tax. As former President Bill Clinton had warned them in August 2008: "I tried that once. It didn't work for me" (Gallaugher 2008, p. 1).

By 2009, climate policy advocates believed that the best legislative option would be to allocate emissions permits within a fixed overall cap, while allowing a market to emerge for unused permits, so those who managed to cut emissions more than required could make money by selling permits to those who had cut less. This was known as the "cap-and-trade" approach. Originally the cap would be set at a generous level, but then would be steadily lowered in future decades to achieve significant emissions reductions. Cap-and-trade had been used successfully to limit SO_2 emissions (a source of acid rain) under the 1990 Clean Air Act Amendments. Even some prominent

Republicans endorsed this approach, including Senator Lindsey Graham from South Carolina, former House Speaker Newt Gingrich, and Senator John McCain, who had been his party's presidential nominee in 2008.

Despite such promising circumstances, Congress again balked, and cap-and-trade failed. Environmentalists blamed lock-step Republican obstructionism, weak presidential leadership, disinformation spread by the fossil fuel industry, and the 2009 economic recession. Some pointed as well to a bungled lobbying strategy by the coalition of environmental organizations and business leaders that were promoting cap-and-trade, the so-called US Climate Change Partnership (Skocpol 2013). Unfortunately, some problems were more fundamental. Congressional institutions gave private industry too many veto points to work with, and just as in 1993, the environmental cause was weakened by an unusual hostility among ordinary Americans to government measures that might increase energy prices.

Advocates for strong policy action to mitigate climate change naively assumed that once Americans were educated to understand the magnitude of the threat, they would accept the necessity of emissions controls, even with some short-term economic cost. By 2009, however, no effort had been spared in educating Americans about the climate threat. In 2007, the IPCC had released a widely discussed Fourth Assessment Report, which said it was "unequivocal" that the earth was warming and that human-induced greenhouse gas emissions were "very much to blame." That same year Al Gore accepted an Academy Award, plus a Nobel Peace Prize shared with the IPCC, for his widely seen film *An Inconvenient Truth*. Gore went on to found the Alliance for Climate Protection, funded at $80–$100 million annually, to engage in nonpartisan persuasion activities. Philanthropic environmentalists also committed over $1.1 billion to a new foundation named ClimateWorks, to promote a stronger American climate change response (Bartosiewicz and Miley 2013).

Despite such education and consensus-building efforts, ordinary American citizens in 2009 remained deeply divided on climate change. A survey of 2,129 adult Americans conducted in the fall of 2008 by researchers at Yale University and George Mason University had shown that 18 percent of Americans were "alarmed" about the reality and seriousness of climate change, and another 33 percent were "concerned," but the rest of the population were either "cautious" (19 percent), "disengaged" (12 percent), or "dismissive" (7 percent). When asked at that time to prioritize a list of 8 issues "now being discussed in Washington, D.C.," global warming was rated by Americans number 7 out of 8, behind illegal immigration, tax cuts, education, social security, terrorism, and their number one issue—healthcare. Only abortion came in behind global warming. Just 21 percent of Americans believed that global warming should be a "very high" priority for the next president and Congress, compared to 45 percent who felt that way about healthcare (Leiserowitz, Maibach, and Roser-Renouf 2009).

Respondents to this survey also expressed opinions on what they thought should be done about global warming. Given 12 different policy options, cap-and-trade came in next to last, barely beating out higher taxes on gasoline. Only 11 percent of American adults "strongly supported" creating a new national market that "allows companies to buy and sell credits to emit greenhouse gases within a national cap," while 23 percent strongly opposed this option. Popular support would have been weaker still if the description of the option had included a reference to the higher energy prices that would result. Opponents of cap-and-trade, who understood these sensitivities, sought to re-brand the proposal "cap-and-tax."

Americans who do not want the government to take strong actions that might raise the price of energy sometimes justify their reluctance by questioning the science. According to the Pew Research Center, 77 percent of Americans agreed in 2006 and 2007 that there was solid evidence the earth was warming, yet only 47 percent of these believers in warming saw most of the effect coming from human activity, and since then Americans appear to have become even less convinced. By 2013 only 69 percent believed that warming was real, and only 42 percent of those blamed human activity (Pew Research Center 2013). This weak and fragile foundation of public support would have made President Obama's 2009 cap-and-trade proposal relatively easy for opponents to block even without the institutional veto points, the economic recession, the obstructionist tactics of Republicans, or the higher priority that Democrats were giving to healthcare.

In June 2009 a Waxman–Markey bill was introduced in the House of Representatives to cap America's greenhouse gas emissions at 17 percent below the 2005 level by 2020. This measure passed in the House, albeit by a close 219–212 vote. Things then fell apart in the Senate, just as in 1993, where a parallel cap-and-trade measure never even made it to the floor. Cap-and-trade would have failed on a floor vote in any case, due to the Senate's filibuster custom, which can require a 60-vote supermajority. At first glance, this again looked like an exploitation of veto points by the fossil fuel industry, which had poured substantial resources into opposing cap-and-trade. During the first three years of the Obama administration, ExxonMobil spent more than $52 million lobbying in Washington (Coll 2012). A closer look shows that the opposition to cap-and-trade was much wider.

The strongest proponents of cap-and-trade were not elected or appointed government officials at all, but environmental advocacy organizations backed with money from private philanthropies. These proponents made considerable progress in the House of Representatives, thanks to a few well-positioned and sympathetic Democratic leaders, including Rep. Henry A. Waxman (D-CA) who chaired the House Energy and Commerce Committee, Rep. Edward J. Markey (D-MA) who chaired a new Energy and Environment Subcommittee of the Energy and Commerce Committee, and also Speaker Nancy Pelosi (D-CA).

Yet top Democrats both in the Senate and the White House were never enthusiastic about pushing hard for cap-and-trade (Bartosiewicz and Miley 2013). Barack Obama had endorsed a cap-and-trade approach during his 2008 campaign for the presidency, but once in office, facing an unexpected financial crisis and recession, his priorities changed.

At a meeting of top White House advisors to set priorities during his first week in office in 2009, Obama barely mentioned energy or environmental issues, or even financial regulatory reform. He made it clear he wanted healthcare reform to be his legacy (Suskind 2011). Both White House Chief of Staff Rahm Emanuel and senior advisor to the president David Axelrod specifically opposed giving priority to climate change policy (Bartosiewicz and Miley 2013). Opinion polls had suggested there would be political risks if the president pushed hard for a measure that would increase energy prices in the middle of a recession. In January 2009 Obama did ask Congress to send him legislation that would include a "market-based cap on carbon pollution," but he then walked away from the issue, inviting Democratic leaders in the House to do what they could.

Meanwhile in the Senate in 2009, top Democrats showed limited enthusiasm for cap-and-trade. The Senate Environment and Public Works Committee, chaired by Senator Barbara Boxer (D-CA), took nine months to produce a draft text. Cap-and-trade had already passed in the House at this point, so Senate Republicans knew they were the last line of defense, and they mounted a strong blocking response, refusing even to vote on Boxer's measure in committee, where it quietly died. Senate Majority Leader Harry Reid (D-NV) tried to revive some support for cap-and-trade by appointing Senators John Kerry (D-MA), Joe Lieberman (an independent who caucused with the Democrats), and Republican Lindsey Graham (R-SC) to write a bill, but Graham soon walked away from his own bill, angry with the White House over unrelated issues, including immigration reform. This new Senate bill needed at least one

Republican vote to get to 60, because Ted Kennedy's Democratic seat in Massachusetts had just gone to a Republican, but that one needed Republican could never be found. Soon Democrats began defecting, led by Senator Max Baucus from the coal state of Montana. Majority Leader Reid himself was up for re-election in 2010, and was trailing in the polls behind a Tea Party candidate strongly opposed to environmental regulations, which reinforced Reid's eventual decision not to take a cap-and-trade measure to the floor (Bartosiewicz and Miley 2013).

Throughout this unsuccessful legislative effort, the proponents of cap-and-trade sought to broaden their support by offering one concession after another. In the House, Waxman wooed coal state Democrats by agreeing that the emissions permits would be distributed free, rather than paid for by industry. Farm-state members were wooed by an agreement that left the entire agricultural sector "uncapped" under the proposed law (Larsen, Kelly, and Heilmayr 2009). Such concessions weakened enthusiasm for the measure among environmentalists.

The failed effort to legislate cap-and-trade in 2009–2010 persuaded President Obama not to raise the issue when running for re-election in 2012. By then the House of Representatives had fallen under Republican control, thanks in part to a Tea Party surge fueled by a combination of corporate and populist rage against the supposed growth of big government, especially healthcare reform, but also cap-and-trade. At Obama's carefully scripted nominating convention in September 2012, the party platform failed to mention cap-and-trade, a contrast from four years earlier, and former Vice President Al Gore did not even attend the event. Responding to written questions about cap-and-trade on one scientific website at the time, Obama changed the subject to his positive support for clean energy (Kuhnhenn and Thomas 2012).

President Obama eventually came back to the climate change issue early in 2013, freed from having any more elections of his own to face. Knowing that members of Congress would still not want to act, Obama decided to experiment with an unprecedented alternative. Rather than seek new legislation, he ignored Congress and tried executive branch rule-making under the existing laws that governed ordinary air pollution. In June 2014, Obama's Environmental Protection Agency (EPA) proposed a regulation to cut carbon pollution from the nation's power plants by 30 percent from the peak 2005 level, by 2030. The fate of this most recent initiative will not be known for some time. The proposal could not become an actual regulation for at least a year, and at that point state-level authorities would still have to write specific regulations before it could come into effect. Challenges at the state level, in the federal courts, in Congress would meantime be mounted by the coal industry.

In advancing this new measure, the president was up against more than just narrow coal state interests. Most American citizens still do not view climate change as a priority concern. One Pew poll in January 2014 showed that Americans ranked global warming as 19 on a list of 20 issues they wanted Congress and the president to deal with. A Wall Street Journal/NBC poll that same month found that climate change ranked dead last on a list of 15 issues, when people were asked what administration priorities should be. Only 27 percent of respondents said that addressing climate change should be an absolute priority, 41 percent said it could be delayed, and 29 percent said it shouldn't be pursued at all (Nelson and Mundy 2014).

To summarize, while most other major industrial countries have set in place some form of a carbon tax or a cap-and-trade system, the federal government in the United States still has not done so. America's distinct political institutions are clearly one reason for this outcome, as is the nation's large fossil fuel endowment, which created the industries that now exploit the weakness of the institutions. Yet the popular indifference of so many Americans toward the climate change challenge suggests that more is going on. In the chapter that follows, some distinct cultural sources for this indifference will be explored.

Veto Points and Obesity Policy

America's efforts to combat obesity have a briefer history than those to combat climate change, but a similar weakness is already visible. The only policy instruments available so far at the federal level have been public exhortation, appeals to volunteerism, and some conditions attached to federal resource transfers to public schools. Federal nutrition subsidies to help the poor have been conditioned on healthy eating in one small case—the WIC program—but not in the vastly larger SNAP program. Federal policy instruments such as taxes, mandates, or direct regulations have gone essentially unused. State and local governments have done more, but only some, and only a bit more.

In the previous chapter we saw that this weak federal response was hard to explain through reference to material endowments. Can it be explained instead through reference to America's distinct governing institutions, including the veto points within those institutions that allow minority opponents to block majority action?

To answer this question, consider three separate arenas of policy action: taxes on caloric soda, restrictions on advertisements of food to children, and menu restrictions in public school cafeterias. Outcomes in these areas have indeed been constrained by veto-minded industry groups taking advantage of the nation's weak constitutional design. Yet this blockage can also be traced to a broad social reluctance to grant the federal government stronger powers in this area.

Opinion surveys tell an important story. In May 2012, a Rasmussen Poll reported that 63 percent of American adults explicitly opposed taxes (state or federal) on soda and junk food, while only 18 percent supported such taxes (Rasmussen 2012). Some of this popular thinking has no doubt been influenced by manipulative and misleading industry campaigns, but some is also genuine and deeply rooted in the nation's culture. Americans do not mind taxes on the consumption of "sinful" products like alcohol and tobacco, but few want the government to use strong measures challenging personal decisions about food.

Caloric Soda

Soft drink consumption is strongly implicated in weight gain worldwide. One multivariate linear regression study of 75 countries in 2013 found that for every 1 percent increase in soft drink consumption in a population, an additional 2.3 adults per 100 persons will become obese, even after controlling for other foods consumed, total calories, income, urbanization, and aging (Basu et al. 2013). The United States, meanwhile, has the second highest per capita consumption of sugary soda in the world, at 31 gallons per year. The highest consumption level now is in Mexico, a country that rivals America's obesity prevalence, with 43 gallons consumed per person every year. The rest of the advanced industrial world is far behind in soda consumption.

The probability of a child becoming obese increases by 60 percent for each extra glass of sugared beverage consumed per day (Brownell and Frieden 2009). A 2011 Harvard School of Public Health study found that sugary beverages came in second only to potato chips and other potato products as food contributors to long-term weight gain in America (Mozaffarian 2011). Between 1977 and 2002, per capita intake of caloric beverages actually doubled in the United States across all age groups (Brownell et al. 2009). Soft drinks are not only more conducive to weight gain than solid foods, they also have little or no nutrient value (Vartanian et al. 2007).

Fortunately, soda consumption has more recently been falling in America. According to *Beverage Digest*, per capita soda consumption in the United States peaked in 1998, and by 2012 it had actually fallen back down to the level of 1987 (Zmuda 2013). Unfortunately, this drop was offset to some extent by increased consumption of energy drinks that contain caffeine as well as sugar, and by noncarbonated sports drinks, which can have as much sugar as carbonated soda. Sales of sugary soft drinks may now be declining, but they remain a large contributor to America's high calorie intake. By one estimate, total per capita energy intake in America in 2009 was about 250 to 300 calories per day higher than it had been several decades earlier, with nearly half the increase accounted for by the consumption of sugared beverages (Brownell and Frieden 2009).

As America's obesity crisis worsened in the 2000s, a community of nutrition scientists, health professionals, policy activists, and health foundations launched a political effort to bring the problem under control using state and federal taxes, particularly soda taxes. By that time 40 states already taxed sugared beverages, but only at low levels for the purpose of generating revenue, rather than at the higher levels needed to alter consumer behavior. Dissatisfied with such limitations, a group of child and healthcare advocates in the state of New York in 2008 proposed an excise tax on sugared beverages large enough (one penny per ounce) to reduce consumption by an estimated 13 percent. Even if 25 percent of the resulting reduction in calorie intake was replaced by other foods, the average person might still lose slightly more than two pounds a year under such a tax (Brownell and Frieden 2009). Governor David A. Paterson included this soda tax in the 2009 budget proposal that he sent to the state legislature in Albany.

The American Beverage Association (ABA) mobilized quickly to veto this proposal, but they had plenty of support from other constituencies. In the first four months of 2009, the ABA spent $9.4 million to oppose the tax in New York, but private grocers and the Teamsters union joined with the beverage industry, creating a new organization named New Yorkers Against Unfair Taxes, which eventually claimed 10,000 citizen and 158 business members. Opposition came as well from state legislators with soda distribution centers and bottling companies in their districts, many of them Democrats. The tax proposal was also opposed by those claiming to speak for low-income

New Yorkers. Triada Stampas, director of government relations for the Food Bank of New York City, testified against the tax (Hartocollis 2010).

The strength of this resistance was significant, especially in a state more tolerant than most regarding consumption taxes. The State Legislature of New York imposes a $4.35 excise tax on every pack of cigarettes sold in the state, the highest levy in the nation, yet this same legislature signaled that it wanted no part of just a 12-cent per can tax on sugary soda. Governor Paterson, who at this point was still planning a 2010 election run, quietly dropped the soda tax idea.

After faltering in New York, soda tax proposals resurfaced at the federal level in 2009, in the early stages of a national healthcare reform debate. Healthcare reform would be expensive, so advocates for a soda tax hoped to promote their plan as both health-improving and revenue-boosting. They estimated that a national tax of 1 cent per ounce on sugar-sweetened beverages would raise $14.9 billion in the first year, which was not a large share of the anticipated $77 billion annual cost of the 2009 healthcare plan then being considered by the Senate Finance Committee, but still a useful amount (Neuman 2009). The advocates freely admitted that a soda tax would be regressive on the poor, yet they explained that low-income, obesity-prone Americans would gain the most in terms of health, both from the subsidized care the tax would help finance and from the nudge toward less soda consumption (Jacobson 2009).

Some Democrats in Congress were initially open to considering such arguments, but the White House was not. In May 2009, when the Democratic-controlled Senate Finance Committee released a list of 14 different ways to help fund healthcare reform, it included what it called "Lifestyle Related Revenue Raisers," such as an alcohol excise tax or a sugar-sweetened beverage excise tax, but when the Obama administration constructed its own list, neither such tax was included (Committee on Finance 2009). Three months later, in July, President Obama did at one point say that a soda tax was "an idea that we should be exploring," but he immediately qualified that by observing that people "don't necessarily want Big Brother telling them what to eat or drink, and I understand that." White House spokesperson Reid Cherlin hastened to add that a soda tax was "not something we've proposed" (Saltonstal 2009). The White House position was largely preordained, given Obama's 2008 campaign promise not to raise "any form" of taxes on families making less than $250,000 a year (Kartch 2009).

Even if Obama had strongly endorsed a soda tax, the idea would never have made it through the Senate Finance Committee, since Chairman Max Baucus (D-MT) was from a sugar beet state, and ranking member Chuck Grassley (R-IO) was from Iowa, the leading supplier of high fructose corn syrup to the soft drink industry (Schweitzer 2011). It also mattered to Grassley that the nation's most significant farm lobby organization, the American Farm Bureau Federation, had submitted a formal notice of opposition. This was a committee-level veto point clearly situated to block any soda tax proposal.

The veto point was there, but nothing really had to be vetoed. The administration had proposed nothing, the House of Representatives had passed nothing, and inside the Senate the soda tax idea had no support. There was no draft legislation to consider, let alone to veto. Soda taxes to reduce consumption had never been endorsed by more than a handful of elected politicians; the idea, even more than cap-and-trade, was primarily promoted by unelected public health advocates, public interest think tanks, and private foundations.

Private beverage and sweetener industries took no chances. They mounted a significant campaign in Congress against the soda tax idea in 2009, just as they had earlier in the New York State Legislature. During the first nine months of 2009, according to the Senate's office of public records, 21 different companies and organizations reported that they had lobbied specifically against soda taxes, spending $24 million in the process. About $5 million of that went to a national advertising campaign aimed at members of Congress and supported by a newly formed coalition called Americans Against Food Taxes. In September 2009, this industry group took out a full-page ad in the *Washington Post,* written as an open letter to Congress saying, "Don't tax our groceries" (Schweitzer 2011). In this case the so-called Americans Against Food Taxes included Coca Cola, Pepsico, and Burger King (Spolar and Eaton 2009). The American Beverage Association spent $7.3 million all by itself, and the National Corn Growers Association also spent $200,000 to oppose the tax. By November 2009, nobody in Congress was talking about a federal soda tax to help pay for healthcare, and in May 2010, a White House task force on childhood obesity explicitly handed the idea back to the states, inviting them to experiment with taxing sugary beverages, should they wish to do so (Gentile 2010).

Again, the organized opposition to a soda tax extended well beyond private industries. Elena Rios, a physician and president of the National Hispanic Medical Association, sided with the beverage makers on the issue because she thought a narrow tax on sugary soda was not the comprehensive approach to health that was needed by her community (Spolar and Eaton 2009). Former President Bill Clinton thought the same. Asked about a soda tax in May 2009, he said, "The better thing to do is to give incentives right across the board for prevention and wellness" (Davis 2009). Clinton preferred to do this by coaxing the industry into voluntary cooperation, a method subsequently embraced by First Lady Michelle Obama as well, in her "Let's Move!" campaign. Clinton's own Alliance for a Healthier Generation had actually reached such a deal with the beverage industry in 2006, reducing the caloric content of drinks sold in school vending machines (Gasparo and Esterl 2014). Industry leaders praised Clinton for being a "stand-up guy" when he criticized the soda tax idea, yet his position was to some extent compromised by financial support the industry had given to his Healthier Generation organization (Leonhardt 2009).

Federal attention to sugar consumption issues eventually returned in 2014, when the FDA initiated an effort to require a separate listing for added sugars on nutrition labels, yet this was a much weaker approach, since the consumers most at risk were unlikely to make good use of the information. It is interesting that strong measures have always been permitted for some non-food consumer products. Congress may have been unwilling to consider a tax on sugary soda to help fund healthcare reform in 2009, yet it was perfectly willing to enact, in that same year, a 62 cent increase (a 158 percent increase) in the federal cigarette tax, to fund an expansion of the Children's Health Insurance Program (CHIP). The same institutional veto points were also present in this case, but they could not be mobilized because polling showed that more than two-thirds of all voters were in support of a significant increase in the federal cigarette tax for the purpose of providing healthcare coverage to uninsured children (Myers 2009). The president, a former smoker himself, signed this new law on the same day it was sent to him by Congress.

When it came to tobacco, then, a parallel legislative concept in the same year, and with the same president and Congress, met a dramatically different legislative outcome. In contrast to food or soda, products such as tobacco, alcohol, and narcotic drugs encounter strict regulation in America. In part this makes sense, since excessive consumption of these other items carries greater risk, and large portions of the population have already decided not to consume them at all. Yet we will see that culture matters as well, because Anglo-Protestant traditions in America continue to view the consumption of these other items as somehow "sinful" in moral terms.

The soda tax idea that failed at the federal level in 2009–2010 has fared only a bit better at the state level. Many states in America do impose taxes on caloric soda, but to raise revenue rather than reduce consumption. Some 33 states currently levy taxes on soft drinks, but at an average level of only 5 percent, which is well below the 15–20 percent level required to have an appreciable effect on consumer behavior (FAO 2013). At the state level, when heavier taxes to alter behavior are proposed, actual voters sometimes participate in the veto-like response. A number of soda tax initiatives formally enacted by state legislatures have been overturned as a result of direct ballot initiatives sponsored by the beverage industry. America is unusual in giving its citizens such direct democracy options.

In 2008 the Maine Legislature passed a significant soda tax of 42 cents per gallon (3 cents per ounce), but then private industry stepped in with a $4 million "Fed up with Taxes" ballot initiative campaign, and voters rejected the tax two years later (Peters 2010). In 2010, the Washington State Legislature imposed a new tax on soft drinks (and candy), and this tax was only 2 cents for every 12 ounces of soda, but even so it was highly unpopular, having to be adopted late one afternoon without any public hearing or input. The American Beverage Association then spent $16.5 million to promote a ballot initiative that promptly overturned the tax.

Ballot issues promoting soda taxes have also failed at the municipal level. In 2012, voters in two midsized California towns (Richland and El Monte) rejected soda taxes by margins of more than 2 to 1 after the ABA spent $3.6 million to help block these measures, using advertisements and paid canvassers. Marion Nestle, a leading food and nutrition expert who is no friend to the beverage industry, highlighted the role that corporate assets had played in the outcome, but then observed something more fundamental about American culture: "appeals to voter concerns about higher prices, job losses, and personal autonomy are more effective than appeals based solely on health considerations" (Nestle 2012).

Finally in 2014, a successful ballot campaign made the city of Berkeley, in California, the first in the country to enact a penny-per-ounce soda tax (30 other cities had tried and failed). Two key factors to this success were the absence of a substantial minority population in this small and mostly white and upscale city, plus a $85,000 donation to the campaign from former New York City Mayor Michael Bloomberg. Mayor Bloomberg's own earlier campaigns against caloric soda in his own city had been less successful. In 2010, New York City sought permission from the US Department of Agriculture to pilot a temporary elimination of caloric soda from purchase eligibility under the SNAP program. This request was refused by the USDA, but it was also immediately criticized by the minority community in New York, as an implicit slur on the food choice habits of SNAP recipients. A subsequent effort in Congress in 2013 to restrict foods for purchase with SNAP benefits was also scrapped, after objections from a strange-bedfellows coalition that included beverage and snack food companies plus anti-poverty groups such as the Food Research and Action Center (Bjerga 2013). The low-income Americans who consume unhealthy foods appear to be just as dedicated to the concept of free choice as the companies that sell the products.

Finally, in 2012, Mayor Bloomberg attempted to use his own hand-picked Board of Health to block sales of soda and other high-calorie drinks in containers larger than 16 ounces. In response, the National Association for the Advancement of Colored People (NAACP) actually brought a lawsuit, alleging that the ban "arbitrarily discriminates against citizens and small-business owners in African-American and Hispanic communities." The NAACP position was compromised by that organization's long ties to big soft drink companies, particularly Coca-Cola in Atlanta, yet members of the City Council's Black, Latino, and Asian Caucus also spoke out against the ban (Grynbaum 2013). In the end, Bloomberg's measure was blocked by a state judge one day before it was set to take effect.

America's inability to adopt strong policies to speed the decline in caloric soda consumption is thus a combined result of veto point exploitation by industry plus broad social opposition. One 2012 survey found that only 22 percent of Americans supported soda taxes (Gollust et al. 2014). A 2013 survey from the

Associated Press and the Center for Public Affairs Research revealed that Americans were willing to support mandatory calorie counts on menus (70 percent approve), and requirements for more physical activity in school (80 percent approve), but 60 percent were opposed to taxes targeting unhealthy foods, and 75 percent opposed Bloomberg-style restrictions on what people can buy. These same Americans did not deny the existence of an obesity crisis, as three-quarters said it was a serious health problem for the nation. Yet for most it was an issue of individual or family responsibility. Only one-third considered it a community problem that governments, schools, healthcare providers, or even the food industry should take responsibility for (Kerr and Agiesta 2013). In Europe and Japan, where greater cultural weight is placed on social responsibility and less on individual responsibility, stronger policy actions against obesity are able to go forward. Institutional veto points were thus a part of the problem in this case, but far from the totality of the problem.

Restrictions on Food Advertising to Children

Many governments around the world place restrictions on the advertising of food to children, but not the United States. As mentioned earlier, the United Kingdom imposed regulations in 2007 to restrict both content and the scheduling for advertisements of foods high in fat, salt, or sugar (known as HFSS). Australia bans food ads meant for children younger than 14 years of age. The Netherlands bans ads for sweets to children younger than 12 (Nestle 2006). For decades, Finland has not permitted any commercial sponsorship of children's programs (Consumer's International 1996). The Flemish region of Belgium disallows any advertising in the five minutes before or after children's programs. Since 1978, the province of Quebec in Canada has banned all advertisements targeting children aged 12 years or younger. In Sweden since 1991, all television advertisements directed to children under 12 are banned by that nation's Radio and Television Act, and all advertisements of food, toys, and other products are also banned both before and after children's programs. Norway bans advertisements aimed at children during children's television programs. The governments of Greece and Denmark also restrict advertising to children (Oommen and Anderson 2008). In 2014, Mexico banned television advertising for high-calorie food and soft drinks between 2:30 PM and 7:30 PM on weekdays, and between 7:30 AM and 7:30 PM on weekends (Gallagher 2014).

In the United States, proposals to restrict food advertising to children are offered but consistently blocked. As early as 1977, two nonprofit organizations—Action for Children's Television and the Center for Science in the Public Interest—petitioned the Federal Trade Commission (FTC) to ban TV commercials for candy and sugary snacks directed at young children, and in the following year a sympathetic FTC commenced public hearings on the issue. The FTC asked for comments on a staff proposal to ban all TV advertising aimed at young children, plus commercials for sugary snack foods aimed at older children. Pushback was immediate. Food and toy companies, ad agencies, and broadcasters quickly filed a lawsuit against the Commission and lobbied Congress to block new rule-making in this area. The result was a (so-called) Federal Trade Commission Improvements Act of 1980, which legally barred the FTC from issuing industry-wide regulations to restrict advertising aimed at children (CSPI 2005). This outcome looks like a clear example of industry using Congress as a veto point, but once again there was more to the story.

At the time, in 1980, this outcome was widely understood not as a veto of the majority will but as a rescue of the nation's freedoms from an overreaching FTC. The *Washington Post*, hardly a pro-industry newspaper, editorialized that the FTC staff proposal had been "a preposterous intervention that would turn the FTC into a great national nanny" (*Washington Post* 1978). Simply on logical grounds the 1980 outcome was hard to depict as a minority industry veto, since it took the form of an affirmative and fully bipartisan legislative step voted by a majority in both houses of Congress. The House and Senate were both under Democratic control at the time, and a Democratic President— Jimmy Carter—signed the measure into law.

The 1978 FTC staff proposal might have seemed like balanced rule-making in Europe, but it was out of step with America's very different cultural and legal traditions. Two years earlier, in an important 1976 legal decision, *Virginia State Board of Pharmacy,* the Supreme Court had granted commercial advertising free speech protections under the First Amendment. Writing for the Court, Justice Blackmun stated the reasons:

> So long as we preserve a predominantly free enterprise economy, the allocation of our resources in large measure will be made through numerous private economic decisions. It is a matter of public interest that those decisions, in the aggregate, be intelligent and well informed. To this end the free flow of commercial information is indispensable. (*Virginia State Board of Pharmacy* 1975, at 765)

It is hard to imagine a European jurist extending this much privilege either to free enterprise or to the freedom of "commercial speech," strong evidence that cultural as well as institutional explanations lie behind America's distinct rejection of restrictions on advertising. European courts and the European Court of Justice have come to embrace a concept of protected commercial speech in the abstract, so there has been some convergence, yet in practice they repeatedly deny that protection by refusing to overrule legislated limitations on commercial advertising (Gassy-Wright 2005).

In 1980, the same year that Congress blocked FTC efforts to restrict advertising, the Supreme Court also laid out what remains a prevailing legal doctrine in America on protected commercial speech. In *Central Hudson Gas & Elec. Corp. v. Public Service Commission,* the Court said that advertising can of course be restricted if it promotes unlawful products, or is found to be false or misleading, but otherwise three difficult hurdles must be jumped before restrictions can be imposed. First, the restriction must satisfy a "substantial" governmental interest. Second, the restriction must advance that interest directly and materially, not just indirectly or speculatively. And third, the restriction must be "[no] more extensive than is necessary to serve that interest" (Redish 2011, p. 13). These *Central Hudson* tests have been relaxed in some cases, such as restrictions on commercial advertisement of legal casino gambling, but not for advertising food and drink. Despite the nation's childhood obesity crisis, then, any advertisement restriction violating *Central Hudson* will risk court nullification on constitutional grounds.

The Obama administration understood this constraint when it set up its White House Task Force on Childhood Obesity in 2009. When the Task Force issued its *Report to the President* in May 2010, it warned that "[any regulatory] efforts must carefully consider freedom of speech interests" (*White House Report* 2010, p. 31). Legally blocked from proposing direct regulations on advertisements, the Obama administration instead opted for voluntary guidelines, to be developed by a newly created Interagency Working Group on Food Marketed to Children.

Not even this weak approach worked. Private industry was strongly opposed, fearing that such guidelines would inevitably be used in a punitive way by the federal agencies that held regulatory jurisdiction over corporate behavior in other areas (Jaffe 2009). When the Working Group released its proposed "principles for food marketing" for comment in April 2011, private industry mobilized in opposition. The top lobbyist for the Grocery Manufacturers Association (GMA) branded the proposed federal guidelines a "dramatic overreach" (Gold and Hennessey 2013, p. 3). Roughly 30 different companies flooded Capitol Hill with lobbyists, spending a reported $37 million and securing from Congress a provision to prevent the Working Group from issuing its guidelines unless it first conducted a cost-benefit analysis, to determine how many food-industry and marketing-related jobs would be lost if the guidelines were followed. This measure effectively killed the guidelines (Nestle 2011; Gold and Hennessey

2013). This might look like an industry-choreographed veto, but it was hardly a narrow minority that prevailed, since the killing requirement was approved by a 329–91 floor vote in the House and a 62–30 floor vote in the Senate (ANA 2012).

Private industry has employed another tactic to preempt federal regulations on advertising food to children. Since 2006, more than a dozen private companies have promoted self-regulation as an alternative, through a Children's Food and Beverage Advertising Initiative (CFBAI). Health advocates have not been impressed with the CFBAI standards, since they allow for a continued marketing to children of Reese's Puffs and Cookie Crisp cereals, some Kool-Aid drink mixes, sugary "fruit" snacks like Fruit Roll-Ups, and other sweet and salty junk foods (CSPI 2011). Industry claims the CFBAI initiative has led to a decline in TV food and drink advertising to younger children ages 2–11, yet advertising both to adolescents and adults has actually increased. Between 2008 and 2010, children's and teens' exposure to sugary soda ads may have doubled, according to one study from the Harvard School of Public Health (Harvard School of Public Health 2013). Self-regulation by industry falls short in this case because real federal regulation cannot be threatened, thanks both to Congress and the Supreme Court.

Frustrated in the effort to constrain advertising of bad foods, the Obama administration next opted to seek voluntary corporate assistance in promoting healthy foods. In 2013 First Lady Michelle Obama began welcoming food industry representatives into the White House in hopes that their marketing skills could be enlisted to promote healthy eating, not only through her "Let's Move!" childhood obesity initiative, but also a new "Drink Up" initiative to promote water consumption, plus a veteran-focused "Joining Forces" initiative. Some of the same industry associations that just recently succeeded in defeating Obama's voluntary guidelines approach, including the American Beverage Association, the Grocery Manufacturers Association, and the National Restaurant Association, were now being treated like part of the team. They enjoyed hearing the First Lady praise their CFBAI initiative (the one that considered Kool-Aid healthy enough to advertise), and they took advantage of their new respectability to brag that the voluntary approach was actually better than government regulation. As the chief lobbyist for the Grocery Manufacturers Association claimed, "We are making progress that, to be quite honest, is faster than what government could accomplish" (Tau and Evich 2013).

The progress made has been hard to measure. The Federal Trade Commission did report that industry spending on food marketing to children declined in 2012, but it remained at $1.8 billion a year, and more of this spending was now going to Internet, tablet, and cell phone marketing, outlets that can be more effective with children because they are more interactive (Wootan 2012). In 2013, Yale's Rudd Center for Food Policy & Obesity released a study comparing advertising in 2013 to 2010, showing that children ages 6–11 did see 10 percent fewer TV ads for fast food. However, Spanish-language advertising to Hispanic preschoolers increased by 16 percent, and fast food marketing via social media and mobile devices, which are the media favored by teens, grew exponentially (Orciari 2013).

Federal School Lunch Policy

Blocked on soda taxes and advertising to children, the Obama administration turned to federal school lunch programs as the best venue for combating obesity. Action was easier to take here because schools are in the public sector, with lunch programs that are significantly dependent on federal funding. In addition, the consumers being pushed toward a reduced calorie intake would not yet be old enough to vote. Still, the reach of this approach would have limits, because even schoolchildren consume the vast majority of their calories outside school. School-age children in America consume twice as many empty calories (from added sugars or solid fats) through fast food restaurant or store purchases versus at school (Poti, Slining, and Popkin 2013). This would also be a more expensive policy approach; improved school lunch menus would cost local school districts more money, thus requiring more federal budget support.

In America, the federal government has played a major role supporting public school meals since 1936, originally as part of an effort to reduce Depression-era crop surpluses on the farm. To the present day, federal school meals programs operate within the Department of Agriculture. These programs, managed by the Food and Nutrition Service (FNS), provide free or reduced price meals to low-income children before school, during school, after school, and also over the summer, at a recent annual total cost of roughly $16 billion, which is paid to states through commodity donations and annual grants. Students are entitled to free lunches if their families' incomes are below 130 percent of a poverty-level income standard established by the Department of Health and Human Services. Students with slightly higher family incomes that are still below 185 percent of the poverty line become eligible for lunch at a reduced price, and other students can purchase slightly subsidized meals as well. From 1977 to 2012, participation in these popular meal programs increased from just over 5 million students to 32 million (New America Foundation 2013).

As these programs grew in size, the federal government began using them to pursue "wellness" objectives. Originally in 2004, Congress had legislated a requirement that participating districts establish, for all schools under their jurisdiction, a local school wellness policy (SWP). When the Healthy, Hunger-Free Kids Act was passed in 2010, Congress took this money-for-wellness approach a giant step further (USDA 2013d). Under this new Act, school food-service operators were required, beginning in 2012, to serve meals that conformed to a complex set of nutrition parameters, including caps on calories and sodium, reduced fat, and mandated portions of grains, fruits, vegetables, dairy, and meat, all based on weekly maximums and daily minimums. These new school lunch menu restrictions became an early centerpiece of First Lady Michelle Obama's "Let's Move!" campaign. Congress was under Democratic control in 2010, so the measure passed despite 153 House Republican votes in opposition. The added budget cost was expected to be $4.6 billion over 10 years, since an extra 6 cents per meal would have to be reimbursed to schools to cover the greater expense of meeting the new requirements.

Spending to give away food will always be an easier obesity-fighting strategy for American political leaders than imposing taxes or outright regulations. Even so, the Healthy, Hunger-Free Kids Act had to make its way through Congress partly by stealth. There was not a single committee hearing or committee vote in the House, and only a voice vote in the Senate (Henderson 2010). This reflected the political sensitivity in America of allowing anyone in the federal government to tell private citizens, even those receiving free government meals, what they should and should not eat. At the time the measure passed, a Rasmussen poll revealed that only 23 percent of Americans thought the federal government should have any direct role in setting nutritional standards for public schools (Rasmussen Reports 2013). Local control of schools is yet another distinctive American trait. The federal government in Washington did not even have a cabinet-level Department of Education until 1979, and many at that time opposed the move as an unnecessary and unconstitutional federal intrusion into local affairs. To the present day, American education is highly localized, lacking the national curriculum and testing systems typical of more centralized European systems. The resulting need to work through many autonomous local school districts complicated the menu reform problem.

Private industry also had concerns. The food and food service industries worried about the new law and expressed their concern to friends in Congress. As a consequence, Congress instructed the USDA at the rule-writing stage to adjust some of the new regulations to lessen the extent of the menu changes required. For example, tomato paste on pizza was allowed extra credit so it could continue to count as a serving of vegetables, and the proposed weekly limit on servings of starchy vegetables was dropped in deference to the potato lobby (Pear 2011). The new law did limit total calories, but because of food industry objections there was no specific cap on sugar (Yang Su 2013).

Despite these changes, the Healthy, Hunger-Free Kids Act has remained under sustained political attack. When the Government Accountability Office investigated the program in 2013, it documented problems with weak student acceptance. In one district, the elimination of some popular menu options such as cheeseburgers and peanut butter and jelly sandwiches led to a three-week student school lunch boycott. When meals became less appealing, some students stopped participating in the program (Brown 2013). Nationwide, according to the USDA, school lunch participation dropped by only 3 percent, yet in one New York school district, four months into the program the number of kids buying lunch dropped by half (Rokita 2013). When paying students refuse to participate, revenue losses can make the program financially unsustainable.

By 2014, one organization that had originally supported the reform, the School Nutrition Association (a so-called lunch ladies lobby, but one with ties to the food industry), had turned against it, after learning from internal surveys that schools were struggling with higher costs and lower participation. In May 2014, Republicans in the House of Representatives, with SNA support, promoted an appropriations measure to give schools operating at a net loss a temporary waiver from the new menu standards (Nixon 2014). First Lady Michelle Obama reacted with disbelief ("Why are we even having this conversation?") and attacked the lunch ladies by name (Confessore 2014). Despite White House veto threats, the House Appropriations Committee approved a temporary waiver, and the SNA amplified its own campaign by warning that the costs of meeting the new federal standards would likely triple in FY 2015.

The nutrition and calorie impacts of the new menu standards were hard to measure. In some cases, participating students did accept lunches with more fruits and vegetables, but then tossed these items away. One school in Florida that studied student behavior saw 321 of its 526 students throw away their mandatory portions of fruits and vegetables (Aguilera 2013). A 2014 study from the Harvard School of Public Health found that fruit selections by students did increase under the new standards, and consumption of selected vegetables increased as well, but 40 percent of selected fruits and 60–75 percent of selected vegetables were nonetheless discarded rather than consumed (Datz 2014).

One problem for schools had been staying under the meat and grain maximums without falling below the calorie minimums. Athletic coaches and student athletes complained that they were not getting enough energy at lunch to remain alert and active in the afternoon. As a result, halfway through the first year of implementation, the USDA increased the meat and grain limits (Brown 2013). In 2014, the USDA also allowed some schools to delay adding more whole grains to meals. Yet another problem was weak control in schools over the "competitive foods" sold through vending machines, school stores, and à la carte in the cafeteria. The USDA published a proposed rule for these foods which went into effect in 2014, but enforcement problems loomed as these items are typically sold in multiple locations and under no central authority (Brown 2013). The new menu rules will almost certainly bring improved nutrition, by increasing fruit and vegetable consumption while reducing sodium and saturated fat intake, but the final impact on obesity might be very small. One study of 19,450 students actually found no difference at all in obesity tendencies between those who went to schools where sweets and salty snacks were sold, versus those in schools where such items were not available (Van Hook and Altman 2012).

In America's public schools, the most under-utilized option in the fight against obesity is not diet but exercise. Calorie consumption among school children has actually been in decline for at least a decade, but physical activity levels have also been in decline. In February 2013, the CDC reported that in 2010, compared to a decade earlier, average daily calorie consumption for boys was already down 7 percent and for girls down 4 percent (Tavernise 2013). Weight was not lost, however, because according to the Obama administration's own Task Force Report on Childhood Obesity, "fewer than one in five high school students meet the current recommendations of 60 minutes of daily physical activity, and a recent study showed that adolescents now spend more than seven hours per day watching television, DVDs, movies or using a computer or mobile device like a cell phone or MP3 player" (White House Report 2010, p. 66). One obvious contributor to this problem had been the demise of high school physical education classes, where daily participation rates had fallen from 42 percent in 1991 to only 25 percent by 1995. Rates are now up slightly, but in 2011 they were still at only a 31 percent level. In that year, only 24 percent of 12th graders in America attended daily physical education classes (CDC 2013a). As of 2012, only 35 percent of all high school districts nationwide required any student testing for fitness (CDC 2013b).

First Lady Michelle Obama's "Let's Move!" initiative conspicuously stressed the importance of physical activity, but at no point did it seek to revive mandatory physical education in school. Her *Healthier US School Challenge* (HUSSC) plan demanded "rigorous standards," to see that schools provided physical activity *opportunities*, but without any actual requirements (Let's Move 2013). As a consequence, between 2007 and 2012, young Americans were moving around less, not more. According to a SFIA/Physical Activity Council survey, the share of inactive 6–12-year olds increased from 16 percent to 20 percent over this period, and the share of inactive 13–17-year olds rose from 17 percent to 19 percent.

Comparisons to Europe are instructive. Mandatory physical education remains a prominent feature of public education across the Continent. According to one comprehensive 2013 study by the EU Commission,

> The importance of physical education is emphasized in the curricula of all European countries, in which it is a mandatory subject throughout the whole of full-time compulsory general education. (European Commission 2013, p. 25)

To explain how mandatory physical education could decline so far in the United States while remaining a pervasive feature of public schooling in Europe, we will once again have to look beyond the distinctiveness of America's political institutions.

Summarizing, in 2009–2010 no new taxes or significant new federal regulations were brought to bear on the nation's obesity crisis, despite a conspicuous decision by a popular First Lady to adopt this as her personal cause. President Obama never formally proposed a soda tax as a means to help fund healthcare reform because he anticipated no support, even from prominent congressional Democrats. Obama's FTC proposed "voluntary" federal guidelines for advertising food and drink to children, but Democrats in Congress voted alongside Republicans to condition these guidelines on a job loss impact assessment, which killed the idea. Congress did enact, and the Department of Agriculture did successfully promulgate, new menu requirements for public schools taking federal funding, but these requirements were weakened by lenient rule-making, subsequent rule adjustments, incomplete student acceptance, and affordability problems for some schools. Opponents remained determined to gut the program by legislating waivers. Meanwhile, the option of reviving mandatory physical education in schools was never seriously pursued.

These weak federal policy responses to the obesity crisis can be attributed in part to America's distinct political institutions, which gave multiple veto points to private industry and to others opposing strong action. Yet the existence of such veto points did not explain the failure of the federal soda tax proposal, since no prominent political leader in Washington, D.C. had ever proposed such a tax in the first place. The existence of veto points does help to explain blockage of the FTC's "voluntary" advertising guidelines, since Congress killed the guidelines following a high pressure lobby campaign by private industry, and since threats of court review were one reason the ill-fated guidelines had only been made "voluntary" in the first place. In the case of school lunch menu reform, America's highly localized system of public education, plus lobby efforts in Congress backed by private industry, again weakened the reform, yet America's distinctive institutions were only one reason for this weakness. A broad public aversion to any nutrition standards imposed by government also came into play.

Considering fuel and food together, America's unusual proclivity for excess can be traced, to some extent, to the nation's distinct political institutions. With fossil fuels, however, the multiple veto points provided by America's institutions were used with success because America's fossil fuel industries are unusually large (a result of natural endowments), and also because taxes on consumption are culturally unpopular in America. In the case of food calories, where natural resource endowments are less important, industry use of institutional veto points to block policy action was consistently prominent, but in most cases the policy actions blocked by private industry lacked broad popular support. Stronger government actions, in each case, were not what a majority of Americans seemed to want. Distinctive elements in America's political culture thus emerge as a final ingredient in the story.

CHAPTER 4

America's Unusual Culture

The United States has exceptional resource wealth, a distinct demographic endowment, and unique governing institutions, but it also embraces an unusual mix of cultural values. Compared to citizens in other rich countries, Americans tend to be more individualistic, less welcoming toward state authority, more trusting of free markets, and far more religious or moralistic. They are also more optimistic about using science and technology to improve their lives. Taken together, these cultural traits heighten the tendency for Americans to overconsume both food and fuel, and help frustrate public policy efforts to impose restraint.

Generalizations about national culture are easy to criticize, because strong cultural differences are of course found within nations as well as between. Within America, blue states differ measurably from red states, and within each of these blue or red states there will always be contrary enclaves of red or blue people. The goal here is to explain differences in national outcomes for obesity and per capita CO_2 emissions, so the measures of culture used will be national averages, drawn most often from cross-national surveys.

As another caveat, clear dividing lines are difficult to draw between America's distinct cultural values and its unusual political institutions. Like chickens and eggs, each of these two factors continuously spawns the other. For example, when political leaders in America created weak governing institutions because they mistrusted state authority, the result was an undependable state, which reinforced the culture of mistrust. Americans have been forced to rely more on themselves and on free markets, so when they have done well under these circumstances attractions to the market are reinforced. Values are also hard to separate from material circumstances. America's cultural optimism emerged in part from its fortunate geology and geography, as a nation rich in natural resources and protected by two oceans from most geopolitical danger.

Differences Between America and Europe

Both Europe and America have a political left and a political right, but Europe's political right can look almost left by American standards. As Mary Ann Glendon has written, ". . . [c]ontinental Europeans today, whether of the right or left, are much more likely than Americans to assume that governments have affirmative duties. . . . By contrast, it is almost obligatory for American politicians of both the right and the left to profess mistrust of government" (Glendon 1992, pp. 524–525). Continental Europe embraces social democracy, an ideology that welcomes extensive state regulation and government programs to increase economic equality and to "buffer citizens from the ups and downs of the economic cycle" (Murray 2013). America, by contrast, embraces an ideology of personal responsibility. Socialism is essentially unknown in America, just as libertarianism is essentially unknown in Europe.

The greater individualism of Americans can be measured. One comparative analysis of IBM employees in 39 countries found that on an index of individualism, the average score across all countries was 51, but in the United States the index score was 91. Evidence that cultural traits drove this outcome can be seen in the fact that Australia, Britain, and Canada were the next three countries on the list, all sharing a common Anglo-Protestant heritage with the United States (Hofstede 2001). The non-Protestant countries on the continent of Europe were well behind. America's individualism typically combines with a greater optimism about our ability to control events. Pew surveys have found that only 36 percent of Americans believe they have little control over their own fate, compared to 41 percent in Britain, 50 percent in Spain, 57 percent in France, and 72 percent in Germany (Pew 2011).

These American traits of individualism and self-confident optimism have long been celebrated, especially by other Americans. Ralph Waldo Emerson, whose motto was "trust thyself," wrote approvingly of individualism as a pathway to self-reliance (Richardson 1995, p. 300). Henry David Thoreau captured the national imagination by moving into an isolated cabin near Walden Pond. On both the right and left, American politicians are comfortable celebrating individual self-reliance. In a campaign address in 1932, Franklin D. Roosevelt described Jeffersonian individualism as "the great watchword of American life" (Roosevelt 1932). Roosevelt's opponent in that same election, Herbert Hoover, liked to champion what he called "rugged individualism" (Hoover 1928).

This value of individual self-reliance co-exists in America with an embrace of "equal opportunity," the nation's distinct brand of social egalitarianism. In contrast to Europeans, with their history of inherited nobility and a titled aristocracy, Americans find it easier to embrace an ideal of equal social worth. Former President Ronald Reagan gave concise expression to this ideal in a speech in 1992: ". . . (W)e are all equal in the eyes of God. But as Americans, that is not enough, we must be equal in the eyes of each other" (Reagan 1992). Reagan's words are doubly interesting because they also reference the greater attachment that Americans maintain toward religion. A 2007 Pew Attitudes Project developed an index of "religiosity," based on the answers to three questions: Do you believe faith in God is necessary for morality? Is religion very important in your life? Do you pray at least once a day? In answering these questions, Americans were 50 percent more religious than Israelis, roughly twice as religious as Canadians, and three times as religious as Western Europeans (Pew 2007). This greater religiosity leaves Americans more prone to see life as a contest between good and evil (Calabresi 2006). In fact, 69 percent of Americans recently claimed to believe in the Devil (Lipset 1996). This makes Americans less tolerant than Europeans of behaviors seen as "sinful" within the traditions of the Protestant church.

Religion notwithstanding, Americans are also more optimistic than Europeans about modern science. As reported by the National Science Foundation, 90 percent of Americans agree that "science and technology are making our lives healthier, easier, and more comfortable," while in the European Union only 66 percent, and in Japan only 73 percent, agree. When asked if "the benefits of scientific research have outweighed the harmful results," 69 percent of Americans say yes, while only 46 percent of Europeans, and 40 percent of Japanese, agree (NSF 2012). Americans are also more likely to believe that we "control our environment." Eighty-two percent of Americans say yes on this question, compared to 77 percent in the United Kingdom and 66 percent in Germany (Hampden-Turner and Trompenaars 1997). Americans believe less in government because they believe so much more in themselves, in their God, and in science.

The Origins of American Culture

The provenance of America's distinct culture is obvious enough. The nation's founders brought to the new land a unique English common law tradition that emphasized limits on government authority (Hannan 2013). The Church of England was also far less hierarchical than the continental Catholic alternative. North America, settled primarily by the English, developed a far more liberal and egalitarian culture than South America, settled by the Catholic monarchies of Portugal and Spain.

America's culture began as a transplant from England, but the colonials were a sufficient distance from the mother country to evolve their own separate and distinct traits. As Alexis de Tocqueville put it in the nineteenth century, "The American is the Englishman left to himself" (Tocqueville 2003). In the new land, communities emerged beyond the authority of the British Crown and the English Church; in fact the Puritans came to America specifically to escape both Crown and Church (Morgan 1967). They believed they were leaving a corrupted homeland to create a New Israel in a new promised land, a distinctly virtuous "City on a Hill," in the words of John Winthrop (Madsen 1998).

As enumerated in Thomas Jefferson's Declaration of Independence, the values that justified America's formal political separation from England were all individual rights against state authority: life, liberty, and the pursuit of happiness. Jefferson later claimed that this was little more than an expression of existing English tradition, yet the motive was to do a better job of honoring that tradition than England itself.

Less high-minded motives also inspired the break toward independence. Colonial Americans were looking west to a resource-rich frontier, one they did not wish to share with a tax-happy Parliament in London. America's independence was founded on an opposition to being taxed, and a unique cultural aversion to taxation persists to the present day, complete with "Tea Party" rallies featuring costumed patriots wearing colonial regalia and carrying muskets.

America's early valuation of individual self-reliance over state authority was then continuously reinforced for two centuries by the dominating presence of a western frontier. The frontier helped nurture Jefferson's vision that an ideal society might be one of independent yeomen farmers living in harmony, without a strong central state. He derived this notion from a theory of English history that imagined pristine (pre-Norman) Saxon tribes living in the forest without any rulers. Jefferson hoped some version of this ideal could now be reborn in the new lands of the American West (Ellis 1996). The importance of a western frontier in supporting America's distinct culture of individualism is most explicitly endorsed by historian Frederick Jackson Turner, who argued in 1893 that when settlers first came to America they arrived thinking like Europeans, but then learned on the frontier to act independently and rely on themselves. They did this from necessity because the frontier was significantly beyond the help of governmental authority. For Turner, the American trait of "dominant individualism" was based not on philosophy but physical necessity:

> American democracy was born of no theorist's dream; it was not carried in the Sarah Constant to Virginia, nor in the Mayflower to Plymouth. It came out of the American forest. . . . (Turner 1920, p. 293)

If Turner is correct, why don't other frontier societies have highly individualistic cultures? In fact, they do. Australia and Canada ranked second and fourth on Hofstede's 39-country individualism scale. Australians are slightly less individualistic than Americans, according to one account, because their frontier always had a more significant governmental presence, while frontier settlements in America were mostly initiated by individual hunters, trappers, prospectors, adventurers, and traders, or farmers moving west primarily on their own initiative (Huntington 2004).

America's distinct culture of individualism and its accompanying mistrust of governmental authority have long been noticed by visitors from Europe. Both Alexis de Tocqueville from France in the 1830s, and Lord James Bryce from England in the 1890s, commented on the exceptional protections given in America to citizen liberties, and the unusual legal limits placed on governmental power. Swedish sociologist Gunnar Myrdal, in 1944, described this mix of values as a distinct "American creed." Political sociologist Seymour Martin Lipset later elaborated in shorthand a summary of the five most important components of this creed: liberty (versus authority), egalitarianism (equality of opportunity—especially in education), individualism (versus collectivism), populism (versus elitism), and laissez-faire (versus socialism) (Lipset 1996).

Needless to say, these creedal values have never come close to being fully realized. America regularly denies a surprising number of its own citizens full liberty (for example, rates of incarceration are far higher than in any other rich country). Equality of opportunity is conspicuously missing as well, with only 52 percent of Black American males graduating from high school compared to nearly 78 percent for White males. As for populism, it is still trumped nearly everywhere by elitism, both on Wall Street and Main Street. Yet when Americans are confronted with such gaps between their ideals and reality, the instinct is not to abandon the ideal but instead to work to improve the reality. Historians have observed repeated cycles of "great awakenings" in American politics, which lead to concerted efforts to bring reality closer to the ideal. The original great awakening in the eighteenth century helped bring on the American Revolution itself; a second great awakening in the 1820s and 1830s led to the abolitionist movement and universal primary education; a third great awakening in the 1890s led to populist pressures for progressive social and political reform at the dawn of the twentieth century; and a fourth great awakening in the 1950s and 1960s led to the civil rights movement, the women's movement, and the gay rights movement (Huntington 2004).

America's Anglo-Protestant creedal values have even persisted despite repeated waves of immigration by both non–Anglos and non-Protestants. Self-selection is one reason. Many individuals are attracted to the United States because they already embrace key elements of the creed. They think like Americans even before they arrive. The rest quickly learn that their chance of being welcomed increases if they assimilate to the creed. If you want to realize the American Dream, it helps to be seen dreaming like an American.

Critics of the United States, and also of the American Dream, can easily point out the dark side of this individualistic, self-reliant culture. Sociologist Robert Bellah worried in 1985 that America's individualism had in fact "grown cancerous." He was writing during the Reagan years, halfway through a so-called decade of greed. Bellah said America's individualism "may be destroying those social integuments that de Tocqueville saw as moderating its more destructive potentialities. . . ." (Bellah et al. 1985, p. xlvii). Bellah later warned against a "national self-idolization" growing out of too many prideful recitations of the creed (Bellah 1991, p. 168).

On America's political right, prideful assertions of exceptionalism are indeed all too common. In 2010, former Republican vice presidential nominee Sarah Palin wrote a book titled *America by Heart: Reflections on Family, Faith, and the Flag*, featuring a chapter titled "America the Exceptional" (Palin 2010). In that same year, Mitt Romney wrote a book celebrating America's exceptionalism, titled *No Apology: The Case for America's Greatness* (Romney 2010). Not to be outdone, Newt Gingrich wrote a book in 2011 titled *A Nation Like No Other: Why American Exceptionalism Matters*. According to Gingrich, Americans should not hesitate to brag about their exceptional values; it isn't hubris, because it's all true (Gingrich 2011). Leaders on the left are far less comfortable with narratives of exceptionalism. When Barack Obama was asked early in his presidency if he believed in America's exceptionalism, he said, "I believe in American exceptionalism, just as I suspect the Brits believe in British exceptionalism, and the Greeks believe in Greek exceptionalism" (Shear 2011).

The continuing importance of American exceptionalism should be an empirical question. Scholars who approach the issue in this fashion find it to be important, but as a "double-edged sword" that brings harm as well as benefit. America's cultural mistrust for governmental authority helps explain why the nation has the highest crime rate in the developed world, and also the lowest level of voter participation (Lipset 1996). America's cult of individual self-reliance makes it difficult to restrict gun ownership, so murder rates in the United States are roughly three times as high as in Western Europe. America's moralism, which inspires policies to criminalize the use of recreational drugs, has left the nation with a per capita prison population five times as large as in Western Europe. America's worship of free markets creates enormous aggregate wealth, but it also tolerates vast and widening gaps in health, wealth, and education. America has rates of homelessness and child poverty many times higher than in other industrial countries. American exceptionalism also contributes to excess in the consumption of both food and fossil fuel.

American Culture and Taxes on Consumption

Culture shapes taxation patterns in America. Because Americans want a smaller state, they insist on lower levels of taxation overall, and because they have an egalitarian streak, they also resist taxes on consumption that would be regressive on the middle class and the poor. Table 4.1 shows that across all sectors and levels, total tax revenues in the United States (federal, state, and local) are smaller as a share of GDP than in any other wealthy country. The second column shows that taxes on consumption also make up an unusually small part of the smaller overall burden.

These extremely low taxes on consumption open a wide door to consumer excess. America has traditionally rejected high consumption taxes on populist grounds: such taxes tend to be

TABLE 4.1. Total Tax Revenue as Percent of GDP, and Taxes on Consumption as Percent of Total Tax Revenues, 2010

	Total Tax Revenue as % of GDP, 2010	Taxes on General Consumption as % of Total Taxation
USA	25%	8%
Australia	26%	14%
Canada	31%	14%
Japan	28%	10%
France	43%	17%
Germany	36%	20%
UK	35%	19%
All OECD	34%	21%

Source: OECD, *Revenue Statistics, 1965–2011.* Paris: OECD, 2012, Table A and Table 28

regressive on lower income citizens, who use a larger share of their income for consumables. It would be technically possible to design a non-regressive consumption tax or to use revenues from a mildly regressive consumption tax to replace revenues from the more regressive payroll taxes currently used to fund Social Security and Medicare, but America has not done this (Brooks 2012).

In the absence of significant consumption taxes, revenue collection in America is surprisingly progressive rather than regressive. Table 4.2 demonstrates that in 2005, compared to all of the other 23 rich countries at that time, America placed a significantly higher tax burden on its top 10 percent of income earners than any other nation.

Of course, one reason for this higher progressivity of revenue collection in America is the nation's much higher level of income inequality. The rich pay a higher percentage in part because they also earn a much higher percentage. Yet even when

TABLE 4.2. Share of Taxes of Highest Income Decile, 2005

Australia	36.8%
Canada	35.8%
France	28.0%
Germany	31.2%
Japan	28.5%
UK	38.6%
USA	45.1%
OECD-24	31.6%

Source: OECD, 2008. *Growing Unequal?* Table 4.5

the OECD corrects for this factor, the United States still collects a larger share of its taxes from high income groups than does any other rich country.

Low consumption taxes in America in part reflect an accident of timing. A number of states began using sales taxes to collect revenue early in the twentieth century, preempting the use of this instrument by the federal government. By the time Washington first considered the idea seriously—in 1941, as one possible way to help cover the looming costs of wartime mobilization—the risk of a competition between federal and state revenue instruments loomed as a problem. Regressivity was the larger deterrent, however. When President Franklin D. Roosevelt came out against a consumption tax in 1941, he said it "violates the ability to pay. It falls more heavily on the poor; it is, in fact, a 'spare-the-rich' tax" (Thorndike 1996, p. 3). These feelings persist to the present day. In 2010, Representative Paul Ryan (R-Wis) proposed an 8.5 percent VAT, but the Senate responded by adopting a nonbinding resolution by an overwhelming 85–13 vote, stating, "it is the sense of the Senate that the VAT is a massive tax increase that will cripple families on fixed income and only further push back America's economic recovery" (Avi-Yonah 2011, p. 1). Ryan responded by shelving the proposal.

Revenue collection is surprisingly progressive in America, but revenue expenditure is not. The large income inequalities generated by free markets in America are less likely to be offset by government programs because those programs are much smaller relative to GDP than in Europe, particularly in areas such as health and welfare. In this respect, the laissez-faire and small government dimensions of the American creed can trump the populist and egalitarian dimensions.

Culture and Climate Change Policy

Turning specifically to the weakness of America's climate change policies, cultural traits such as laissez-faire, populism, and opposition to government authority play critical roles. Surprisingly, America's greater faith in science and technology is also important. Just as surprisingly, America's greater individualism is less important.

Individualism

Frustrated policymakers sometimes blame America's weak climate change policies on the nation's culture of individualism. Ron Binz, President Barak Obama's nominee in 2013 to chair the Federal Energy Regulatory Commission (FECR), speaking in 2012, stressed the need for Americans to think in more collective terms about greenhouse gas emissions: "We have a bias toward individualism in this country which can work for great things, but it can also at times prevent us from doing societal things, and there's really no substitute for doing that right now" (Binz 2012). Yet Americans do "societal things" all the time, through churches, book clubs, and private charities, just not through the federal government. The cultural trait Binz should have focused on was opposition to taxation and government authority, not individualism as such.

Individualism is not even the reason Americans prefer large, energy-inefficient single family homes or private auto transport. These things are better explained by the nation's greater material wealth, its greater land area available for suburban sprawl, and its much lower energy prices. If Americans prefer suburban living for cultural reasons, it has to be a culture more of the family than the individual. More Americans do live alone today compared to the past, with 32 million living solo in 2012 compared to 27 million in 2000, yet most of these are urbanites, not suburbanites. Individualists seeking an escape from family obligations and neighborhood scrutiny will never be comfortable in the suburbs. The tug of the suburbs is stronger in America compared to Europe in part because the tug of marriage is stronger. International surveys reveal that Americans are more likely than most foreigners to put the institution of marriage ahead of individual happiness (ISSP 1991).

As for the Americans who do live solo in cities, this kind of individualism actually helps *reduce* CO_2 emissions. In densely populated New York City, where solos make up roughly half of all residential households, per capita greenhouse gas emissions are two-thirds below the average for the nation as a whole (World Bank 2011). This is because the dwellings are smaller and are joined rather than separated, and because many urban individualists do not drive cars at all. The nation's most committed solo drivers are not urban individualists but family-oriented suburban commuters. Nor is individualism the reason these suburbanites fail to carpool; the most powerful reasons instead are convenience, plenty of parking, and easily affordable gasoline (Baldassare, Ryan, and Katz 1998).

America's private auto culture has begun to weaken in any case. Younger Americans today are driving less than their parents did, with fewer bothering even to get a license (Schwartz 2013). Miles of driving in the United States peaked in 2007 at 3 trillion, and began what is now the longest measured decline since the Second World War (Dezember and Glazer 2013).

Some hope this will presage a cultural shift in America away from suburban dwelling as well. In 2013, journalist Leigh Gallagher predicted "the end of suburbs" in America, due to changes in family structures, more costly oil, and a renaissance of urban living among younger people (Gallagher 2013). In that same year, however, 14 of the nation's 20 largest cities saw their growth slow or their populations fall outright compared to the year before (Shah 2014). More than half of all Americans live in the suburbs today, and four out of five home buyers are still seeking detached single-family houses (Klotkin 2013).

Resistance to Government Authority

A more powerful cultural reason for excess fossil fuel consumption in America is social resistance to centralized government authority. Culturally, Americans are far less comfortable than citizens in other rich countries with the intrusive governmental mandates, taxes, or regulations needed to reduce greenhouse gas emissions. Most Americans are not hostile to receiving benefits from the government, which is why a substantial welfare state has actually emerged in the United States since the late twentieth century (Novak 2008). Yet Americans retain their distinct disapproval of governmental efforts to coerce a change in personal consumption behavior. In November 2011, a Pew Global Attitudes survey asked Americans and Europeans which was more important: "freedom to pursue life's goals without state interference," or "state guarantees that nobody is in need." In America, 58 percent opted for freedom, and only 35 percent opted for state guarantees. In Britain, the preference was roughly reversed: 38 percent opted for freedom, while 55 percent opted for state guarantees. On the Continent, the divergence from America was even more extreme. In Germany, France, and Spain, 62 percent opted for state guarantees over freedom (Pew 2011).

Americans tolerate nominal consumption taxes as a device to raise public revenue, but only at the state level, where the revenues will be spent locally. They are also willing to accept taxes on behaviors traditionally considered to be "sinful" such as smoking and drinking, which many Americans abstain from in any case. But taxes to coerce less consumption of either energy or food are typically off the table. President Clinton's Btu tax proposal in 1993 failed in part due to industry objections, but the measure was also unpopular with a wide range of ordinary Americans. Recall that in February 1993, before private industry had launched its campaign against the Btu tax idea, a Yankelovich survey found that only 23 percent of Americans favored new taxes on energy (Kempton, Boster, and Hartley 1995). When Democrats in Congress took a second run at coercing reduced fossil fuel consumption in 2009, they tried to hide their intent behind the "market-oriented" aspects of a cap-and-trade system, yet support evaporated as soon as consumers noticed that the measure would increase energy prices. The more information Americans got about cap-and-trade, the less they liked it (Blumenthal 2009).

Congress knew all along that cap-and-trade would be politically toxic if it came to be seen as driving up energy costs for middle-class Americans. In an attempt to cover itself against this risk, the Senate in April 2009 voted 65–33 for an amendment preempting consideration of any measure that would raise energy costs in any way for Americans with $200,000 or less in adjusted gross income. With this measure the Senate was implicitly ruling out cap-and-trade, yet not a single senator spoke against it, and even 18 Democrats voted in favor (OTI 2009). This was not a vote rejecting the reality of climate change, but it was a vote rejecting any policy response that might limit the freedom of Americans to pursue life's goals without coercive state interference.

While a small increase in energy costs can be unacceptable to Americans if it comes from government action, substantial increases are routinely tolerated so long as they appear to come from the free market. Between 2004 and 2008, gasoline prices at the pump doubled; Americans grumbled, but most accepted the pain as a market outcome. In laissez-faire America, harm that appears to come from the market can be seen as fair, but if imposed by the government it becomes unjust and intolerable.

Laissez-faire

Americans are far more comfortable with a corporate-led economy compared to Europeans. Socialist parties in Europe attract strong voter support and lead or enter government coalitions on a regular basis, while in America socialism scarcely exists at all. America's early history as a settler colony lacking an entrenched and hereditary ruling class is one explanation. As political scientist Walter Dean Burnham said, "no feudalism, no socialism" (Burnham 1974, p. 718). Friedrich Engels observed in 1890 that Americans are born conservatives, ". . . because America is so purely bourgeois, so entirely without a feudal past and therefore proud of its purely bourgeois organization" (Engels 1890, p. 467).

In both Europe and Japan, wealth and status traditionally derived not from success in private business but from land inheritance within a titled nobility, or from military and administrative appointments offered by church or state. In such societies, individuals from the profit-making business class were often looked down on as vulgar or even immoral (Lipset 1996). Not so in America, where those who create profit-making business firms are celebrated as visionaries and are even given special thanks for "creating jobs." In America, governmental interference with the private sector has always been seen as just that—interference. In Thomas Jefferson's first inaugural address in 1801, he declared, "A wise and frugal government, which shall restrain men from injuring one another, shall leave them otherwise free to regulate their own pursuits of industry and improvement, and shall not take from the mouth of labor the bread it has earned. This is the sum of good government" (Jefferson 1801).

Deference to business firms and free markets remains to the present day a distinctly American cultural trait. Even at the depths of an economic recession in March 2009, nearly 70 percent of Americans responded to a Pew survey by agreeing that "people are better off in a free-market economy, even though there may be severe ups and downs from time to time." In 2010, 37 percent of Americans agreed "strongly" with the view that a free market economy was the best system, compared to only 19 percent in the United Kingdom, 6 percent in France, and just 2 percent in Japan (Globespan 2011).

These cultural differences help to explain why private business firms have always been given greater space in America to control the extraction, refining, and marketing of fossil fuels. In wartime the government can ration or redirect fuel resources, but not in peacetime. Things are dramatically different in Europe. Following the Second World War, state-owned enterprise accounted for a significant fraction of all economic activity in countries such as the United Kingdom, Germany, France, Austria, Portugal, and Sweden, and this included the petroleum sector. As late as the mid-1970s, Norway and Britain were creating new government energy companies (Statoil and BNOC, respectively) to handle North Sea oil. A wave of privatizations eventually eliminated outright public ownership for most European oil corporations (the United Kingdom went first, privatizing BP in 1977), but oil companies in Europe nonetheless enjoy far less autonomy than oil companies in the United States (Bortolotti and Milella 2006).

Populism

A populist element within America's culture also helps block strong action against climate change. In America, where even poor people drive automobiles, taxes on fossil fuels are seen as regressive and thus objectionable on cultural grounds (Sterner 2011). Regressivity also became a significant political problem for cap-and-trade. By one calculation, the 2009 Waxman-Markey cap-and-trade bill would have imposed a cost burden (relative to income) four times greater on poor American households in the bottom income quintile versus well-to-do households in the highest income quintile. This became a constant embarrassment to Democratic supporters of the idea (Grainger and Kolstad 2009). In March 2009, Berkshire Hathaway CEO Warren Buffett (an early supporter of Barack Obama) criticized cap-and-trade as "pretty regressive," and the White House was never able to deny this troublesome aspect of the plan. Asked about Buffett's remark, Obama's press secretary Robert Gibbs could only say the president looked forward to "working with Congress to put a solution together" (Galbraith 2009). Giving up on cap-and-trade proved to be the solution.

Technically, there were other options. A cap-and-trade measure could have been based on the sale or auction of the emissions permits, creating a new revenue stream, and some of the revenue could then have been used to extend tax breaks to citizens in the middle and bottom ends of the income spectrum. Yet this approach would have made cap-and-trade look even more plainly like a new tax, violating another cultural taboo. Advocates for cap-and-trade originally did hope to sell or auction the permits, but this part of the plan had to be dropped by the sponsors of the bill early in 2009 to get the measure through the House of Representatives (Viard 2009).

Climate science denial, which is a rejection by ordinary Americans of an elite scientific consensus, may also have a populist component. According to Gallup Poll results in 2007–2008, only 49 percent of Americans at that time believed that climate change was caused by human activity, compared to 59 percent of Germans, 63 percent of French, 65 percent of Italians, 71 percent of Spaniards, and 91 percent of Japanese (Pelham 2009). Climate science denial actually increased in America between 2006 and 2009, when the percentage who believed the earth was warming "because of human activity" declined from 47 percent to 36 percent (Pew 2009). Yet America's populism must be weighed here against its traditionally strong faith in science and technology. In America, scientists have prestige ratings comparable to nurses, doctors, firefighters, and teachers, and they rank ahead of military and police officers (NSF 2012). In some ways, Americans are more trusting of science than Europeans. As David G. Victor has pointed out, 58 percent of Europeans say scientists cannot be trusted to tell the truth because they depend on industry for money, and more than half of Europeans think scientists gain power from their knowledge that is dangerous (Victor 2014).

Religiosity

America's greater religiosity is a stronger cultural source of climate science denial than populism. The same religious groups that work to promote creationism in public school curricula in America also work to discredit climate science. A so-called Cornwall Alliance for the Stewardship of Creation, a coalition of more than 1,500 conservative individuals and religious clergy, was formed in 2005 to promote "An Evangelical Declaration on Global Warming," stating that the Earth and its ecosystems, "created by God's intelligent design and infinite power," are resilient and self-regulating, and that "recent global warming is one of many natural cycles of warming and cooling in geologic history" (Cornwall Alliance 2013). Acting on these beliefs, a Seattle-based creationist think tank, the Discovery Institute, co-authored a Louisiana Science Education Act, which opened the classroom door to climate science denial (Stewart 2012). Yet the religious spectrum is broad in America, so liberal churches simultaneously espouse stronger measures against climate change, as one means to preserve God's creation and protect the poor. The Interfaith Climate Change Network, a collaborative effort between the National Council of Churches and the Coalition on the Environment and Jewish Life, follows precisely this approach.

The strongest source of climate science denial in America is not culture at all, but a disinformation campaign financed by the fossil fuel industry, based on a hope that if the science can be challenged, new taxes and regulations will be avoided. Denialists tend to be disproportionately White, male, and conservative, which normally describes an elite, pro-science demographic, not a populist demographic (NSF 2012). Fossil fuel industries use conservative think tanks and Republican politicians to promote contrarian studies that sow seeds of doubt regarding climate science (McCright and Dunlap 2011). One report by the Union of Concerned Scientists found that Exxon-Mobil alone spent roughly $16 million between 1998 and 2005 on a campaign to sow doubts about the reality of climate change (Kolmes 2011). What makes Europe and Japan different on this issue is not less religion or less cultural populism, but the absence of a powerful domestic fossil fuel industry with both means and motive to spread such disinformation.

Faith in Science and Technology

While many Americans say they reject the science of human-induced climate change, they are far more inclined than Europeans to trust that science and technology will provide a response, a factor that lowers America's climate anxieties. In the spring of 2013, the Pew Research Center surveyed respondents in 39 different countries, to learn their views on a variety of "global threats." In this survey, only 40 percent of Americans considered climate change a "threat," compared to 54 percent of Canadians and Europeans, 56 percent in Asia and the Pacific, and 65 percent in Latin America (Pew 2013b). This lower sense of threat reflects greater confidence among Americans that a scientific or technical workaround will become available, should the crisis ever become severe.

One example is seen in America's greater faith in unproven technologies, such as the carbon capture and storage (CCS) techniques being developed to capture and liquefy carbon from burning coal, then pump it deep underground. In Germany, the introduction of such CCS systems met massive social and political resistance, so in 2013 the idea was essentially scrapped (Rueter 2013). In the United States, the idea remains alive thanks in part to $3 billion worth of federal assistance contained in the 2009 economic stimulus package, plus considerable private sector enthusiasm. In 2014, in Mississippi, the Southern Company was building the world's first new power plant to employ an "integrated gasification combined cycle" that captures and stores most of its own carbon. The Southern Company had been willing to sustain a $1.1 billion loss to shareholders in order to push this unproven project forward (Kunzig 2014). America's optimism that a new technology can be found to burn coal cleanly undercuts its inclination to discipline coal consumption.

A more extreme example of America's technological optimism is its growing interest in "climate engineering." Rather than reducing or capturing greenhouse gas emissions, engineers might slow warming trends at a lower cost by injecting sunlight-reflecting aerosols into the stratosphere, a technique known as solar radiation management, or SRM. This possibly dangerous approach enjoys growing support from America's political right, most prominently from the American Enterprise Institute (AEI 2013).

In sum, America's distinct culture has contributed to the nation's excessive consumption of fossil fuels in multiple ways. Individualism, anti-science populism, and religiosity are not the most important factors, however. More important is America's trust in private markets, its faith in innovative new technologies, and its opposition to coercive governmental actions that might raise energy costs for the middle class.

Culture and Overeating

When considering the cultural sources of excessive food consumption in America, individualism does become the most useful place to start. Americans are the most individualistic people in the industrial world, followed in order by people from Australia, Britain, and Canada. All of these highly individualistic Anglo-Protestant countries experience an obesity prevalence well above the OECD average. The OECD average is 17.8 percent, but the average for Canada in 2010 was 24.2 percent, for Australia 24.6 percent, for Great Britain 26.1 percent, and for the United States 35.9 percent (OECD 2013b). Individualism leads to eating behaviors less disciplined by social or family routines. Once modernity makes food ubiquitous and continuously available, unstructured eating and in some cases nearly continuous eating becomes a problem in individualistic societies. Eating in America today is driven by highly individualized and personalized psychological inclinations (Oliver 2006). Americans eat alone while at work, alone while commuting to work in the car, alone at the food court while shopping, alone at home while watching TV, and alone in front of the refrigerator both before and after normal mealtime. Eating while driving is also a distinctly American habit. A remarkable 17 percent of all meals ordered at restaurants in America are now eaten in cars (Nassauer 2012). Fast food restaurants sell fried chicken in containers custom-designed to fit automobile cupholders, and auto steering wheels now mount snacking trays.

Regularly scheduled at-home family meals are of diminished importance in America. Only 66 percent of 15-year-olds in America eat the main meal of the day together with their parents "several times a week," which ranks the United States 23rd out of 25 industrial countries on this scale. Once again, the other four Anglo-Protestant countries cluster at the bottom along with the United States, ranking 18, 19, 22, and 24. By contrast, in France and Italy more than 90 percent of 15-year-olds still report family meals at least several times a week. The demise of family meals has also diminished the eating of healthy foods. Americans today eat salad with a meal on average only about 36 times a year, which is 20 percent less often than in 1985 (Nassauer 2011). A decline in family meals has also been linked to increased substance abuse, slower language development, and reduced academic achievement (Fiese and Schwartz 2008).

Eating away from home is now more common for every American income group. Among low-income Americans, the share of food calories consumed away from home has increased from 5 percent to 28 percent since the 1960s; among middle-income Americans from 8 percent to 31; and among high-income Americans from 12 percent to 35 percent. More eating away from home coincides with higher calorie intake. Between 1965–1966 and 2007–2008, overall daily energy intake increased in America by 152 food calories per day for low-income groups, 110 calories a day for middle-income groups, and 118 calories a day for high-income groups (Smith, Ng, and Popkin 2013). Among those adults in America who eat fewer breakfasts or dinners at home, obesity is more prevalent (Ma et al. 2003). Americans also eat their food quickly, averaging just 12 minutes for breakfast, 28 minutes for lunch, and 24 minutes for dinner, according to the research firm NPD Group, Inc.

Unstructured eating takes over in America in part because disciplines have also weakened in other areas. Teenagers in the United States are now permitted to spend 40–50 percent of all their waking hours engaged in "discretionary behavior," compared to 35–40 percent in Europe and only 25–35 percent in Japan (Larson 2001). Because food is so abundantly available, some of this discretionary behavior includes eating between meals.

More Egalitarian Gender Relations in America

The reduced frequency of structured home meals in America is in part a result of increased female participation in the paid workforce. Between 1950 and 1999, the percent of married women who participated in the workforce in America increased from 24.2 percent to 74.4 percent, thus diminishing the full-time availability of at least one parent in the home to prepare meals (Costa and Kahn 2001). As a result, between

1965–1966 and 2007–2008, the proportion of American women who cooked declined from 92 percent to 68 percent, and among those who did cook, the time devoted to meal preparation declined from 112.8 minutes a day to 65.6 minutes a day (Smith, Ng, and Popkin 2013). These declines were partly offset by the greater time men spent cooking, but as of 2008, only 42 percent of men cooked, and these men averaged only 45 minutes a day in meal preparation.

The absence of a parent in the home also means less discipline over the snacking urges of children, and fewer opportunities to supervise active outdoor play. Economists have calculated that in a child's lifetime, each 10-hour increase in average weekly hours worked by the mother will increase the probability that the child is obese by about 1 percentage point (Anderson, Butcher, and Levine 2003). Another study finds that for each additional five-month period of a mother's employment, a child of average height can be expected to gain one extra pound over and above normal growth. Sixth graders with working mothers are six times more likely to be overweight than those with stay-at-home moms (Morrissey et al. 2011).

America led the post–World War II international women's movement in part because this cause resonated so strongly with the nation's belief in equal opportunity. The other Anglo-Protestant countries, the United Kingdom, Canada, Australia, and New Zealand, were also more progressive in creating equal opportunities for women to enter the paid workforce. What makes America different today, however, is not female employment outside the home so much as a lack of social services from the state to support working women. Female labor force participation in the United States in 2009, for women aged 25–64, was actually lower than in Slovenia, Germany, the United Kingdom, Australia, Austria, New Zealand, Finland, Canada, Sweden Netherlands, Denmark, Switzerland, Norway, and Iceland (OECD 2011a). Yet in these other countries, maternal employment was less likely to result in unstructured eating because of stronger government support for things like childcare (Jaumotte 2003). When maternal employment is supported with more generous state-funded day-care facilities, the result is not higher obesity prevalence. More important than the employment of the mother can be the absence of a father. The percent of households in America headed by a single parent has tripled since 1960; married couples now make up less than half of all households. The United States ranks last on a 27-nation OECD scale when it comes to the percentage of children living with two married or cohabiting parents. Only 71 percent of children in America have two married or cohabiting parents, compared to an 84 percent average for the OECD as a whole (OECD 2011a). This can be significant, since single-parent preschoolers in America have an obesity rate of 21.5 percent, versus 17.6 percent for two-parent preschoolers (Anderson and Whitaker 2010). When counting overweight as well as obese children, those from single-parent households have a 41 percent prevalence rate versus just 31 percent from dual parent households (Huffman et al. 2010). Calorie intake is higher and vegetable consumption lower among children from single-parent families, versus children from two-parent families (Rasmussen et al. 2006).

Can this lower prevalence of two-parent homes in America be linked to the nation's culture of individualism? Since other Anglo-Protestant countries are clustered with the United States at the bottom of OECD rankings for this trait, a link is plausible. Yet the highest rates of single-parent homes in the United States are found not among supposedly individualistic white Anglo-Protestants, but instead among African Americans. This takes us back to the contribution that race and race relations have made to America's higher rates of obesity.

Racial Minorities and Obesity in America

In an earlier chapter we observed that disadvantaged racial minorities in America have a higher obesity prevalence than White

Americans, consequently pushing up the national average. This effect is largely absent in Europe and Japan because the disadvantaged minority populations in these countries are so much smaller. We must now ask if there is something beyond social disadvantage linked to the race prejudice of Whites that contributes to this effect. One reason to suspect so is the significant difference in obesity prevalence between men and women within minority communities, as seen in Table 4.3.

These data show that among men in the United States, there has never been more than a small difference in obesity prevalence between Whites, Blacks, and Mexican Americans. Among women, however, the differences have always been pronounced. If high obesity among minorities derives from social disadvantage, we must seek to understand why minority women experience more of this disadvantage than minority men. Alternatively, we must seek an explanation less closely tied to race prejudice and disadvantage.

There is no single agreed-upon explanation for high rates of obesity among African American women compared to White

TABLE 4.3. Prevalence of Obesity among US Adults Age 20 and Over

Men	1988–1994	2009–2010
Non-Hispanic White	20.3	36.2
Non-Hispanic Black	21.1	38.8
Mexican American	23.9	36.6
Women		
Non-Hispanic White	22.9	32.2
Non-Hispanic Black	38.4	58.5
Mexican American	35.4	44.9

Note: Based on NHANES, which includes a household interview and physical examination for each survey participant.

Source: Fryar, Carroll, and Ogden 2012, Table 3

women. Some argue that cultural differences have reduced the intensity of weight-loss motivation among African American women, while they increase that intensity among White women (Baturka et al. 2000). Psychologists can present evidence suggesting that overweight Black women tend to be less susceptible to a thin body ideal than overweight White women (Chithambo and Huey 2013). In addition, public health officials point to differential frequencies of breastfeeding, to differentials in numbers of children, and to differentials in average age at first pregnancy (Friday 2012). Even genetic factors have not been ruled out (Kumanyika 1987).

Among African American women who are single parents, however, social and economic disadvantage is an unavoidable explanation. Single-parent African American families headed by females earn only 36 percent as much as two-parent black families, a shocking level of poverty that is typically accompanied by poor health and low education (Mather 2010). These women lack the money, the knowledge, and frequently also the time needed to feed themselves and their children properly. For these single parents, time can be as large a factor as dollar costs. A 2010 study of low-income single parents in the journal *Family Medicine* compared the dollar cost per calorie of meeting national dietary guidelines with whole foods from local supermarkets versus "convenient" foods from fast-food outlets. Dollar costs per calorie for the healthy diet were actually lower than for the convenience diet, but time costs of healthy eating were much higher (McDermott et al. 2010).

Even if we knew exactly why minority women in America are more prone to obesity, it would be hard for political leaders to act on that knowledge. So delicate is this issue, there may be no political space to take any targeted actions at all. If White Americans begin to design government initiatives that appear to target obesity prevalence among minority women, this will be rejected, and possibly for good reason, as yet another round of White racism.

Laissez-faire and Personal Responsibility

Most Americans view health as a personal or a family responsibility, not a state responsibility. This explains why the public share of medical services spending in the United States in 2011 was just 50 percent, compared to an average of 78 percent for the OECD countries together (OECD 2013c). Because the American state carries this smaller share of health cost burdens, it is less motivated to take the policy measures—such as taxes imposed on sugary soda—that might lighten those burdens. Children in America who become obese incur 47 percent more medical costs over a lifetime on average, compared to children of normal weight, but this does not trigger a strong policy response because the state pays only part of the cost (Finkelstein et al. 2014).

Food and beverage companies in America invoke personal responsibility as their strongest message when resisting health-targeted taxes and regulations. Claiming to speak for personal freedom versus government authority, the industry depicts anti-obesity policy measures as actions of a "food police" or a "nanny state" (Kwan and Graves 2013). In 1996, a group of food companies and restaurant chains formed a nonprofit organization named the Center for Consumer Freedom (CCF), which made "protecting personal responsibility" its motto. If young children are not old enough to make good decisions, "parental" responsibility becomes the fall-back. According to CCF, health campaigners calling for taxes on soda and junk food are "eroding our basic freedoms—the freedom to buy what we want, eat what we want, drink what we want, and raise our children as we see fit" (CCF 2014).

This framing of the issue is acceptable to a majority of Americans. A Harris Interactive/HealthDay poll released in April 2013 revealed that 57 percent of adults in the United States opposed taxes on sugary drinks and candy, while only 22 percent were in favor. Humphrey Taylor, chairman of the Harris Poll, characterized this specific result as "a strong vote against the nanny state" (Norton 2013). The dominance of personal responsibility thinking in America can also be seen in the $61.6 billion that individual Americans spend every year on diet pills, diet books, dietary supplements, diet websites, meal replacement programs, and commercial weight loss centers, even when such measures seldom bring lasting results. In 2012, 108 million Americans reported that they were on a diet. People on serious diets typically lose 5 to 10 percent of their starting weight in the first six months, but then the backsliding begins. Within four or five years, one-third to two-thirds of these dieters actually regain more weight than they originally lost (Mann 2007).

Populism

The food and beverage industry also protects itself from anti-obesity taxes and regulations by invoking populist values, reminding voters that taxes on junk food and soda will be regressive on the poor. In 2010, the American Beverage Association asserted that a tax on common grocery items like beverages would be "regressive, and disproportionately hurt the most those who can least afford it" (ABA 2010). Concerns over populist equity have been enough to turn even some strong anti-obesity campaigners away from championing soda taxes. Adam Drewnowski, director of the Center for Public Health Nutrition at the University of Washington, believes that taxing soda would be unfair because soda consumption in America is correlated with poverty. He has said it would be callous for wealthy Americans who do not drink soda to impose taxes on poor Americans who do (Drewnowski 2009).

If restrictions on soda or junk food consumption are proposed in the United States, accusations of both elitism and racism frequently get in the way. When Mayor Bloomberg attempted to ban large sugary drink sales, dozens of Hispanic and African American civil rights groups joined in opposition.

When the Bay Area city of Richmond, California, attempted to put a 1-cent-per-ounce tax on sugar-sweetened beverages, the Richmond chapter of the NAACP argued that the proposal was paternalistic and that lawmakers had failed to consult with their community before sending the ballot issue to voters. When the measure eventually did reach the voters, they rejected it. A former Richmond councilman who led efforts for the tax, a retired cardiologist, said later, "They claimed it was racist—that here I was, a white doctor, trying to impose a regressive tax on black people. Even though we had data showing it would improve the health of African-American children, it was hard to get that message out" (Confessore 2013).

Religiosity

Unexpectedly, even America's culture of greater religiosity may contribute to its obesity problems, although the evidence can be mixed and sometimes ambiguous. One Northwestern University study tracked 2,433 young men and women for 18 years and found that those who attended church or a Bible study group once a week were 50 percent more likely to become obese by middle age. This study controlled for differences in race, sex, education, income, and baseline BMI (Paul 2011). In another study, conservative Protestant males were found to be approximately five pounds heavier, compared to men who reported no religious preference, even after controlling for demographics, health behaviors, social support, and stress (Kim, Sobal, and Wethington 2003). In this study, however, much of the relationship between religion and obesity was described as the result of lower smoking rates among religious persons. An earlier 2006 study examined religious affiliation plus four different dimensions of religiosity (attendance, salience, media practice, and consolation). This study found that high levels of religious media practice and affiliation with the Baptist denomination increased the risk of obesity for women, yet attendance at actual religious services was associated with a lower incidence of obesity (Cline and Ferraro 2006).

According to data gathered in 1994, when America's obesity crisis was still at an early stage, differences in religious affiliation led to dramatic differences in obesity prevalence. At that time, obesity prevalence among Baptists was 30 percent, compared to 22 percent for fundamentalist Protestants, 17 percent for Catholics, 7 percent for those with no religion, and just 1 percent for Jews (Cline and Ferraro 2006). Supplementary analyses pointed to education and race as being key to such outcomes, as less educated citizens and African Americans tended to be more heavily affiliated with Baptist or fundamentalist religious groups.

Historically, Protestant traditions have sought to discipline personal behavior regarding tobacco, alcohol, gambling, sexual activity outside marriage, dancing, card playing, and even theater-going, but not food. In the American church today, where celebrations of good works and fellowship are too often accompanied by excess consumption of highly caloric pot-luck style foods, religious leaders are now waking up to the problem. The National Baptist Convention, which represents nearly 10,000 churches, has begun encouraging "no fry zones" in church kitchens (Robertson 2011). Megachurch pastor Rick Warren, at one point nearly a 300-pounder himself, published a diet book in 2013 titled *The Daniel Plan,* named for the biblical prophet who challenged himself to eat only vegetables. Warren asked followers to join him in using this plan to drop weight, and 15,000 signed up (Wolfe 2014).

America's Protestant heritage does strongly support a range of government actions to constrain the consumption of things considered sinful by the church. A constitutional amendment was briefly used early in the twentieth century to attempt a ban on the sale of alcohol, and high "sin taxes" continue to be imposed on tobacco. Recreational drug use and illicit gambling also encounter stiff criminal penalties in America, along with prostitution. If backed up by Protestant rectitude, the government in

America can take strong action. In the case of cigarette smoking, TV ads were banned, sales taxes were increased, warning labels were required on packages, and then local bans were placed on smoking in public places. Finally, punitive lawsuits were brought against tobacco companies. As a result, smoking rates among adults fell from 42 percent in 1965 to 20 percent today. Similar actions are unlikely to be taken against junk food and caloric soda in America, absent a touchstone within the Protestant faith tradition.

America's campaign against cigarette smoking was a major public health achievement, yet it did have the unintended effect of worsening the nation's obesity crisis. Persons who quit smoking typically gain weight as a result, an average 4.4 kilograms for males and 5.0 kilograms for females in the first year (Flegal et al. 1995). Americans smoke less than Europeans, so this is a contributing factor to the nation's higher obesity prevalence. Today only 15.1 percent of the American adult population still smokes daily, compared to 19.5 percent in Japan, 21.5 percent in the United Kingdom, 21.9 percent in Germany, 23.1 percent in Italy, and 23.3 percent in France (OECD 2013b). Such differences do not reflect anything durable in the culture, however, since half a century ago it was Americans who smoked more than Europeans (Forey et al. 2011). Frequency of cigarette use is more responsive to a balance between income gains (which increase use) and health concerns (which decrease use), than to religious or cultural strictures (Cutler and Glaeser 2006).

Smoking notwithstanding, cultural factors do contribute to the nation's high prevalence of obesity. America's individualism has led to unstructured and undisciplined eating patterns, and a cultural preference for free market outcomes and personal responsibility over state authority blocks a government policy response. As political scientist J. Eric Oliver explained in 2006, public policy efforts to coerce behavior change in areas such as diet and exercise "contradict the core principles of our liberal, democratic society" (Oliver 2006, p. 178). Populism and egalitarianism do their part as well, by helping to block policy responses that might seem regressive on the poor or paternalistic toward minorities. Even the nation's stronger embrace of religion may add to the problem, by exempting most excess food consumption from church criticism.

Summarizing, America's unique culture has been identified in this chapter as a significant contributor to the nation's distinct tendency to overconsume both fossil fuels and food calories— especially food calories. This comes on top of earlier confirmed contributions from America's distinct material, geographic, and demographic endowment, plus its unusual governing institutions. Again, we find America's overconsumption to be seriously overdetermined. Campaigners against CO_2 emissions and obesity who wish to change America's damaging habits will find themselves up against an iron triangle of resisting forces. What course of action is likely to be taken, in the future, should these problems persist or worsen? The next chapter shows why America, unable to escape its habits of excess, may look instead for better ways to adapt and live with that excess.

CHAPTER 5

America's Response to Excess

When threatened by their own overconsumption, societies can either find a way to consume less, or they can continue the excess and look for new ways to cope with the consequences. The first response is conventionally labeled *mitigation* and the second *adaptation*. It is often wise to pursue both strategies at the same time, but the psychology of each is quite different. If prospects brighten for successful adaptation, less energy will usually go into mitigation.

For both CO_2 emissions and obesity, mitigation has always seemed the better first response. Stabilizing the climate through timely reductions in greenhouse gas emissions is a more attractive long-run strategy than struggling to stay ahead of increased climate disruption with self-protective measures, because the protections required will become steadily more costly if emissions are allowed to continue unchecked. Responding to obesity by encouraging reduced calorie intake and increased physical activity ("diet and exercise") is likewise far better than spending more every year on medical interventions, given the cost and difficulty of providing treatment to ever larger numbers of people with weight-linked ailments.

In the United States, as we have seen, these more sensible mitigation responses have been difficult for political leaders to pursue. The nation's unusual material and demographic circumstances, its easily paralyzed political institutions, and also its unusual cultural traits have so far in each case blocked an effective mitigation response. The strong policy instruments needed to bring excess consumption under control in the United States—such as taxes, regulations, and mandates—have not been available for use. With the mitigation pathway blocked, political leaders will be tempted to shift more resources and psychological energy toward the second-best path of adaptation. In this chapter, we show that in America a significant policy pivot toward adaptation is already taking place.

The adaptation pathway is distinctly attractive to America's political leaders because it can be pursued without recourse to coercive consumption taxes, regulations, or mandates. Adaptation will not require asking Americans to do *less* of anything. Instead, it presents opportunities to do new things that many Americans will be good at and can even profit from. Developing improved coastal protection systems, new drought-tolerant farm crops, improved bariatric surgeries, and new blockbuster diet drugs will be challenges welcomed by America's innovative and responsive private market institutions. Meeting these challenges will require increased government spending, but little or no direct infringement on the personal freedom of citizens. The required governmental spending will be relatively easy to support because benefits will be immediate, tangible, visible, and locally captured. Adaptation investments will be seen as creating rather than destroying jobs.

The purpose here is not to endorse adaptation over mitigation. In an ideal world, investments in mitigation would come first, and second-best adaptation approaches would play only a backup role. Putting adaptation first can be a damaging and even a disastrous long-term strategy, given the open-ended cost of trying to live with increasing climate disruption or with a population experiencing continued personal weight gain. Yet because the adaptation strategy is so well tailored in the short run to America's material, institutional, and cultural circumstances, it will present an irresistible temptation to America's political class.

The Politics of Mitigation versus Adaptation

The concerned activists who campaign against America's damaging overconsumption of both fuel and food have always preferred mitigation, sometimes to the point of rejecting any consideration of adaptation options. The purity of their motivation makes them hostile to any second-best approach, partly for the good reason that any investment made in adaptation could diminish the perceived urgency of mitigation. Despite their strong and pure motives, these concerned activists have so far failed in America to secure the taxes, regulations, or mandates needed to make significant progress toward sufficient mitigation of either CO_2 emissions or obesity. The most they have been able to win from the federal government are weak or even sham measures, based only on public exhortation, voluntarism, or subsidies designed to buy (or rent) a few mitigating behaviors at the margin. Weak half-measures of this kind are doubly dangerous, because they can create a complacent status quo. The political class will exaggerate the value of these measures to maintain public support, as will some activist organizations, that point to these measures as concessions they have won. What they have not won is significant mitigation.

For climate change, the political class in America has protected itself from accusations of inaction by spending public resources to subsidize the deployment of some non-fossil sources of energy such as solar and wind power, even though the impact on CO_2 emissions has been negligible. For obesity, the political class spends public resources to promote less caloric food in public schools, even though school menus are only a small part of the problem. Such approaches fit well with America's culture and institutions because no voting-aged adults are being coerced into a lifestyle change, yet as strategies to mitigate overconsumption they are manifestly unpromising. Solar and wind technologies for electric power have price and reliability disadvantages that are still much too large to support a voluntary scale-up. Likewise with non-coercive pathways toward obesity mitigation: even if more healthy foods become available in school lunch cafeterias, or in so-called food deserts, Americans who prefer to eat for convenience, taste, or emotional gratification, rather than for health, will continue doing so.

Mitigation activists in America hold out a hope that today's sham efforts are just a politically necessary prelude to stronger and more effective future measures. The combined weight of America's material, institutional, and cultural circumstances suggests this may be a vain hope. As climate and obesity problems worsen for Americans, today's weak policies are likely to be followed less by improved mitigation efforts and more by an implicit policy shift toward adaptation. America's mitigation policies will probably strengthen a bit, and they will probably remain the aspirational focal point in most public policy discussions, but in terms of actual resource commitment they will probably be supplemented by steadily larger and more determined efforts at adaptation.

Climate Change: Failed Mitigation

Climate activists in America have not yet been able to secure the policy measures needed to reach a significant CO_2 mitigation target. They have gained some mitigation indirectly and at the margin through government subsidies to promote non-fossil ("renewable") energy sources from solar radiation and wind, after having watched Germany take this path with some effect. Yet the political conditions necessary for Germany's progress are missing in the United States, and even the German success falls well short of a climate-stabilizing mitigation standard.

Germany's policy, launched in 2000 and known as the *Energiewende* ("energy turn"), was founded on a governmental guarantee—for a 20-year period—of high fixed prices for those who generate power from solar and wind. Thanks to these price guarantees, the renewable share of electric power generation in Germany did increase considerably, to reach 23 percent by 2013 (Economist 2014). The key policy instrument was a coercive mandate imposed on utility companies, obliging them to pay higher rates to renewable power providers (EIA 2013a). The utilities have covered this added cost by passing higher rates along to their energy customers.

Trying to adopt a policy of this kind in America is a nonstarter, given the much higher electricity costs that would result. In Germany, the average electricity-using household now pays an extra $355 a year to subsidize renewables. Substantial exemptions have been given to German industries in the name of job protection and export promotion, but they are still left paying nearly three times as much for electricity as industrial users in the United States (Eddy and Reed 2013). These higher costs have strained political acceptability even in Germany. Chancellor Angela Merkel's 2011 decision to begin shutting down the nation's nuclear power plants in the aftermath of the Fukushima reactor accident in Japan created a power deficit in the country that soon drove prices to damaging levels. Germany's minister for economic affairs and energy sounded the alarm in January 2014, telling attendees at a Berlin conference that the country was facing "dramatic de-industrialization" if its energy costs could not be reduced (Eddy 2014).

A second reason that America cannot follow Germany is institutional and jurisdictional. Power utilities are primarily regulated at the state level in America. Some state governments have been ready to encourage wind and solar through so-called renewables portfolio standards (RPS), but these states have hoped to lower costs to consumers by using price competition between renewable energy generators, not German-style high price guarantees that increase costs. Many RPS schemes even include a price cap specifically intended to protect consumers from any pass-through of higher renewables costs (Rickerson and Grace 2007). As of 2013, 29 states had legislatively mandated RPS requirements, but only five were promoting renewables with mandated feed-in tariffs that followed the design of those used in Germany—California, Oregon, Washington, Vermont, and Maine (CAR 2014; EIA 2013b).

Even if America could follow Germany's approach, the mitigation payoff would be small and uncertain. When Germany began shutting down its nuclear power plants after 2011, wind and solar were unable to scale up to fill the new deficit (even with the high fixed price guarantee), so Germany was pushed back toward fossil fuels, and specifically toward dirty coal, which was cheaper than natural gas. In 2012, power generation from natural gas in Germany declined and coal-fired plants increased their output. Coal's share in German electricity production actually increased from 43.1 percent to 44.7 percent, and total German greenhouse emissions rose by 1.6 percent. By one calculation, even if Germany's current push for solar and wind power continues, the share of total electricity generated from renewables in 2022 will be no greater than it was in 2010, assuming that nuclear sources remain shut down (Boisvert 2013).

In the United States so far, the federal government has been promoting renewables in the most expensive and least effective way possible, which is by offering tax breaks and subsidies to private firms that deploy panels and turbines using already available technology. The Bush administration initiated this approach with the Energy Policy Act of 2005, hoping to gain more energy independence for America (greenhouse gas mitigation was a distant secondary concern). When a financial crisis and recession struck in 2008–2009, the Obama administration increased the subsidies as an economic stimulus to promote "green jobs."

Between 2007 and 2010, the total value of America's subsidies and direct financial interventions in energy markets doubled, from $17.9 billion up to $37.2 billion (CAR 2014). Many of the tax breaks funded private investments that were going to be made anyway during this period of extremely high oil prices (OECD 2010a). Between 2009 and 2012, the Department of Energy guaranteed $16 billion in renewable energy loans through a so-called 1705 program, yet most of the guarantees went to companies with ample financial resources of their own, or for low-risk projects (Rugy 2012). The higher-risk projects often failed. The Solyndra company, a manufacturer of advanced solar panels, received a $535 million loan guarantee through the 1705 program to build a factory outside San Francisco, but then went bankrupt in 2011 amid falling solar panel prices.

In the one renewable fuel sector where Congress did actually impose a mandate—to produce biofuels from plants—the consequences for CO_2 mitigation were even less significant. Congress had been promoting the use of fermented corn ethanol for auto fuel since 1978, by offering tax credits to blenders. The original political motive was energy independence, plus help for corn farmers and the ethanol industry, not mitigation of greenhouse gas emissions. Indeed, a life-cycle analysis of corn-based ethanol production shows it does nothing at all to mitigate climate change (Fargioine 2008). Biofuel promotion was nonetheless ramped up dramatically under the Energy Independence and Security Act of 2007, when Congress added a quantitative mandate requiring at least 15 billion gallons of ethanol from products like corn by 2015. The greenhouse gas mitigation impacts have been nil.

Public subsidies to spur larger investments in solar and wind did bring a rapid capacity increase in America, but from only a tiny base, so the share of America's energy consumption satisfied by non-hydro renewables increased from only 4.7 percent in 2008 to just 6.5 percent in 2012 (CAR 2014). Even if these subsidies continue for decades, the CO_2 mitigation gains will continue to be small. In its Annual Energy Outlook 2013, the US Energy Information Administration estimated the net impact on America's energy-related CO_2 emissions if the policies on renewables in place at that time remained in place to 2040. EIA calculated three future scenarios: a basic Reference Case with current policies terminating as their sunset dates arrived; a No Sunset case, where tax credits for renewable energy sources and other measures are not terminated; and an Extended Policies Case, which includes everything in the No Sunset case plus additional updates to things like federal equipment efficiency standards. In both the Reference Case and the No Sunset Case, America's energy-related CO_2 emissions increase rather than decline between 2011 and 2040 (in fact, in 2013 they did increase, by 2.9 percent). In the Extended Policies Case there is a decline of 2.8 percent relative to the reference case, but no decline in absolute terms, as seen in Figure 5.1 (EIA 2013b).

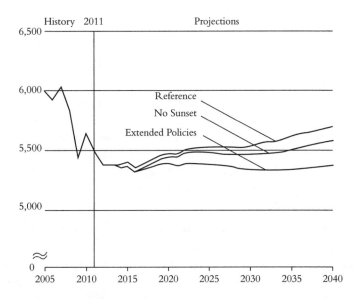

FIGURE 5.1. Energy-Related Carbon Dioxide Emissions in Three Cases, 2005–2040 (million metric tons) **Source:** EIA Outlook 2013, Figure 18

An alternative mitigation strategy, the experimental carbon capture approach mentioned in the previous chapter, also faces serious limits. Since 2008, the US government has spent nearly $6 billion to explore CCS, yet the most advanced techniques currently available still drive up the cost of generating electricity by between 30 percent and 80 percent, blocking a voluntary scale-up (Sarewitz and Pielke 2013). In 2011, American Electric Power had to cancel a big carbon-capture project because state regulators were not willing to let the company pass these much higher costs along to its customers. As for nuclear power, reviving this option has been off the table politically in America since the 1979 Three Mile Island accident.

President Obama in several instances has pursued mitigation without Congress, both through tighter regulations imposed on auto fuel efficiency and also on power plants. Regarding auto fuel efficiency, gains were made. In 2012, the EPA and the Department of Transportation promulgated new rules that would require automakers to double the average fuel economy of new cars and trucks by 2025, under the Corporate Average Fuel Economy (CAFE) program. This CAFE program had originally been launched during the energy crisis of the 1970s, not as a climate change policy but as a means to reduce America's dependence on foreign oil. The program operates by imposing payment penalties on auto firms that fail to meet the standard. One National Academy of Sciences study in 2002 found that without the standard, annual motor vehicle fuel consumption in the United States would have been 14 percent higher (NAS 2002). The new rules set in place in 2012 may reduce national carbon emissions by 180 million tons per year by 2020, which would equal 3 percent of America's current total carbon emissions (Davenport 2014b). Chrysler and GM tactfully decided not to fight this new imposition of government authority, in part because they had just received a taxpayer-financed federal bailout.

There will be stronger resistance to President Obama's efforts to use unilateral EPA rule-making to reduce emissions from power plants. The "adversarial legalism" in American politics is likely to slow, weaken, or possibly even block executive action here. Obama's EPA proposal announced in June 2014 will require new state-level rules, sometime after 2015, to reduce carbon pollution from power plants by 30 percent from 2005 levels, by 2030 (EPA 2014). This measure looked stronger than it really was, since it only addressed power plants and since America's carbon emissions from power plants had already fallen by 14 percent from the peak level of 2005, mostly in response to a market-driven transition from coal to natural gas. So the country was already nearly halfway to the new EPA goal on the day it was announced. This new EPA proposal also had some soft edges at the state level, where multiple paths would be permitted to reach the goal, including measures not linked to power generation, such as adding insulation to buildings and trading permits across state borders.

Even if fully achieved by 2030, the required power plant emissions reductions would not be as large as the earlier auto fleet emissions reductions (Eilperin 2014). Global carbon dioxide emissions might be reduced by only 1–2 percent (Economist 2014). Nonetheless, Obama used the EPA proposal as the foundation for a new public promise, made in November 2014 in Beijing, to cut United States emissions 26–28 percent below 2005 levels by 2025.

Obama's partisan critics viewed this as a legacy-seeking effort by a weakened lame duck president to dump a costly and unrealistic plan into the lap of a successor. The US Chamber of Commerce immediately objected to the new plan, claiming it would lower the US GDP by $51 billion a year and reduce disposable income for US households by a total of $586 billion through 2030 (US Chamber of Commerce 2014). Even as his own party was about to lose control of the Senate in 2014, Obama invited political challenge by ignoring the opposition. Neither the office of House Speaker John Boehner (R-OH) nor the office of Senate Minority Leader Mitch McConnell (R-KY) had been contacted before the June 2014 EPA announcement, and the pledge made in Beijing in November was to most a surprise. (Nelson and Lee 2014). Accordingly, push back was strong. Rep. David McKinley (R-WV) proposed a so-called Protection and Accountability Regulatory Act, with support from 66 other House Republicans and one Democrat, designed to nullify both the EPA's new carbon emissions rule for existing power plants as well as an earlier EPA rule applying to new plants. Senate Minority Leader (soon to become the Majority Leader) McConnell threatened legislation to block the new rule, unless guarantees could be given that it would not cost jobs, slow economic growth, or inhibit the delivery of electrical power.

The new EPA rule may also encounter challenge in federal court. In 2007, the Supreme Court did rule that CO_2 could be considered a pollutant under the Clean Air Act, so long as the EPA could demonstrate that continued emissions would harm human health and welfare, and the EPA did publish such an Endangerment Finding in 2009. Yet on technical grounds, the EPA is not permitted to regulate a pollution source at the state level under Section 111(d) of the Clean Air Act (which the rule proposed to do) if the agency was already regulating that source at the national level under Section 112 of the Act. Immediately after the new rule was proposed, the Attorney General of West Virginia threatened to sue the EPA on these grounds, should the rule ever come into effect (Kasperowicz 2014). The rule also could be challenged as arbitrary and capricious, since it sought to control CO_2 emissions from power plants but not from other stationary sources, such as office buildings or schools (Singer 2013).

At the very least, the measure will encounter delay at the state level. The president's original hope had been for a draft regulation on existing plants by June 2014, a final version by June 2015, and then a requirement that states submit plans for carrying out the rule by June 2016. Since state environmental agencies typically take two or three years to write new regulations, this timetable was never realistic (Davenport 2014b). The end of the story will not be known until after President Obama has left office. Coal interests will work hard to block or weaken the measure between now and then.

Pivot toward Climate Adaptation

As significant mitigation efforts continue to be weakened or stalled in the United States, and scarcely undertaken at all in China or the rest of the non-OECD world, adaptation to actual climate disruptions will begin to seem more urgent and this alternative approach will gain luster. In April 2014, the IPCC reported that "despite a growing number of climate change mitigation policies," global greenhouse gas emissions from all anthropogenic sources had increased by 1.0 gigatonnes of CO_2 equivalent each year between 2000 and 2010, which was more than twice the average annual increase seen during the earlier 1970–2000 period (IPCC 2014, p. 5). The IPCC concluded that without added mitigation efforts, the result would be a global mean surface temperature increase from 3.7 to 4.8 °C by 2100 compared to preindustrial levels, which is roughly twice the 2 °C increase deemed safe (IPCC 2014, p. 8). Facing such projections, even the most enthusiastic advocates for mitigation might begin thinking more seriously about adaptation. In the United States, where there have always been fewer mitigation enthusiasts in the first place, adaptation options become particularly tempting.

Advocates for mitigation who claim it is not too late can point to economic models showing that the economic cost of holding warming to less than 2 °C is entirely affordable. In 2014, the IPCC estimated that the mitigation needed to hold CO_2-equivalent atmospheric concentrations to no more than 450 parts per million by the year 2100 might depress global consumption growth rates only slightly. Compared to baseline growth rates between 1.6 percent and 3 percent per year, growth under such a mitigation regime might be reduced by only 0.04–0.14

percentage points. This would constitute a significant cumulative sacrifice over time, but it would be scarcely noticeable, year by year (IPCC 2014, p. 17). Yale economist William Nordhaus agrees with the math, that warming could be kept below the 2 °C UN target at a relatively small cost of only 1.5 percent of world income, but this requires making two far-fetched political assumptions: 100 percent participation by countries, and 100 percent efficient policies (Nordhaus 2013). Modeling efforts that make more realistic assumptions suggest that if the goal is to reduce the *economic costs* of climate change, adaptation will probably be cheaper than mitigation through the rest of the twenty-first century (Bosello et al. 2010).

America's political leaders put little trust either in economic models or climate models, but extreme weather events get their attention, and the response to such events has recently emphasized adaptation over mitigation. First, a punishing summer drought in the Midwest in 2012 damaged farm production, then later that year superstorm Sandy devastated miles of coastline along the Jersey Shore. Following these events, America's leaders discovered that the nation's material circumstances, political institutions, and distinct culture were all well suited to an adaptation response.

Responding to Extreme Weather

The investments needed to protect most Americans from accelerating climate change will be surprisingly affordable in the short run, thanks to the nation's vast wealth plus its relatively limited risk exposure. With long coastlines, America might seem highly vulnerable to sea level rise, but compared to most other countries and regions it is not. Comparing populations vulnerable to sea-level rise in low-elevation coastal zones (LECZ), North America in 2010 had only half as many exposed individuals as Europe, and Europe in turn had only one-tenth as many as in Asia (Wheeler 2011). Considering agriculture,

America's farming sector will be vulnerable to climate change over the long run, but it is currently only 1 percent of the nation's economy, and in the short run climate change could actually boost America's rain-fed yields by as much as 5–20 percent, according to the IPCC, by providing increased moisture, longer growing seasons, and more carbon fertilization for crops (EPA 2013). In one study of vulnerabilities to climate change in 171 countries, conducted in 2010 by the British firm Maplecroft, the United States ranked 129. In this study, the 44 most vulnerable states were all from the non–OECD world, with the top 10 being Bangladesh, India, Madagascar, Nepal, Mozambique, the Philippines, Haiti, Afghanistan, Zimbabwe, and Myanmar (ClimateWire 2010).

In its 2014 assessment, the IPCC looked hard to find critical economic vulnerabilities beyond coastal flooding to climate change in the United States. The additional risks included shrinkage of glaciers and reduced water in spring snowpack in the western mountains, an earlier peak flow in snow-dominated river systems, increased wildfires, a northward shift in Atlantic fish species, changed migration of salmon, and changes in mussel beds along the West Coast (IPCC 2014b). Needless to say, shifts in mussel beds will pose little threat to most of America's citizens and its industrial and service sector economy. William Nordhaus calculates that if global warming continues, with a temperature increase of 2.5 °C by 2070, roughly 90 percent of the American economy will remain only "lightly or negligibly impacted." The most heavily impacted sectors—farming, forestry, and fishing—make up just 1.2 percent of the American economy (Nordhaus 2013).

Given this relatively low exposure to risk, plus the nation's unmatched material wealth, America will find self-protective adaptation to climate change a tempting policy option. If mitigation fails completely, of course, climate impacts will eventually reach catastrophic tipping points, such as a collapse of large ice sheets in Greenland, or massive changes in ocean circulation.

Yet up to that point, an adaptation approach may remain more attractive, politically, than a forced-pace mitigation approach based on the non-fossil energy technologies available today. The costs of adaptation will be high, but they can partly be financed at low political cost through a private sector that will provide increased corporate R&D to develop drought-resistant crop seeds, innovations for cooling systems for buildings, new financial instruments to insure against risk, and much more. The political challenge will center on delivering taxpayer-financed public goods, such as elevated road infrastructures, more porous pavements, new artificial storm surge barriers, and revamped wastewater treatment facilities (Bosello et al. 2010).

America's government will most likely fund such projects on an ad hoc basis following specific disaster events. The American political system responds with considerable energy and generosity to highly publicized episodic hardships. For example, within two months following superstorm Sandy in 2012, Congress had passed the Disaster Relief Appropriations Act of 2013, known as the "Sandy Supplemental," providing roughly $50 billion in funding to support a Jersey Shore rebuilding effort, one that included substantial investments in future resilience. A Hurricane Sandy Rebuilding Task Force was also created by Executive Order, with instructions to guide the rebuild in a manner mindful of "both current and future risks," an unmistakable reference to adaptation needs in light of continuing sea level rise and increased climate instability (White House 2012).

Post-disaster circumstances not only mobilize vast public resources; thanks to a destruction of the existing built environment, disaster events clear the physical path for more resilient infrastructure upgrades. After Sandy, New Jersey's Department of Environmental Protection (DEP) established higher elevation standards for new buildings, and also for reconstructed buildings if the structure was located in a flood zone and had been declared substantially damaged. Disaster events also facilitate important rule changes. New York City experienced extended power losses after Sandy, so the City Council one year later approved new rules requiring existing hospitals and nursing homes in flood zones to install hookups to temporary generators (Navarro 2013). In addition, New York's Public Service Commission ordered Consolidated Edison, a power company serving the city and some suburbs, to spend $1 billion on improved resilience in the event of future weather shocks. Population resettlement is another adaptation option more easily pursued post-disaster, partly through private market responses (flood insurance rates go up), but also through public funding of prudent retreats from the shore. In February 2013, post-Sandy, New York Governor Andrew Cuomo used $400 million in federal funding to offer a buyout plan: sell your destroyed home to the state at pre-disaster value, then the state will demolish it and not allow the land to be redeveloped.

Some of the ad hoc rebuilding efforts after Sandy were less well considered. The US Army Corps of Engineers made plans to spend up to $5 billion on largely temporary shore restoration schemes, dredging and pumping sand onto eroded beaches that were only destined to erode again (Young 2013). Yet post-calamity approaches to adaptation have a proven track record. In Holland, it took a disastrous North Sea flood in 1953, killing 1,800 people, to prompt the completion of the Delta Works system of dikes and storm surge barriers that now protect low-lying areas against flooding. In the case of Sandy, only 117 deaths were officially recorded, yet the geographic scale of the damage created opportunities to replace a highly vulnerable built environment with something more resilient.

Most of the investments needed for adaptation to climate change will be region-specific, or even site-specific, making them well suited to America's highly decentralized political institutions. Site-specific investments fit perfectly into the "pork barrel" nature of so much public spending in America. The US Congress is different from most European parliaments; it is a body of individuals who seek re-election by delivering tangible benefits to specific geographic communities. In Europe, district-level benefits are less important than party labels, and often candidates run for office "at large" in proportional representation systems disconnected entirely from local geography (Lancaster and Patterson 1981). In America, members of Congress survive in office by bringing federal money back to the district, through defense contracts, bridge and highway projects, VA hospitals, farm subsidies, sewage treatment plants, Small Business Administration loans, or FEMA outlays (Shepsle and Weingast 1981). Relatively weak central control within the executive branch amplifies this tendency, by giving empire-building bureaucrats opportunities to cultivate direct relationships with their congressional funders. It is not an accident that so many federal agencies were assigned new and specific missions post-Sandy, including the Department of Agriculture, the Army Corps of Engineers, the Small Business Administration, the Department of Homeland Security, the Federal Emergency Management Agency, the Department of the Interior, the Department of Health and Human Services, the Department of Defense, the Department of Transportation, and also the Department of Housing and Urban Development (H.R. 152 2013). For the budgets of these separate agencies, Sandy was not a disaster at all.

The Obama administration came to Washington eager to promote mitigation, but following the early failure of cap-and-trade it began seeing political opportunities in the alternative domain of adaptation. As early as 2010, Obama's interagency "Climate Change Adaptation Task Force" presented recommendations for how the nation might live with climate change (FedCenter.gov 2014). The 2012 summer drought, followed by Sandy, then reinforced the attraction of adaptation strategies, and when presenting his new second-term "Plan to Fight Climate Change" in June 2013, Obama added a telling new component:

We're going to need to get prepared. And that's why this plan will also protect critical sectors of our economy and prepare the United States for the impacts of climate change that we cannot avoid. . . . That means stronger seawalls, natural barriers, hardened power grids, hardened water systems, hardened fuel supplies. . . . So the budget I sent Congress includes funding to support communities that build these projects, and this plan directs federal agencies to make sure that any new project funded with taxpayer dollars is built to withstand increased flood risks. (White House 2013)

Later in 2013, Obama signed a new executive order (13,653) that renamed his task force the Council on Climate Preparedness and Resilience, and he directed federal agencies to make it easier for states and communities to get federal funds for rebuilding with greater climate resilience. He also created a bipartisan high-level task force of state and local leaders to offer advice to the federal government on expediting this kind of assistance (Gillis 2013). Obama's May 2013 National Climate Assessment report warned that "the pace and magnitude of projected change emphasize the need to be prepared for a wide range and intensity of climate impacts in the future," and it included a 35-page section on adaptation (USGCRP 2014, p. 671). In March 2014, Obama then unveiled a new website, climate.data.gov, to give local communities further help in preparing for climate change impacts, and when the president's 2015 budget proposal was announced, it included $1 billion for a Climate Resilience Fund, coastal resilience funding for the Commerce Department, infrastructure vulnerability funding for the Energy Department, and expanded funding for the US Geological Survey to monitor, research, and analyze climate resilience (Ritter 2014). Presidential surrogates said that Obama remained committed to greenhouse gas mitigation, but a policy expansion into the more welcoming terrain of adaptation was clearly underway.

Adaptation responses to climate change are not always politically unifying. In 2014, the state of California faced its worst drought in modern history, one that reduced normal river water deliveries to the Central Valley by one-third, placing even irrigated farms under stress. This agricultural emergency in California was more difficult for politicians to manage than the 2012 summer drought in the non-irrigated Midwest, because irrigation water is delivered through semi-public infrastructures that must allocate use among competing interests, so getting more water to farms in the short run can mean taking it away from urban users or from environmentally fragile systems such as the San Joaquin–Sacramento River Delta (Medina 2014). In response to the California drought, Obama nonetheless emphasized adaptation options. Visiting a farm in Fresno, the president warned that the changing climate was going to bring more weather-related disasters like droughts and wildfires, and he announced his plan to ask Congress for $1 billion in new funding for "climate resiliency," plus the creation of seven regional "climate hubs" to help farmers and rural communities respond to climate change risks. Also in 2014, Congress enacted a new Farm Bill, expanding subsidy entitlements and crop insurance to compensate farmers for weather damage and providing a new Livestock Forage Disaster Program.

Many of America's most distinct cultural traits are well suited to this policy shift toward adaptation. While effective mitigation requires taxes or regulations that Americans typically dislike, adaptation can operate well enough through public investments or subsidies, plus private sector initiatives. Americans are less likely to complain about big government when it is employing people, building useful things, or delivering tangible benefits. The adaptation approach also fits with the nation's unusual optimism about technology. Most Americans acknowledge that today's technologies have generated threats to the planet and even to their own future well-being, but they reflexively believe that tomorrow's technologies will be an improvement. Particularly compared to Europeans, Americans believe it is possible to adapt to climate risks with improved weather prediction and storm-monitoring systems, improved systems for back-up power, new crop varieties developed to grow under higher temperatures, or new public health initiatives to protect vulnerable populations under more prolonged heat stress (Macauley and Morris 2011; Macauley 2011).

The sons and daughters of pioneers and frontiersmen, Americans like to win battles against nature. As noted earlier, 82 percent of Americans believe they can control their environment, while only 66 percent of Germans feel that way (Hampden-Turner and Trompenaars 1997). Relying on technologies not yet developed is an uncertain prospect, but Americans are also more tolerant of uncertainty. Geert Hofstede, a Dutch social psychologist, has constructed an index of "uncertainty avoidance" that measures the inclination of societies to cope with anxiety by minimizing uncertainty. Since Americans feel less need to minimize uncertainty, they score a relatively low 46 on this index, while Germans score 65, the French score 86, and the Japanese score 92 (Hofstede 2001).

Emphasizing an adaptation strategy in the short run will also be politically tempting because it can be promoted as giving America's scientists and innovators more time to develop the low-carbon technologies needed to make serious mitigation affordable in the long run. Today's low-carbon technologies are not yet competitive with the fossil fuel alternatives, so trying to scale them up with subsidies is costly. The temptation becomes to postpone scale up and adapt for now, holding off on mitigation until better low-carbon alternatives have been developed. Concerned activists say that we do not have to postpone mitigation, pointing to a 2001 IPCC assertion that atmospheric CO_2 concentrations can be stabilized at acceptable cost using "known technological options" (IPCC 2001, p. 8). For most elected politicians, however, the more attractive path might be to adapt for now, then force a scale up mitigation only after improved technologies become available.

If political leaders take this approach, it will stand no chance of success without a significant change in the way America funds energy research. Until now, public investments in clean energy research have been driven too much by fossil fuel prices and too little by greenhouse gas emissions risks. Government investments in renewable energy R&D increased in the 1970s when petroleum prices spiked, but then fell back to a lower level throughout the 1980s and 1990s after oil prices declined, even though the lower oil prices were worsening climate threats by encouraging higher consumption. When petroleum prices returned to a high level in 2008, public R&D on renewables was revived at least temporarily. A strategy to postpone mitigation until better technologies are available will be a complete sham without public sector R&D investments that are high, sustained, and disconnected from fossil fuel prices (IEA 2010).

Isabel Galiana and Christopher Green have called for funding this sort of public R&D through a "fee" on carbon emissions large enough to generate adequate revenue but not so large as to trigger political resistance by reducing economic growth (Galiana and Green 2010). One model to follow could be America's Interstate Highway Trust Fund, which is constantly replenished from a dedicated revenue stream based on a small 18 cent per gallon federal gasoline tax. Once improved low-carbon technologies are ready for use at scale, the fee could then be increased to speed the uptake. This research-led approach to mitigation would also increase options for international cooperation. Today's coal-dependent rising powers, such as China and India, will probably not go beyond domestic pollution control measures sacrifice economic growth to reduce emissions until energy generation from low-carbon sources comes down sharply in cost. If an American-led R&D project delivers lower cost alternatives, prospects for international cooperation will improve. The new technologies, developed in America's laboratories, could be licensed and sold around the world, generating export-led commercial prosperity for the United States.

Pursuing adaptation in the short run while investing in new technologies for tomorrow will be tempting for elected politicians, but it has always been anathema to committed climate activists. Even following superstorm Sandy, one content analysis of the annual reports and websites of major climate advocacy groups in America showed scant reference to adaptation (Luers, Pope, and Kroodsma 2013). Some climate activists do not even want to buy time through a market-driven switch from coal to natural gas. In 2014, Bill McKibben, founder of 350.org., and Mike Tidwell, director of the Chesapeake Climate Action Network, wrote that gas is "just coal by another name" and that it "needs to stay in the ground" (McKibben and Tidwell 2014, pp. 2–3). This point of view helps rally the environmental base, but it finds little cultural resonance with a broader range of Americans because it is technologically pessimistic rather than optimistic, implicitly statist rather than individualistic or laissez-faire, and regressive because it implies higher energy prices for the poor and middle class.

Climate activists pursuing brute force mitigation with today's technologies will also meet resistance in America because the international cooperation necessary for successful mitigation is still missing. The 1997 Kyoto Protocol agreement on mitigation did nothing to discipline emissions from countries like China or India; when it formally expired in 2012, it was covering barely 20 percent of total global greenhouse gas emissions (Nordhaus 2013). Governments went to Copenhagen in 2009 to produce a follow-up to Kyoto, but they could reach no agreement on emissions caps or carbon taxes, only on an aspiration that temperatures not rise more than 2 °C, and on a 2015 target date for a new agreement, the content of which remained unspecified and the enforcement of which would be pushed back to 2020. In 2013, China and India both warned that they would not be making any emissions reduction commitments within this new treaty framework, further exposing the futility of the exercise (Shorr 2014).

In 2014, India's environment minister rejected out of hand any thought that India would agree to cut its rapidly increasing carbon emissions: "What cuts? That's for more developed countries. The moral principle of historic responsibility cannot be washed away." With 20 percent of Indians still lacking any access to electricity, his attitude was understandable (Davenport 2014d). At a meeting with President Obama in Beijing in November 2014, China's President Xi Jinping finally did promise "to intend to achieve the peaking of CO_2 emissions around 2030," implying at least another decade and a half of emissions growth from by far the world's single largest emitter.

Seeing so little international action on mitigation, vulnerable poor countries have already shifted more of their own negotiating energies to demands for adaptation assistance (Davenport 2014c). Self-protective adaptation is where a growing share of United States policy efforts are likely to go as well.

Obesity: Alternatives to Diet and Exercise

Anti-obesity advocates in America have also preferred mitigation over adaptation, for medical, economic, and social reasons that are convincing on their own terms. Adapting to obesity is a distant second-best option, both for the individuals who retreat to this choice and also for society at large. Medical treatments and surgeries are available to help extremely overweight people enjoy longer and more productive lives, but the money costs are high, the treatments can be risky and unsure, and even when successful they will fail to protect the obese from social stigma and workplace discrimination.

Yet strong policy responses to obesity have so far been blocked in America by the nation's material and demographic circumstances, its easily paralyzed political institutions, and also a cultural preference for individual over social responsibility. If effective mitigation policies remain out of reach politically, we can expect interest to grow in second-best options such as medical treatments, physical accommodation, and improved social acceptance.

Relying on treatment rather than prevention is, after all, the distinctly American way of providing healthcare. By one calculation, 70 percent of the illnesses being treated in the United States could have been prevented (Lieberman 2013). Emphasis on treatment over prevention helps explain America's much higher per capita costs of healthcare. In 2011, the United States spent $8,508 per capita on healthcare, two and a half times more than the OECD average. America uses up 18 percent of its GDP on health spending, twice the OECD average (OECD 2013c). Overinvesting in treatment while underinvesting in prevention has also left the United States with inferior health outcomes. Out of 17 wealthy countries, the United States ranks 16 in life expectancy at birth for women, and dead last for men (IOM 2013).

Relying on treatment is therefore suboptimal, yet this has become the American way. As obesity has spread in America, diseases linked to obesity have become far more prevalent. For example, between 1990 and 2010, the number of Americans with diabetes tripled. The nation's response was not to mitigate obesity, but to adapt to the new reality by developing and delivering improved treatments to control blood sugar, cholesterol, and blood pressure. Medical costs for diabetes treatment in America now total $176 billion per year. On the other hand, these treatments get positive results. Thanks to costly interventions plus other things like a decline in smoking, medical outcomes for diabetic patients in America have significantly improved (Tavernise and Grady 2014). Between 1994 and 2010, even while obesity prevalence among diabetic Americans was rising from 35 percent to 57 percent, age-adjusted death rates among diabetics declined from 36 percent to 17 percent (CDC 2014).

Mitigation would be a far better starting point than treatment, but aggressive treatment can be a good choice if mitigation is out of reach. Treating diabetes is expensive in America, but $176 billion a year is just 6 percent of total national medical costs, so the treatments have so far been affordable. If the goal is to reduce healthcare costs in America, obesity mitigation will deliver relatively small benefits. As of 2006, spending on obesity-related conditions accounted for just 8.5 percent of

Medicare spending, 11.8 percent of Medicaid spending, and 12.9 percent of private-payer spending (HSPH 2012).

Because strong mitigation options will likely remain off the table politically in America, it will be tempting to look for ways to accept obesity and adapt. The adaptation measures available will include improved medical treatments for diseases linked to obesity, improved pharmaceutical options to control weight gain and its consequences, improved physical accommodation for heavy people, and measures to increase social acceptance for those who are overweight. Adaptation responses such as these will not prevent a steady increase in public health burdens, but they will be politically attractive because they allow individual Americans to retain control over their personal diet and exercise choices.

Emphasizing the disease complications from obesity rather than obesity itself will even have a medical logic, since obesity measured in terms of BMI is technically a physical condition, not a medical condition. A high BMI is frequently accompanied by type 2 diabetes and cardiovascular disease, but often it is not. Dr. Robert Lustig, an expert on childhood obesity, has pointed out that "[t]wenty percent of obese people have completely normal metabolic signatures," while conversely, "up to 40 percent of normal weight people have the exact same metabolic problems that the obese do; they are just not obese" (Aliferis 2013, p. 1). Particularly for diabetes, BMI alone cannot be blamed. One study of 175 countries published in 2013 found that diabetes was linked to sugar consumption, independent of body weight. Sugar proved to be 11 times stronger than total calories in explaining diabetes around the world (Basu et al. 2013a). The American Medical Association nonetheless voted in 2013 to categorize obesity by itself as a "multi-metabolic and hormonal disease state." This medically suspect designation was politically useful, because it opened the way for obese citizens to seek larger benefits from the government, for prevention but also for treatments and adaptation.

The medicalization of obesity in America reflects a growing influence for something called "the obesity community," a collection of professional and advocacy organizations with a strong interest in expanding insurance coverage and government benefits for those who have become obese. The leading groups in this community include the Obesity Action Coalition (OAC), which lobbies Congress for more obesity treatment support; the American Society of Metabolic and Bariatric Surgery (ASMBS), another treatment-oriented group; and the American Society of Bariatric Physicians (ASBP), again oriented toward surgical treatments. The Obesity Society (TOS) is a leading scientific body dedicated to prevention as well as treatment, plus research (TOS 2013). Favoring a prevention-first approach is the Academy of Nutrition and Dietetics, an organization supported by public health professionals who are naturally worried about taxpayer costs as well as health outcomes. The political balance within this obesity community has shifted significantly beyond prevention, toward favoring treatment and adaptation.

The dividing line between obesity treatment (adaptation) and prevention (mitigation) is not always clear. Diet and exercise are the traditional ways to mitigate, but weight can also be brought down with drugs or surgeries. Medical treatments for disease outcomes linked to obesity are the traditional way to adapt, but physical accommodations, social acceptance, and workplace protections are adaptive as well. In America, where policies to reduce calorie consumption and promote physical activity have been hard to promote, all of these other approaches have been on the rise.

Weight-loss Drugs

In the United States, legitimate weight-loss drugs prescribed by physicians have so far enjoyed only limited uptake. Roughly 70 million Americans are obese, yet only 2 million or so take prescribed weight-loss drugs, with the vast majority using just a single appetite-suppressor named phentermine, now available for short-term use in generic form. Many patients try prescription drugs but then give up quickly, either because they have secured only a small benefit or because of the expense. Money is an issue for those of retirement age, because Medicare Part D—the prescription drug benefit—lists weight-loss drugs among those it will not pay for. Roughly one-third of Americans with private insurance do have coverage for such drugs, but often with copayments of $50 a month (Pollack 2013a).

In addition, very few weight-loss medicines have been approved by the FDA for long-term use, and few Americans take these drugs because the benefits tend to be modest. Orlistat (sold as Xenical) came on the market in 1999 and usually brings a 5–10 pound loss of weight over six months. It promotes weight loss by reducing the absorption of fats and fat calories from food, but it also inhibits absorption of vitamins A, D, E, and K. One milder version of this medicine is approved by the FDA for over-the-counter use (sold as Alli). Physicians prescribe Orlistat for obese patients who have not been successful at losing weight with diet and exercise, plus seriously overweight patients who have developed weight-related medical problems such as diabetes or high blood pressure (NIH 2014). In 2011, the FDA refused to approve another weight-loss drug named Contrave, pending longer-term studies to clarify heart attack risks (Pollack 2011).

After a hiatus of more than a decade, in 2012 the FDA finally approved two new medicines for longer-term weight management: lorcaserin hydrochloride, sold as Belviq, plus a combination of previously approved medicines (phentermine and topiramate) sold as Qsymia. Roughly half of the obese patients who take Belviq experience at least a 5 percent body weight loss within a year. For Qsymia, 62 percent will do this well (NIH 2013). In clinical trials, patients went from an average of 220 pounds to 207 on Belviq, and 227 pounds to 204 pounds on Qsymia. When drug use is discontinued, however, the benefits disappear. The arrival of Belviq and Qsymia did not bring a substantial increase in total numbers of diet drug users in America; in their first 10 weeks on the market, weekly prescription sales of Belviq only reached 4,000, and for Qsymia roughly 1,000. By contrast, prescription sales of Viagra in the first three months reached 2.9 million, and drugs to lower cholesterol are taken today by something like 20 million Americans (Harper 2011).

FDA-approved obesity drugs can deliver genuine medical benefits beyond a reduction in weight. Particularly when used in combination with diet and exercise, they help lower blood sugar, blood pressure, and triglycerides (other fats in the blood). For the obese, a weight loss of 5 to 10 percent often reduces inflammation as well, improves how a patient feels, and increases mobility (NIH 2013). Yet diet drugs do bring side effects, ranging from stomach pain and diarrhea (from Xenical), to headaches, dizziness, nausea, and constipation (Belviq), and tingling hands and feet or sleep loss (Qsymia). Neither Belviq nor Qsymia won approval from the European Medicines Agency, and Belviq was rejected initially even by the FDA's advisory panel, because of a risk of tumors found in animal studies (Consumer Reports News 2013). In 2010, a weight-loss medicine named Meridia was taken off the market when evidence surfaced that it could increase risks of heart attack and stroke (NIH 2014).

The vast majority of weight loss pills in America are not medical drugs but non-prescription substances sold over the counter as dietary supplements. These are classified neither as foods nor drugs, so the FDA has no consistent role in their regulation. One study of 15,000 adults found that 7 percent had used at least one non-prescription weight-loss product, translating into 17 million people in the United States overall. The heaviest users (a 30 percent use rate) were young obese women (Blanck, Khan, and Serdula 2001). Many of these products are stimulants, and some carry serious risks. Ephedra, an extract from plants, brings short-term weight loss, but it also causes high blood pressure and stresses the heart, so the FDA stepped in to ban the sale of dietary supplements containing ephedra in 2004.

Other supplements—such as Hoodia, from an African cactus—
have been marketed without any scientific evidence of efficacy.
Some diuretics and herbal laxatives are also known to deliver
weight loss, but water rather than fat is being lost, and potassium
levels in the body can fall, causing heart and muscle problems
(NIH 2014). Americans continue to employ these risky non-
solutions to weight gain because they are less expensive than
actual medical drugs, and because they conveniently require no
prescription. Most long-term users of non-prescription weight-
loss products do not even discuss the practice with their physician (Blanck et al. 2007).

On balance, weight-loss drugs have thus brought little aggregate benefit so far. The market for a safe and genuinely effective weight-loss drug would be quite large in the United States,
possibly eclipsing the market for cholesterol-lowering drugs like
Lipitor, which peaked at $13 billion in annual sales before going
out of patent. So far, no prescription drug for obesity has ever
reached an annual sales level of even $1 billion (Pollack 2013).
Pharmaceutical firms are working hard, in alliance with the
obesity community, to loosen some of the standards that the
FDA employs in approving obesity drugs, but until now with
little success. Spotty insurance coverage also continues to hold
down levels of prescribed use.

Obesity Surgeries

Surgical treatments for obesity carry high cost and significant
risk, yet for those in greatest need this has emerged as a valuable option. Advocates even claim that the permanent health
gains secured through surgery can bring enough of a reduction
in long-term medical costs to make this option essentially self-
financing for the severely obese.

The most frequently performed weight loss surgery is called
"gastric bypass," a two-step procedure that first staples the
stomach into a smaller pouch, and then reconnects this smaller

stomach to the digestive system farther downstream, after bypassing part of the small intestine so as to reduce food absorption. Once re-engineered in this fashion, the human digestive system secretes fewer appetite-triggering hormones, so food intake declines and weight loss ensues. In one 2004 study, patients with an average BMI of 41 experienced an average 23 percent loss of weight two years after surgery and held on to a 16 percent weight loss 10 years later. In control groups, average weight continued to increase (Sjostrom et al. 2004). Another 2004 study found that obese patients with a clustering of metabolic syndrome risk factors experienced a cure rate of 95.6 percent after surgery (Lee et al. 2004). One meta-analysis found that a substantial majority of patients with type 2 diabetes, hypertension, and obstructive sleep apnea experienced complete resolution or improvement after bariatric surgery (Buchwald et al. 2004). A 2014 study demonstrated that three years after surgery, more than 90 percent of diabetes patients required no insulin (Marchione 2014). Studies carefully excluding people with medical conditions other than morbid obesity show the mortality rate for the treatment group five years after surgery is only 0.68 percent, versus 6.17 percent for a control group, representing an 89 percent reduction in relative risk of death (Christou et al. 2004).

The bariatric surgery option has so far been restricted to those with a BMI above 40, or to those with a BMI between 35 and 40 when serious obesity-related medical conditions are also present. Individuals with an obese BMI between 30 and 35 do not qualify under current medical society guidelines, and individuals with a BMI of 35–40 who are healthy do not qualify either (United Health Care 2014). Even so, few who do qualify elect the procedure, despite documented benefits. More than 30 million Americans currently qualify for bariatric surgery, yet only about 200,000 undergo the procedure every year, less than 1 percent (MacVean 2012). Reliance on this approach has nonetheless increased, from 1.4 surgeries per 100,000 Americans in 1990, up to 22.4 by 2007 (Whiteman 2013). As of 2008, there were roughly four times as many bariatric surgery operations performed in the United States as in all of the European countries combined, and more than two thousand times as many as in Japan (Buchwald and Oien 2009).

Diet control remains important after surgery. If a gastric bypass patient consumes foods that are high in sugar, the result can be diarrhea, nausea, and/or reflux. Just the same, mortality and major complication rates from gastric bypass are already no worse than for other major abdominal procedures, and as safety standards continue to improve, the readiness of primary care physicians to recommend surgery is likely to continue increasing (Xu 2012). Convenience and choice are also improving. Already most bypass surgeries are performed laparoscopically without a need for large incisions, and one new technique even allows "sleeves" to be implanted through the mouth without surgery, to block food absorption by lining part of the small intestine (Healy 2011). Another popular option is to implant an adjustable gastric band around the stomach, like a belt, but this less expensive method results in less weight loss, and there is a higher probability of weight being regained.

Incomplete insurance coverage is the strongest factor blocking wider use of weight loss surgery, but this too might change. The National Institute of Diabetes and Digestive and Kidney Diseases reports that the typical cost of bariatric surgery can run from $20,000 to $35,000, making it a difficult choice for the non-insured. Currently, roughly two-thirds of large employers in the United States cover bariatric surgery, but many small employers do not, and most private insurance Certificates of Coverage, and many Summary Plan Descriptions, explicitly exclude benefit coverage for bariatric surgery (United Health Care 2014). Also, when coverage is provided, patients must not only meet the BMI conditions or the obesity-related medical conditions; they must also show—with documentation—that they made a motivated effort over a minimum of six months to lose weight through a structured diet program, and they must undergo a psychological evaluation to rule out mental disorders (United Health Care 2014).

Political advocates for the obese continue working to make both surgical and pharmacological options more available and affordable, and progress has been made. In 1999, the Internal Revenue Service ruled that expenses for weight loss treatments were eligible for medical deductions on individual tax returns. In 2006, Medicare was persuaded to cover surgeries so long as the patient was suffering from other health problems related to weight, and so long as the procedure was undertaken at a certified center (Stein 2006). Another major victory came in 2013, with the AMA's decision to classify obesity as a disease, as this allowed the obesity community to demand improved access for drugs and surgeries based on medical necessity. The Social Security Administration also defines obesity as a disease today, which makes it a qualifying impairment for disability claims.

Passage of the 2010 Affordable Care Act (ACA) gave advocates another opportunity to demand expanded protections for the obese, and they secured further gains. The ACA includes a mandate requiring state health exchanges to cover a minimum set of Essential Health Benefits (EHB), but it allows states to decide whether metabolic and bariatric surgery will qualify as EHBs. The initial expectation in 2013 was that 23 of the 50 states would eventually go forward to qualify these surgical procedures as EHBs (Health Central 2013). The ACA also provided valuable new inducements for mitigation, since it required insurance coverage for obesity screening and counseling while allowing employers to charge obese workers 30 percent to 50 percent more for health insurance if they declined to participate in a qualified wellness program (Begley 2012). Medicare began reimbursing physicians for obesity counseling in 2011, and millions of obese Americans enrolling in health marketplace exchanges in 2014 were entitled to intensive behavioral counseling with no patient cost-sharing, plus at least one prescription drug for obesity treatment.

This increased medicalization of obesity is unpopular with insurance companies, who worry about having to pass on higher costs to policyholders. On the other hand, there can be offsetting benefits if surgery coverage results in fewer policyholders needing extended treatments for diabetes and cardiovascular disease. Wider access to surgical and pharmacological options will in any case resonate with important cultural values in America, including equal opportunity, populism ("people should decide, not doctors"), and most of all technological optimism. If surgery is the surest and most convenient way to reduce exposure to serious medical risks, Americans will want access to this technical option, and they will demand access for more than just a privileged few.

Non-health Needs

Health risks are extreme for those with a BMI of 40 or above. For the 83 percent of obese Americans with a BMI not above 40, health should also be a concern, but equally pressing issues can include physical inconvenience, social stigma, and workplace discrimination. Responding to these non-health issues is another emerging component of America's adaptation response to obesity.

Regarding workplace discrimination and physical inconvenience, the American government is slowly moving toward classifying obesity as a disability under the Americans with Disabilities Act (ADA) of 1990. Under this act, individuals classified as "disabled" are protected against discrimination in the workplace, and are also promised any "readily achievable" accommodation that might be needed for them to gain access to schools, public transportation, and newly constructed public commercial facilities.

In 2008 the ADA was strengthened through enactment of an Americans with Disabilities Act Amendments Act (ADAAA), which broadened the definition of what constitutes a disability.

While the ADAAA did not explicitly extend a disability classification to the obese, new opportunities to do so were created in 2011, when Interpretive Guidance for this 2008 law omitted some earlier language which had said, ". . . except in rare circumstances, obesity is not considered a disabling impairment." This opened more space for court actions to protect the obese, and in 2012, the EEOC did successfully bring suit in two cases against employers who had discriminated against severely obese individuals (ACC 2013). Following the AMA decision of 2013 to label obesity as a disease, it seemed only a matter of time before the courts would routinely consider at least some degree of obesity (severe or otherwise) a disability under the ADA. In 2013 the Association of Corporate Counsel began advising employers to begin considering workers who were obese, or morbidly obese, as entitled to protection under the ADA (ACC 2013).

Workplace discrimination is a more salient issue for obese women in America than for men. In the American workplace in 1981–1998, obese men earned 5 percent less than men with normal weight, but obese women suffered a 13 percent wage penalty. These penalties were too large to be explained by either lower labor productivity or higher absentee rates (Baum and Ford 2004; Cawley 2011). After 1998, even though the number of obese Americans in the workforce continued to increase, the wage penalties also increased (Lempert 2007). The more commonplace nature of the condition may not be lowering workplace discrimination, but it may be lowering social discrimination. Market research by the NPD Group, over the 20-year period from 1985 to 2005, showed the percent of Americans who found overweight people less attractive had steadily dropped from 55 percent to 24 percent (Choi 2006). Activists demanding "fat acceptance" are not yet satisfied with this trend, but in a telling way America's extremely high prevalence of obesity may itself be an indirect indicator of social acceptance. If the social stigma were higher, personal efforts to lose weight would possibly be more widespread, determined, and effective (Garcia and Quintana-Domeque 2006).

Workplace protection under the ADA will cut two ways for obese Americans, as it may discourage employers from hiring them in the first place. In America, there is not yet any blanket legal prohibition against this. Moreover, there is a debate within the obesity community over the wisdom of accepting a stamp of being "disabled," even though the language of the ADA says you only need to be *regarded* as having an impairment to qualify. A stronger benefit from the ADA might come through the reasonable efforts it will require to provide physical accommodation for the obese in public spaces and in newly constructed public commercial facilities. Public transportation is another issue. In 2011 the US Coast Guard raised the average assumed weight of commercial passengers from 140 pounds to 185 pounds following several deadly boating accidents linked to excess passenger weight (McKay 2012). Public transport by aircraft is explicitly excluded from coverage under the ADA, so airplane seat accommodations are not determined by federal law.

America's private sector is already responding to the accommodation needs of obese citizens. Office chairs once rated for no more than 300 pounds are now being replaced with new products ($1,300 each) that can handle up to 600 pounds. Some hospitals have spent up to $5 million to accommodate the obese with supersized beds, open MRI machines, and toilets bolted to the floor instead of the wall. Funeral homes now offer much larger caskets (Neporent 2013). Movie theater seats are six inches wider than they were in the 1980s, revolving doors two feet wider, and more automobiles today have rearview cameras, good for safety but also convenient for drivers who cannot turn around (Datko 2012). When Yankee Stadium was rebuilt in 2008, the seats were widened by one to two inches.

There are important medical as well as social and ethical reasons not to stigmatize obesity. In those cases where the condition is genetic, it would be shameful to attach a stigma. In cases where the stigma could induce unwise eating behaviors such as bulimia, it becomes medically dangerous. Limiting stigma in this area should be more manageable in America, as it is the populist, egalitarian thing to do. The already diverse look of America's multi-racial and multi-ethnic population prepares the nation for a future of also accepting and accommodating fellow citizens who become seriously overweight.

Summary

So far, America has responded both to climate change and obesity in a weak but characteristic way. In each case, the federal government has stopped short of using its most powerful policy instruments to coerce behavior change, either from individual citizens or private companies. As a result, little in the way of mitigation has been achieved. As mitigation has faltered, political leaders in America have begun directing greater energy toward adaptation, a tempting policy path because it requires little or no coercion. When pursuing adaptation, damaging old behaviors are not corrected; instead, they are made safer or more acceptable by layering on new behaviors. Having failed to do their share in mitigating greenhouse gas emissions, America's leaders are now turning to the task of protecting the country against damaging climate change effects. Having failed to correct the diet and exercise habits of obese Americans, the federal government is beginning to devote more energy to treating the medical conditions that afflict these citizens, supporting access to appropriate drugs or surgeries, and extending improved physical accommodations for the obese, plus larger protections against workplace discrimination.

The consistent bias in American policy against mitigation and in favor of adaptation nonetheless presents itself differently in these two cases. In the case of climate change, the policy bias against mitigation reflects the anticipated economic cost of reducing fossil fuel consumption quickly using today's technologies and an improbability of effective international cooperation, versus the tangible benefits (including political benefits) waiting to be captured in the short term through public investments in self-protection. In the case of obesity, the bias against mitigation does not come from high cost, since Americans would actually save money by eating less and exercising more. Nor does it come from an improbability of international cooperation, since obesity trends elsewhere make no difference inside America. Instead, strong policies to mitigate obesity are off the table in America because they would be seen as statist and coercive (violating a culture of individual freedom), elitist and discriminatory (coercing the greatest behavior change from the poor, or from racial minorities), and perhaps unnecessary (in a society that trusts science and medicine to solve problems without requiring a lifestyle change).

If America continues to move toward an adaptation posture for both climate change and obesity, what will be the consequence for the rest of the world? This will be the subject of our next, and final, chapter.

America's Excess and the World

Is there any good news for the rest of the world in America's food and fuel gluttony? Will America's decision not to use its strongest policy instruments to mitigate excess consumption, pivoting instead toward adaptation, be harmful or beneficial to others? America's fuel habits will be far more damaging abroad than its food habits. America's self-protective adaptation response to climate change will present serious new dangers for other nations, but America's efforts to adapt to obesity will not harm others, and may even provide a benefit, through sharing of new medical treatments to manage the condition. The adaptation response to obesity does have clear drawbacks, but mostly for Americans themselves.

Climate Change

Other nations will be hurt in many ways if the US government leaves its climate change mitigation policies unimproved and begins moving instead down a path of self-protective adaptation. An American policy posture of this kind will make the already difficult task of stabilizing atmospheric CO_2 concentrations effectively unattainable.

Successful climate stabilization requires, at a minimum, simultaneous policy disciplines by the two largest CO_2 emitters: China and the United States. Disciplines have recently been attempted by some significant European governments, particularly Germany, but credible policies to mitigate are currently not in place in America, and China's new pledge to seek an emissions peak by 2030, even if fulfilled, is not the same as a pledge to cut. If the United States were to forego greater progress on mitigation and move instead toward self-protective adaptation, China's motives to mitigate would be undercut, and eventually even Europe's disciplines might weaken. If America turns away from mitigation, increasingly disruptive climate change will come sooner and hit harder. Eventually, even the United States will be unable to self-protect, as in the event of a major sea level rise caused by ice sheet loss (IPCC 2014b).

America's pivot toward short-term climate adaptation would have benefits for others only if accompanied by a much stronger public research commitment to improve low-carbon energy technologies. If breakthrough science can be delivered this way, even China might eventually make a strong move away from dirty fossil fuels. An American R&D commitment of this kind differs dramatically from today's practice of trying to scale up existing renewable power sources. The federal government tripled its spending on clean energy between 2009 and 2014, but less than 20 percent of that spending actually went for R&D. Federal R&D funding for energy is only one-third as high as for health, and only one-seventh as high as for defense (Sargent 2013). Without much stronger resource commitments, the research-led approach will have little promise.

Even if the needed science breakthroughs take place, America will be uniquely challenged participating in the international agreements needed for an effective scale up. America had some good reasons to dislike the Kyoto Protocol, with its reliance on national emissions caps. A better approach might have been to seek agreement on specific policy actions, perhaps beginning with club-style cooperation among major emitters (Victor 2011). As one example, governments could agree on national obligations to tax carbon (Cooper 1998). With this approach, less wealthy countries like China and India would not be asked to cap their emissions at a lower level of development, locking in their wealth disadvantage. Governments would capture their own tax revenues, which they could use domestically to finance R&D, compensate losers, balance budgets, reduce other tax burdens, or all of the above. National political leaders should also prefer this kind of international agreement because compliance would be based on something they control—a specific policy action—rather than overall emissions levels, which they do not control (Nordhaus 2009).

It is easy to imagine such improvements to the failed Kyoto approach, yet realism suggests that America will remain an impediment to progress under almost any negotiation design. America is poorly equipped to join global multilateral agreements thanks to the eighteenth-century stipulation in its Constitution requiring a two-thirds Senate vote for treaty ratification. This antiquated requirement has already blocked America's participation in numerous international treaties on environmental issues over the years. Since 1975, the United States has failed to ratify the Bonn Convention of Migratory Species, the Convention on Biological Diversity, the Convention on the Law of the Sea, the Kyoto Protocol, the Rotterdam Convention on Hazardous Chemicals and Pesticides, and the Stockholm Convention on Persistent Organic Pollutants (Anderson 2002). Not participating in global multilateral agreements is just one more inconvenient feature of American exceptionalism (Moravcsik 2005).

A final barrier to the pursuit of an internationally coordinated mitigation strategy based on tomorrow's technologies will be opposition from America's climate change activists. These activists deserve great credit for alerting America to the risks ahead, but they remain inflexibly opposed to a research-led approach that would innovate first and then scale up mitigation later. Activist and author Bill McKibben has insisted that we begin mitigating immediately, whatever the economic cost. McKibben ridicules any delayed mitigation approach as "grotesque" and even "farcical." He implicitly acknowledges that America's political class is not yet ready to mitigate at scale, but investments in new science are not his solution. Instead, he calls for an unlikely new social movement, "an in-the-streets surge that labels the fossil fuel companies as the enemies to a workable future, guilty of a 'crime' . . ." (McKibben 2011, p. 8). Given these inflexible views among climate activists, a research-led strategy would probably enjoy support only from a few economists, plus the research scientists and institutes that would get the money.

Disruptive climate change is thus unlikely to be avoided, given the posture of the United States. This will imply growing risks for the large portion of humanity currently lacking affordable options to adapt. The damages most difficult to avoid will come from sea level rise and glacial melting. In 2013 the IPCC estimated that if emissions continue to increase rapidly, as will happen if America pivots toward adaptation, sea level will rise between 0.45 and 0.82 meters by the end of the twenty-first century (IPCC 2013). To appreciate the social risks of such a change, consider that a one-meter rise would put 17.5 percent of the current territory of Bangladesh permanently under water, would eliminate half of that nation's rice-producing land, and would force 20 million people to relocate (Guzman 2013). Glacial melting, which the IPCC describes as already speeding up, will simultaneously threaten freshwater supplies for more than one billion people in Asia who now depend on mountain glacier and snowpack systems for steady water flows. According to the IPCC, almost all of the world's glaciers are already shrinking.

Unabated climate change will also damage agricultural production in tropical countries, where high heat and drought already place severe constraints on crop growth. In 2009, the International Food Policy Research Institute modeled scenarios based on the IPCC's 2007 Fourth Assessment Report and projected that by 2050 wheat production in the developing world would be 34 percent lower with climate change, compared to a scenario without climate change. In South Asia specifically, where most of the world's hungry people still live, wheat production was projected to be an alarming 49 percent lower in 2050 with climate change, compared to a no climate change scenario (Nelson et al. 2009).

The World Bank estimates that poor countries may need as much as $100 billion each year to try to offset the effects of climate change, and in 2009 the world's wealthy countries actually promised $30 billion to make a "fast start" on this kind of financing over the next three years, plus a scaling up to $100 billion by 2020. This was never realistic. In 2013, Todd D. Stern, the State Department's chief climate change negotiator, said that "fiscal reality" would not allow the $100 billion figure to be reached (Davenport 2014c). In fact, the IPCC removed a reference to the $100 billion climate aid fund from the policymakers' summary of its 2014 report, at the urging of the United States. Wealthy countries spend generously for self-protection, but not for someone else's protection. Of the roughly $35 billion that wealthy countries claimed to have spent on climate aid in 2010–2012, only $5 billion went toward adaptation (Plumer 2013a).

If accelerating climate change brings worsening outcomes to developing countries, Americans may eventually find it difficult to turn a blind eye. Yet at this point the tempting alternative for the United States will be another kind of technical fix. American scientists are already developing various geoengineering options, such as injecting droplets of sulfur dioxide into the stratosphere, to reflect 1 percent or more of solar radiation back out into space, or perhaps fertilizing parts of the ocean with iron dust to encourage the growth of phytoplankton, which are tiny plants that take CO_2 out of the atmosphere. Until now, such approaches have been difficult even to talk about due to the troubling uncertainties that range from weather destabilization to ozone loss. Even if solar radiation and warming could be reduced this way, CO_2 would continue to accumulate in the atmosphere, leading to continued acidification of the oceans, causing harm to coral reefs and marine life. Yet the political allure of geoengineering comes from the quick lowering of temperatures it can bring, and the extremely low dollar cost, perhaps only a few billion dollars annually (Keith 2013).

When Mount Pinatubo erupted in 1991, volcanic ash formed a reflective aerosol cloud that reduced by 10 percent for two years the amount of sunlight reaching the Earth's surface. As a result, average temperatures fell by about 0.9 °F, roughly the same amount that average temperatures had risen over the previous 100 years. In 2006, Paul Crutzen, a Nobel laureate scientist who dismisses international cooperation on mitigation as a "pious wish," called for additional research on geoengineering. In 2009, even President Obama's science advisor, John Holdren, said the United States no longer had the luxury of keeping geoengineering options off the table. In March 2013, the National Academy of Sciences partnered with the CIA to fund a 21-month, $630,000 evaluation of various geoengineering techniques (McCormick 2013). Proponents of geoengineering argue that even a small foray into solar radiation management (SRM) could buy the time needed to develop cleaner energy sources, or improve carbon capture and storage options. A further weakening of America's resolve to mitigate is the obvious danger in such talk.

Sadly then, an American shift toward climate change adaptation will bring no hidden benefit at all for the rest of the world. The nation that originally did the most to create this global problem will make matters worse for others if it concentrates on protecting itself.

Obesity

In contrast to fuel consumption, America's continued overconsumption of food inflicts harm almost entirely on Americans at home. This might seem fitting, but it is poor, poorly educated, and non-White Americans who pay the highest price. Obesity in America emerges as just one more example of the nation's larger problem with social, health, and welfare inequality. The groups in America most likely to become obese—racial minorities, single-parent households, and those with only a high-school education or less—are also those least likely to have adequate medical care, and therefore least able to adapt to the condition. Obesity in America is twice as high among children whose parents lack a high-school degree, so it tends to worsen prospects for those already in trouble. Adaptation and treatment options may work well enough for upper-income and college-educated Americans, who have ready access to medical services and more often get the social reinforcement needed to avoid becoming obese in the first place. For the poor, an adaptation and treatment approach will generate poor results. Fortunately, at least, obesity prevalence in the United States does little to increase obesity prevalence in foreign countries. America's bad outcome at home might even help others, if it fosters new treatment options, or if it offers to others a timely warning not to go down America's path.

It is sometimes argued that America is "exporting" its obesity crisis to other countries, via the foreign advertising campaigns of its private food companies, or through Washington's trade and investment promotion policies that presumably operate on behalf of such companies (Clark et al. 2012). American companies and US trade and investment policies do indeed play a prominent role in bringing US-style foods—packaged and processed, energy dense, and hyper-convenient—to consumers in other countries, and some added increment of obesity is no doubt one result. In some cases, the American corporate role is particularly visible, as with the doubling of US food company investments in Mexico between 1994 and 1999, following completion of the North American Free Trade Agreement (NAFTA), or in Thailand where PepsiCo's Frito-Lay company more than doubled its promotional spending to advertise potato chips and other energy-dense snack foods between 1999 and 2003 (Hawkes 2006).

Yet it is hard to depict the resulting health risks as an export from America, since the primary driver is rapid income growth and a more sedentary urban lifestyle among the local consumers within these countries. These consumers are becoming more like us, but not because of us. Mexico and Thailand both urbanized rapidly in the 1990s, quickly producing a large, young, and more prosperous customer base for unhealthy food. Even if American companies had stayed away, these customers would have soon attracted large food company exports and investments from someone else. Europe, for example, also has private firms that manufacture, advertise, and sell unhealthy snack foods around the world. Europe's association of snack food manufacturers, the ESA, has 54 members.

Washington's market-opening trade and investment policies play a role in some cases, but smaller than imagined. In Mexico, the arrival of international food companies selling unhealthy snacks was most definitely accelerated by the 1994 North American Free Trade Agreement (NAFTA), but it was the government of Mexico that originally requested this agreement, in 1990, not the government of the United States (Hufbauer Schott 2005). Some try to blame obesity in Mexico on American farm subsidies, which purportedly "dump" cheap American food into neighboring countries, yet we saw in Chapter 3 that America's farm support programs tend on balance to make food in the United States, including all sweetened products, artificially expensive, not artificially cheap. Biofuels policies in America, which mandate the use of corn for ethanol production, specifically cause America's corn exports to Mexico to be expensive, not cheap. In 2007, a mass demonstration was even staged in Mexico City to protest the high price of corn.

When urbanizing societies liberalize their rules governing foreign trade and investment, which all tend to do, international companies do arrive to sell products that contribute to an increase in obesity prevalence, but the increase in calorie intake will primarily be driven by income growth, not a sudden availability of exotic food choices. The lower physical activity levels associated with urban living play an important role as well. In addition, if the governments of these countries do not wish to open their borders to international food companies, they have a proven and respected sovereign right to refuse. In the case of food retailing in India, WalMart negotiated for years with the government in Delhi hoping to gain access for its large supermarkets, but finally in 2013 the company had to walk away because the terms of entry demanded by India were too onerous (Munroe 2014). Even without WalMart, India's problems with obesity are continuing to increase. Partly this is due to imported food, but in India the problem is high-fat cooking oil imported from Argentina and Brazil, not snack foods or soda imported from the United States (Hawkes 2006).

A broader view also shows that American-style food excess need not be the fate of every high-income country, even those accustomed to borrowing cultural traits from the United States. In Japan, where the most popular sport (baseball) is an American import, and where Hollywood films continue to enjoy a high market share, fast food restaurant chains from the United States have long had a strong and visible presence. McDonald's hamburgers first came to Japan in 1971, and the country now has three times as many McDonald's restaurants as Canada, the United Kingdom, or Germany. Burger King and Wendy's also have a large place in the Japanese market. Despite all this, Japanese eaters manage to control calorie intake and avoid obesity, in part because of the higher prices consumers must pay, especially for beef, and also because Japan has a strong national culture of food restraint. So as the composition of the Japanese diet continues to evolve in the modern age, average per capita food energy intake consistently remains below 1,900 calories a day, compared to more than 2,500 in the United States (Smil and

Kobayashi 2012). Despite four decades of exposure to American fast food, Japan's rate of obesity is the lowest in the OECD world, and its life expectancies are the longest, at 79 years for men in 2011, and 86 years for women.

While rising obesity rates in foreign countries will be hard to attribute to the United States in the years ahead, America is likely to become a leading global source of useful new treatments. If the United States begins investing more to develop medical treatments for its own citizens who have become obese, such treatments will also deliver major benefits beyond America's borders.

Whether or not obesity is a disease, it certainly qualifies as a medical condition, and America has long been a global leader in finding effective treatments for potentially damaging medical conditions. Even though America's own health gains (e.g., reductions in infant mortality) have lagged behind those of Europe, Australia, or Japan, no country has been more innovative in basic medical science, diagnostics, and therapeutics. One count of Nobel Prize winners in medicine and physiology over a recent 40-year period found that 60 percent were from the United States, versus just 42 percent from the European Union, Switzerland, Canada, Australia, and Japan combined (Whitman and Raad 2009). Discovery is more likely to take place in America because research budgets are larger and the research environment is far more competitive and meritocratic. If the world needs more basic medical science in order to understand and combat obesity, it should be pleased to see America's labs playing the lead role.

America is also the top innovator in diagnostics and therapeutics. One count of the top 27 such innovations (those most frequently featured in published literatures over the past 25 years) found that 20 of the 27 and 9 of the top 10 had benefited significantly from work performed in the United States. In comparison, the European Union plus Switzerland (with a combined population 50 percent larger than the United States) contributed significantly to only 14 of these 27 innovations, and only 5 in the top 10 (Whitman and Raad 2009).

When it comes to developing pharmaceutical products specifically, America once again has an unusually strong record. Americans pay much more for drugs than citizens in other advanced countries, in part because the nation's less centralized health system leaves them without the collective bargaining power needed to hold prices down. So monetary returns to pharmaceutical innovations are much higher in America, but at least this encourages more research, specifically inside the United States. Of the top 15 pharmaceutical firms by revenue, eight are based in the United States, six in Europe, and one in Japan. When these firms innovate useful new drugs, the benefits can then be felt worldwide. Some better-insured foreign patients will even benefit more than Americans.

America's obesity crisis is still a comparatively recent development, yet researchers in the United States have already developed a growing inventory of possibly exportable new treatments. GI Dynamics in Lexington, Massachusetts, has developed an "EndoBarrier" sleeve inserted through the mouth and stomach, then placed at the upper portion of the small intestine. This noninvasive and reversible treatment emulates the effect of bariatric surgery, and in 2010 Europe actually moved ahead of the United States in approving its use (Johnson 2011). Another Boston-based company, Gelesis, has been testing a product named Attiva, which is a capsule filled with superabsorbent particles made up of food components which expand into larger gelatinous particles that fill the stomach, helping people feel full longer. In 2011, a team of researchers at the National Institute on Aging reported that a new experimental drug named SRT-1720 enabled obese mice to live 44 percent longer (Wade 2011). In 2012, a scientist from Braasch Biotech in South Dakota published results from an "obesity vaccine" trial that reduced body weight in mice by 10 percent (Zielinska 2012). In 2014, a research team at Harvard and MIT partnered with two

American drug companies, Amgen and Pfizer, in discovering a rare genetic mutation that protects obese people from contracting type 2 diabetes. Amgen and Pfizer immediately launched programs aimed at developing drugs to mimic the impacts from this mutation (Kolata 2014). When it comes to obesity, American innovators are willing to try almost anything. In 2013, a team of scientists at the Washington University School of Medicine in St. Louis found that microbe transplants from the gut of a lean person would prevent mice from gaining weight (Ridaura et al. 2013). Companies are studying the biology of grizzly bears to learn how they manage to maintain a benign medical state despite a seasonal condition of extreme obesity just before hibernation (Corbit 2014). In 2014, a company named HAPILABS even introduced a $100 digital utensil—named the HAPIfork—that reprimands overeaters with a vibrating buzz and a blinking red light if they lift the fork too soon between bites (Stern 2014). Food companies also get into the act. General Mills has developed an extrusion cooker that permits the manufacture of Cheerios with less sugar, yet with no sacrifice of what cereal scientists call "bowl life." How do they do it? "Wouldn't Kellogg's like to know," says a senior vice president at General Mills (Kummer 2012, p. 90).

Conclusion

America's inability to reduce excessive food and fuel consumption at home will therefore generate divergent outcomes for the rest of the world. In the difficult area of climate change, America's policy drift toward self-protective adaptation will undercut its already weak efforts to reduce CO_2 emissions, thus significantly increasing climate risks for others who lack self-protection options. In the area of obesity, however, lax mitigation efforts in America will not diminish mitigation options for governments abroad, and the new treatments that American researchers are likely to develop will be available for export, ensuring an international benefit.

This may seem to be a Janus-faced outcome, but America has in fact failed equally and in the same way on both fronts. The impact on others is divergent only because America's performance remains critical to the global outcome for climate change, but not for obesity. The manner in which America has been falling short on both fronts is not only identical, but identically unattractive. In each case, America's approach is a form of *sauve qui peut*. In response to climate change, America pivots toward adaptation to protect itself, and itself alone. With obesity, America's embrace of personal rather than government responsibility works well enough for the nation's more fortunate citizens, those better educated to avoid the condition and better able to afford medical treatments. For Americans with less education and fewer resources, particularly disadvantaged minorities, personal responsibility without stronger public policy action will remain inadequate. Conclusions such as these, which point to flaws in national character, are painful to reach but impossible to avoid.

References

Advertising Standards Authority (ASA), 2012. "ASA Hot Topic: Food and Drink," www.asa.ora.uk

Aguilera, Jasmine, 2013. "School Lunches Healthier; Are Kids Happy?" News-Press Washington Bureau, July 29, http://www.news-press.com/article/20130730/NEWS01/307300031/School-lunches-healthier-kids-happy-

Aldy, Joseph E., 2013. "Eliminating Fossil Fuel Subsidies," The Hamilton Project, February, http://www.brookings.edu/~/media/research/files/papers/2013/02/thp%20budget%20papers/thp_15waysfedbudget_prop5.pdf

Aliferis, Lisa, 2013. "Study: Sugar—Independent of Obesity—Causes Diabetes," February 28, http://blogs.kqed.org/stateofhealth/2013/02/28/study-its-the-sugar-not-obesity-that-causes-diabetes/

Allaire, Maura, and Stephen Brown, 2012. "U.S. Energy Subsidies: Effects on Energy Markets and Carbon Dioxide Emissions." Prepared for The Pew Charitable Trusts, Philadelphia, August, http://www.pewtrusts.org/our_work_report_detail.aspx?id=85899411349

Alston, Julian M., Abigail M. Okrent, and Joanna Parks, 2013. "Effects of U.S. Public Agricultural R&D on U.S. Obesity and its Social Costs," RMI-CWE Working Paper No. 1302, Robert Mondavi Institute Center for Wine Economics, UC Davis, January.

Alston, Julian M., Daniel A. Sumner, and Stephen A. Vosti, 2008. "Farm Subsidies and Obesity in the United States: National Evidence and International Comparisons," *Food Policy* 33: 470–479.

American Beverage Association (ABA), 2010. "ABA Responds to Latest Study on Soda Taxes," December 10, http://www.ameribev.org/news-media/news-releases-statements/more/233/

American Enterprise Institute (AEI), 2013. "Solar Radiation Management: An Evolving Climate Policy Option," May 29, http://www.aei.org/events/2013/05/29/solar-radiation-management-an-evolving-climate-policy-option/

Anderson, J. W., 2002. "U.S. Has No Role in UN Treaty Process," *Resources*, Issue 148, Summer, http://www.rff.org/Publications/Resources/Documents/148/148_treaty_process.pdf

Anderson, Kym, and Yujiro Hayami, 1986. *The Political Economy of Agricultural Protection*. Sydney: Allen & Unwin.

Anderson, Patricia M., and Kristin F. Butcher, 2006. "Childhood Obesity: Trends and Potential Causes," *The Future of Children* 16(1): 19–45.

Anderson, Patricia M., Kristin F. Butcher, and Philip B. Levine, 2003. "Maternal Employment and Overweight Children." *Journal of Health Economics* 22: 477–504.

Anderson, Sarah E., and Robert C. Whitaker, 2010. "Household Routines and Obesity in US Preschool-Aged Children," *Pediatrics,* February 8, http://pediatrics.aappublications.org/content/125/3/420

Andreyeva, Tatiana, Michael W. Long, and Kelly D. Brownell, 2010. "The Impact of Food Prices on Consumption: A Systematic Review of Research on the Price Elasticity of Demand for Food," *American Journal of Public Health* 100 (2): 216–222.

Arnould, Eric J., and Craig J. Thompson, 2005. "Consumer Culture Theory (CCT): Twenty Years of Research," *Journal of Consumer Research* 31 (March): 868–882.

Associated Press (AP), 2007. "Singapore to Scrap Anti-Obesity Program," *Washington Post,* March 20, http://www.washingtonpost.com/wp-dyn/content/article/2007/03/20/AR2007032001145.html

Association of Corporate Counsel (ACC), 2013. "Obesity as a Disability under the ADA: Is It More Likely Now Than Before?" Lexology, September 11, https://www.google.com/#q=Obesity+as+a+disability+under+the+ADA%3A+is+it+more+likely+now+than+before%3F

Association of National Advertisers (ANA), 2012. "2013 Continuing Resolution Blocks IWG Advertising Guidelines," http://www.ana.net/content/show/id/24226

Ausubel, Jesse H., Iddo K. Wernick, and Paul E. Waggoner, 2012. "Peak Farmland and the Prospect for Land Sparing," *Population and Development Review* 38 (Supplement). http://phe.rockefeller.edu/docs/PDR.SUPP%20Final%20Paper.pdf

Avi-Yonah, Reuven S., 2011. "The Political Pathway: When Will the U.S. Adopt a VAT?" http://www.taxanalysts.com/www/freefiles.nsf/Files/AVI-YONAH-26.pdf/$file/AVI-YONAH-26.pdf

Baldassare, Mark, Sherry Ryan, and Cheryl Katz, 1998. "Suburban Attitudes Toward Policies Aimed At Reducing Solo Driving," *Transportation* 25: 99–117.

Bartosiewicz, Petra, and Marissa Miley, 2013. "The Too Polite Revolution: Why the Recent Campaign to Pass Comprehensive Climate Legislation in the United States Failed," Prepared for the Symposium on
the Politics of America's Fight Against Global Warming, co-sponsored
by the Columbia School of Journalism and the Scholars Strategy Network, Harvard University, February 14.

Bassett, David R., et al., 2008. "Walking, Cycling, and Obesity Rates in
Europe, North America, and Australia," *Journal of Physical Activity and
Health* 5: 795–814.

Basu S., McKee M., Galea G., Stuckler D., 2013. "Relationship of Soft
Drink Consumption to Global Oversight, Obesity, and Diabetes: A
Cross-National Analysis of 75 Countries," *American Journal of Public
Health* 103(11), March 14.

Basu, Sanjay, Paula Yoffe, Nancy Hills, and Robert H. Lustig, 2013. "The
Relationship of Sugar to Population-Level Diabetes; Econometric
Analysis of repeated Cross-Sectional Data," *PLoS One* 8(2): e57873.
DOI: 101371/journal.pone. 0057873.

Baturka, N., P. P. Hornsby, and J. B. Schorling, 2000. "Clinical Implications of Body Image among Rural African-American Women," *Journal
of General Internal Medicine* 15: 235–241.

Baum, C., 2012. "The Effects of Food Stamp Receipt on Weight Gained
by Expectant Mothers," *Journal of Population Economics* 25(4): 1307–1340.

Baum, Charles L, and William F. Ford, 2004. "The Wage Effects of Obesity: A Longitudinal Study," *Health Economics* 13. http://amosyang.net/
wp-content/uploads/2012/10/wageobesity.pdf

BBC News, 2009. "Room to Swing a Cat? Hardly," *BBC Magazine*, UK,
August 15, http://news.bbc.co.uk/2/hi/uk_news/magazine/8201900.stm

Begley, Sharon, 2012. "As America's Waistline Expands, Costs Soar,"
Reuters, April 30, http://www.reuters.com/article/2012/04/30/
us-obesity-idUSBRE83T0C820120430

Bellah, Robert N., 1991. *Beyond Belief: Essays on Religion in a Post-
Traditionalist World*. Berkeley: University of California Press.

Bellah, Robert N., Richard Madsen, William M. Sullivan, Ann Swindler,
and Steven M. Tipton, 1985. *Habits of the Heart: Individualism and Commitment in American Life*. Berkeley: University of California Press.

Berg, A. Scott, 2013. *Wilson*. New York: Putnam.

Binz, Ron, 2012. Remarks at Statewide Sustainability Roundtable,
November 9, University of Denver, Sturm College of Law, http://
www.sustainablecolorado.org/programs/education/roundtables/
statewideroundtable

Bjerga, Alan, 2013. "Mars Inc. to Libertarians Thwart Food Stamp
Health Limits," *Bloomberg,* December 2, http://www.bloomberg.com/
news/2013-2012-02/mars-inc-to-libertarians-thwart-health-limits-on-
food.html

Blanck, Heidi, et al., 2007. "Use of Nonprescription Dietary Supplements for Weight Loss Is Common among Americans," *Journal of the American Dietary Association* 107(3): 441–447.

Blanck, Heidi, Laura Khan, and Mary Serdula, 2001. "Use of Nonprescription Weight Loss Products," *Journal of the American Medical Association* 286(8): 930–935.

Blumenthal, Mark, 2009. "The Problem With Polling Cap and Trade," *National Journal.com*, November 2, http://www.nationaljournal.com/njonline/the-problem-with-polling-cap-and-trade-20091102

Boisvert, Roger, 2013. "Green Energy Bust in Germany," *Dissent*, Summer, http://www.dissentmagazine.org/article/green-energy-bust-in-germany

Bollinger, Bryan, Phillip Leslie, and Alan Sorensen, 2010. "Calorie Posting in Chain Restaurants," National Bureau of Economic Research, August, http://www.nber.org/papers/w15648

Boone-Heinonen, Janne, et al., 2011. "Fast Food Restaurants and Food Stores," *Journal of the American Medical Association,* July 11, http://archinte.jamanetwork.com/article.aspx?articleid=1106078

Bortolotti, Bernardo, and Valentina Milella, 2006. "Privatization in Western Europe; Stylized Facts, Outcomes, and Open Issues," Fondazione Eni Enrico Mattei, October.

Bosello, Francesco, Carlo Carraro, and Enrica de Cian, 2010. "Market- and Policy-Driven Adaptation," pp. 222–276, in Bjorn Lomborg, ed., *Smart Solutions to Climate Change: Comparing Costs and Benefits.* New York: Cambridge University Press.

Broadberry, Stephen, and Alexander Klein, 2011. "Aggregate and Per Capita GDP in Europe, 1870–2000: Continental, Regional, and National Data With Changing Boundaries," Department of Economics, University of Warwick, Coventry, UK.

Brooks, Steve, 2012. "Taxing Spending: The Case for a National Consumption Tax," Texas Enterprise, McCombs School of Business, University of Texas.

Brown, Kay E., 2013. "School Lunch: Modifications Needed to Some of the New Nutrition Standards," Testimony before the Subcommittee on Early Childhood, Elementary, and Secondary Education, Committee on Education and the Workforce, House of Representatives, June 27. GAO-13-708T.

Brownell, Kelly D, Thomas Farley, Walter C. Willett, Barry M. Popkin, Frank J. Chaloupka, Joseph W. Thompson, David S. Ludwig, 2009. "The Public Health and Economic Benefits of Taxing Sugar-Sweetened Beverages." *The New England Journal of Medicine* 361 (October 15): 1599–1605.

Brownell, Kelly D., and Thomas R. Frieden, 2009. "Ounces of Prevention—
The Public Policy Case for Taxes on Sugared Beverages." *New England
Journal of Medicine* 360 (April 30): 1805–1808.

Brownson, R. C., et al., 2005. "Declining Rates of Physical Activity in
the United States: What Are the Contributors?" *Annual Review of Public
Health* 26: 421–443.

Buchwald, H., Y. Avidor, E. Braunwald, et al., 2004. "Bariatric Surgery:
A Systematic Review and Meta-analysis." *Journal of the American Medical
Association* 292(14): 1724–1737.

Buchwald, Henry, and Danette Oien, 2009. "Metabolic/Bariatric Surgery
Worldwide 2008," *Obes Surg*, published online November 3, DOI:
10.1007/s11695–11009–0013–5.

Burnham, Walter Dean, 1974. "The United States: The Politics of Het-
erogeneity," in Richard Rose, ed., *Electoral Behavior*. New York: The
Free Press.

Cabe, Delia, 2001. "Buying Into the Future," *Radcliffe Quarterly* (Fall):
10–17.

Cain, Derrick, 2014. "Nearly One-Third of U.S. Food Got Dumped in
2010, USDA Says," Agri-Pulse, February 25, https://www.google.
com/#q=%E2%80%9CNearly+one-third+of+U.S.+food+got+
dumped+in+2010%2C+USDA+says

Calabresi, Steven G., 2006. "A Shining City on a Hill: American Exceptionalism and the Supreme Court's Practice of Relying on Foreign
Law," *Boston University Law Review* 86: 1335–1416.

Calvin, K., A. Fawcett, and J. Kejun, 2012. "Comparing Model Results
to National Climate Policy Goals: Results from the Asia Modeling Exercise," *Energy Economics* 34(Supplement 3): S306–S315.

CAR, 2014. *United States Climate Action Report*. Sixth National Com-
munication of the United States of America Under the United Nations
Framework Convention on Climate Change. U.S. Department of State,
http://www.state.gov/e/oes/rls/rpts/car6/index.htm

Carraro, Carlo, and Emanuele Massetti, 2012. "When Should China Start
Cutting Its Emissions?" www.voxeu.org, April 25.

Cawley, John, 2011. "Why the Overweight Earn Less." *New York Times,*
November 29, http://www.nytimes.com/roomfordebate/2011/11/28/
should-legislation-protect-obese-people/the-obesity-wage-penalty

Center for American Progress (CAP), 2010. "Eliminating Tax
Subsidies for Oil Companies," May 13, http://www.americanprogress.
org/issues/green/news/2010/05/13/7756/eliminating-tax-subsidies-
for-oil-companies/

Center for Consumer Freedom (CCF), 2014. "What Is the Center for
Consumer Freedom?" http://www.consumerfreedom.com

Center for Science in the Public Interest (CSPI), 2005. "Liquid Candy: How Soft Drinks Are Harming Americans' Health," June, http://www.cspinet.org/new/pdf/liquid_candy_final_w_new_supplement.pdf

Center for Science in the Public Interest (CSPI), 2011. "President Urged Not to Retreat on Kids' Food Marketing," September 2011, http://cspinet.org/new/201109271.html

Centers for Disease Control and Prevention (CDC), 2011. "Losing Weight," Division of Nutrition, Physical Activity and Obesity, August 17.

Centers for Disease Control and Prevention (CDC), 2012. "Adult Obesity Facts," http://www.cdc.gov/obesity/data/adult.html

Centers for Disease Control and Prevention (CDC), 2012a. "What Causes Overweight and Obesity?" Division of Nutrition, Physical Activity and Obesity, April 27. http://www.cdc.gov/obesity/adult/causes/index.html

Centers for Disease Control and Prevention (CDC), 2013a. "Physical Activity Facts," February, http://www.cdc.gov/healthyyouth/physicalactivity/facts.htm

Centers for Disease Control and Prevention (CDC), 2013b. *Results from the School Health Policies and Practices Study, 2012.* Washington, D.C.: US Department of Health and Human Services, Centers for Disease Control and Prevention.

Centers for Disease Control and Prevention (CDC), 2014. http:/www.cdc.gov/diabetes/statistics/mortalitydka/fratedkadiabtotals.htm

Chaney, Tiffany, and Paul Emrath, 2006. "U.S. vs. European Housing Markets," National Association of Home Builders, May 5, http://www.nahb.org/generic.aspx?sectionID=734&genericContentID=57411&channelID=311&print=true

Chithambo, Taona P., and Stanley J. Huey, 2013. "Black/White Differences in Perceived Weight and Attractiveness among Overweight Women," *Journal of Obesity* 2013, http://dx.doi.org/10.1155/2013/320326

Choi, Candice, 2006. "Fewer People Say Overweight People Are Less Attractive, Survey Finds," Associated Press, January 23, http://usatoday30.usatoday.com/news/health/2006-2001-11-weight-survey_x.htm

Christou, N. V., J. S. Sampalis, M. Liberman, et al., 2004. "Surgery Decreases Long Term Mortality, Morbidity, and Health Care Use in Morbidly Obese Patients." *Annals of Surgery* 240(3): 416–423.

Clark, Sarah E., et al., 2012. "Exporting Obesity: U.S. Farm and Trade Policy and the Transformation of the Mexican Consumer Food Environment," *International Journal of Occupational and Environmental Health* 18(1): 53–64.

ClimateWire, 2010. "Nations: Bangladesh, India Most Vulnerable to Climate Change," October 21, *ClimateWire,* http://www.eenews.net/stories/1059941272/print

Cline, Krista M. C., and Kenneth F. Ferraro, 2006. "Does Religion Increase the Prevalence and Incidence of Obesity in Adulthood?" *Journal of the Scientific Study of Religion* 45(2): 269–281.

Cohen, Lizabeth, 2003. *A Consumers' Republic: The Politics of Mass Consumption in Postwar America.* New York: Vintage Books.

Coll, Steve, 2012. "Gusher: The Power of ExxonMobil," *The New Yorker,* April 9, pp. 28–37.

Committee on Finance, US Senate, 2009. "Baucus, Grassley Release Policy Options for Financing Comprehensive Health Care Reform," Newsroom, US Senate Committee on Finance, May 18, www.finance.senate.gov

Confessore, Nicholas, 2014. "How School Lunch Became the Latest Political Battleground," *New York Times Magazine,* October 7, http://www.nytimes.com/2014/10/12/magazine/how-school-lunch-became-the-latest-political-battleground.html

Confessore, Nicholas, 2013. "Minority Groups and Bottlers Team Up in Battles over Soda," *New York Times,* March 12, http://www.nytimes.com/2013/03/13/nyregion/behind-soda-industrys-win-a-phalanx-of-sponsored-minority-groups.html?pagewanted=all

Congressional Budget Office (CBO), 2005. "Policies That Distort World Agricultural Trade: Prevalence and Magnitude," August, CBO, http://www.cbo.gov/sites/default/files/cbofiles/ftpdocs/66xx/doc6614/08-22-doha.pdf

Consumer Reports News, 2013. "Weight-Loss Pill Belviq Is Now Available, But We Say Skip It," *Consumer Reports News,* June 13, http://www.consumerreports.org/cro/news/2013/06/weight-loss-pill-belviq-is-now-available-but-we-say-skip-it/index.htm

Consumers International, 1996. "A Spoonful of Sugar. Television Advertising Aimed at Children: An International Comparative Survey," November. http://www.consumersinternational.org/media/308610/a%20spoonful%20of%20sugar%20-%20television%20food%20advertising%20aimed%20at%20children-%20an%20international%20comparative%20survey.pdf

Cooper, Richard N., 1998. "Toward a Real Global Warming Treaty," *Foreign Affairs,* March/April, http://www.foreignaffairs.com/articles/53807/richard-n-cooper/toward-a-real-global-warming-treaty

Corbit, Kevin, 2014. "A Grizzly Answer for Obesity," *New York Times,* February 11, http://www.nytimes.com/2014/02/12/opinion/a-grizzly-answer-for-obesity.html

Cornwall Alliance, 2013. "An Evangelical Declaration on Global Warming," Accessed December 29, http://www.cornwallalliance.org/articles/read/an-evangelical-declaration-on-global-warming/

Costa, Dora L., and Matthew Kahn, 2001. "Understanding the Decline in Social Capital, 1952–1998," NBER Working Paper 8295, May, http://www.nber.org/papers/w8295

Cox, Wendell, 2009. "Examining Sprawl in Europe and America," *Reason*, January 16, http://reason.org/news/show/1003218.html

Cross, Gary. 2000. *An All-Consuming Century: Why Commercialism Won in Modern America.* New York: Columbia University Press.

Cutler, David M., and Edward L. Glaeser, 2006. "Why Do Europeans Smoke More Than Americans?" NBER Working Paper No. 12124, March, http://www.nber.org/papers/w12124

Dahl, Robert A., 2002. *How Democratic Is the American Constitution?* New Haven, CT: Yale University Press.

Dargay, Joyce, Dermot Gately, and Martin Sommer, 2007. "Vehicle Ownership and Income Growth, Worldwide: 1960–2030," *The Energy Journal* 28(4): 143–171.

Datko, 2012. "As We Get Fatter, Products Get Bigger," *Health Insurance*, May 15, http://money.msn.com/health-and-life-insurance/article.aspx?post=d0d68ec7-bc2d-432e-a7b2-3be3b6e3ad03

Datz, Todd, 2014. "Study Shows Kids Eating More Fruits, Veggies," *Harvard Gazette,* March 4, http://news.harvard.edu/gazette/story/2014/03/study-shows-kids-eating-more-fruits-veggies/

Davenport, Coral, 2014. "Obama to Take Action to Slash Coal Pollution," *New York Times*, June 2, p. A1.

Davenport, Coral, 2014b. "EPA Staff Struggling to Create Pollution Rule," February 4, http://www.nytimes.com/2014/02/05/us/epa-staff-struggling-to-create-rule-limiting-carbon-emissions.html

Davenport, Coral, 2014c. "Climate Study Puts Diplomatic Pressure on Obama," *New York Times,* April 1, p. A3.

Davenport, Coral, 2014d. "Emissions From India Will Increase, Official Says," *New York Times*, September 24, http://www.nytimes.com/2014/09/25/world/asia/25climate.html?_r=0

Davis, Teddy, 2009. "Bill Clinton: Soda Tax Isn't the Way to Go," May 14, ABC News.

Department of Transportation (DOT), 2011. Office of Highway Policy Information, Federal Highway Administration. www.fhwa.dot.gov/ohim/onh00/bar4.htm

Dezember, Ryan, and Emily Glazer, 2013. "Drop in Traffic Takes Toll on Investors in Private Roads," *Wall Street Journal*, November 20, http://online.wsj.com/news/articles/SB10001424052702303482504579177890461812588

Drewnowski, Adam, 2009. "Obesity, Diets, and Social Inequalities," *Nutrition Review*, May, http://www.ncbi.nlm.nih.gov/pubmed/19453676

Duesenberry, James, 1949. *Income, Saving and the Theory of Consumption Behavior*. Cambridge, MA: Harvard University Press.

Dzioubinski, Oleg, and Ralph Chipman, 1999. "Trends in Consumption and Production: Household Energy Consumption," United Nations, Department of Economic & Social Affairs, DESA Discussion Paper No. 6, April, New York.

Economist, 2014. "Obama's Green Gamble," June 7, http://www.economist.com/news/united-states/21603482-presidents-new-climate-rule-will-change-america-he-hopes-it-will-change-china-and

Eddy, Melissa, 2014. "German Energy Official Sounds a Warning." *New York Times*, January 21, http://www.nytimes.com/2014/01/22/business/energy-environment/german-energy-official-sounds-a-warning.html?_r=0

Eddy, Melissa, and Stanley Reed, 2013. "Germany's Effort at Clean Energy Proves Complex," *New York Times*, September 19, p. A5.

Ellis, Joseph J., 1996. *American Sphinx: The Character of Thomas Jefferson*. New York: Vintage.

Elperin, Juliet, 2014. "Why Obama's Car Rules Trump His New Climate Proposal," *Washington Post*, June 2, http://www.washingtonpost.com/blogs/the-fix/wp/2014/06/02/why-obamas-car-rules-trump-his-new-climate-proposal/

Energy Information Administration (EIA), 2013. "U.S. Energy-Related Carbon Dioxide Emissions, 2012," October 21, http://www.eia.gov/environment/emissions/carbon/

Energy Information Agency (EIA), 2013a. "Feed in Tariff: A Policy Tool Encouraging Deployment of Renewable Electricity Technologies," May, http://www.eia.gov/todayinenergy/detail.cfm?id=11471

Energy Information Agency (EIA), 2013b. *Annual Energy Outlook 2013*, Department of Energy, EIA0383, April 15, http://www.eia.gov/forecasts/aeo/pdf/0383%282013%29.pdf

Engels, Friedrich, 1890. "Engels to Sorge," in Karl Marx and Frederick Engels, *Selected Correspondence, 1846–1895*, trans. Donna Torr. New York: International Publishers, 1942.

Environmental Protection Agency (EPA), 2013. "Climate Change: International Impacts & Adaptation," Environmental Protection Agency, June 21, http://www.epa.gov/climatechange/impacts-adaptation/international.html

Environmental Protection Agency (EPA), 2014. Carbon Pollution. Emission Guidelines for Existing Stationary Sources: Electric Utility Generating Units. 40 CFR Part 60, http://www.eenews.net/assets/2014/06/02/document_gw_01.pdf

Erlandson, Dawn, 1994. "The BTU Tax Experience: What Happened and Why It Happened," *Pace Environmental Law Review* 12(1): 173–184.

Etzioni, Amitai, 2012. "The Crisis of American Consumerism," *Huffington Post*, September 4, 2012, http://www.huffingtonpost.com/amitai-etzioni/the-crisis-of-american-co_b_1855390.html

European Commission, 2013. "Physical Education and Sport at School in Europe," Education, Audiovisual and Culture Executive Agency, Eurydice Report, March, Brussels.

European Union, 2013. "VAT Rates Applied in the Member States of the European Union," European Commission, taxud.c.1(2013)69198—EN, January 14.

Eurostat, 2012. "File: Energy Dependency Rate, EU-27, 2000–2010." http://epp.eurostat.ed.europa.eu

Fan, M., 2010 "Do Food Stamps Contribute to Obesity in Low-Income Women?" *American Journal of Agricultural Economics* 92(4): 1165–1180.

Fargione, Joseph, et al. 2008. "Land Clearing and the Biofuel Carbon Debt," *Science* 319(5867): 1235–1238.

FedCenter.gov, 2014. "Climate Change Adaptation," https://www.fedcenter.gov/programs/climate/

Federation of Tax Administrators (FTA), 2014. "State Sales Tax Rates and Food & Drug Exemptions," January 1. http://www.taxadmin.org/fta/rate/sales.pdf

Field to Market, 2012. "Environmental and Socioeconomic Indicators for Measuring Outcomes of On-Farm Agricultural Production in the United States." http://www.fieldtomarket.org/report/national-2/PNT_NatReport_Corn.pdf

Fiese, Barbara H., and Marlene Schwartz, 2008. "Reclaiming the Family Table: Mealtimes and Child Health and Wellbeing." *Social Policy Report* XXII, No. IV. Society for Research in Child Development.

Finkelstein, Andrew, et al., 2014. "Lifetime Direct Medical Costs of Childhood Obesity," *Pediatrics*, April 7, http://pediatrics.aappublications.org/content/early/2014/04/02/peds.2014-0063.abstract

Finkelstein, Eric A., 2012. "Obesity and Severe Obesity Forecasts Through 2030," *American Journal of Preventive Medicine* 42(6): 563–570, http://www.ajpmonline.org/article/S0749-3797%2812%2900146-2900148/abstract

Finnish Energy Industries, 2010. Energy Taxation in Europe, Japan, and the United States. Summary of the Energy Taxation Survey of Electricity, Fuels, District Heat and Transport in the EU and EFTA Countries, Japan and the United States. Released by Finnish Energy Industries in November 2010. http://energia.fi/sites/default/files/energy_taxation_ineurope_japan_and_the_united_states.pdf

Hoeller, Peter, and Markku Wallin, 1991. "Energy Prices, Taxes and Carbon Dioxide Emissions," *OECD Economic Studies* 17 (Autumn 1991): 91–105.

Fischer, R. A., Derek Byerlee, and G. O. Edmeades, 2009. "Can Technology Deliver on the Yield Challenge to 2050?" Paper produced for the FAO Expert Meeting on How to Feed the World in 2050, Rome, June 24–26.

Flegal, K. M, M. D. Carroll, C. L. Ogden, and L. R. Curtin. 2010. "Prevalence and Trends in Obesity among U.S. Adults, 1999–2008," *Journal of the American Medical Association* 293(15): 1861–1867.

Flegal, Katherine, et al., 1995. "The Influence of Smoking Cessation on the Prevalence of Overweight in the United States," *New England Journal of Medicine* 333(18): 1165–1170.

Food and Agriculture Organization (FAO) of the United Nations, 2013. *The State of Food and Agriculture 2013: Food Systems for Better Nutrition.* Rome, http://www.fao.org/docrep/018/i3300e/i3300e.pdf *Foreign Affairs*, March/April.

Forey, Barbara, Jan Hamling, Peter Lee, and Nicholas Wald, 2011. *International Smoking Statistics.* ISS WEB Edition, http://www.pnlee.co.uk/iss.htm

Fouquet, Roger, and Peter Pearson, 2006. "Seven Centuries of Energy Services: The Price and Use of Light in the United Kingdom (1300–2000)." *Energy Journal* 27(1): 139–177.

Frank, Robert H., 1999. *Luxury Fever: Weighing the Cost of Excess.* Princeton, NJ: Princeton University Press.

Friday, Leslie, 2012. "Exploring the Causes of Black Women's Obesity," *BU Today*, November 29, http://www.bu.edu/today/2012/exploring-the-causes-of-black-womens-obesity/

Fryar, Cheryl D., Margaret D. Carroll, and Cynthia L. Ogden, 2012. "Prevalence of Overweight, Obesity, and Extreme Obesity among Adults: United States, Trends 1960–62 Through 2009–10," National Center for Health Statistics, September, http://www.cdc.gov/nchs/data/hestat/obesity_adult_09_10/obesity_adult_09_10.pdf

Galbraith, Kate, 2009. "Buffett: Cap-and-Trade Is a 'Regressive' Tax," *New York Times,* March 9, http://green.blogs.nytimes.com/2009/03/09/buffett-cap-and-trade-is-a-regressive-tax/?_r=0

Galiana, Isabel, and Christopher Green, 2010. "Technology-Led Climate Policy," pp. 292–339, in Bjorn Lomborg, ed., *Smart Solutions to Climate Change: Comparing Costs and Benefits.* New York: Cambridge University Press.

Gallagher, James, 2014. "Mexico Restricts Soft Drink TV Ads to Fight Obesity," *BBC,* July 16, http://www.bbc.com/news/world-latin-america-28325105

Gallagher, Leigh, 2013. *The End of the Suburbs: Where the American Dream Is Moving*. New York: Portfolio.

Gallaugher, Wes, 2008. "Bill Clinton's Recommendations to Ease the USA into a Green Economy." *Sustainable Edmonds: Local Actions for Global Challenges,* August 19, http://sustainable-edmonds.org/2008/08/bill-clintons-recommendations-to-ease-the-usa-into-a-green-economy/

Gantner, Leigh, 2007. "Food Advertising Policy in the United States," Case Study #4–1 of the Program: "Food Policy for Developing Countries: The Role of Government in the Global Food System," Per Pinstrup-Anderson and Fuzhi Cheng, eds., Ithaca, NY: Cornell University Press.

Garcia, Jaume, and Climent Quintana-Domeque, 2006. "Obesity, Employment and Wages in Europe," *Advances in Health Economics and Health Services*, Research Issue 17: 187–217.

Gardner, Bruce L., 2002. *American Agriculture in the Twentieth Century*. Cambridge, MA: Harvard University Press.

Gasparro, Annie, and Mike Esterl, 2014. "Tougher Food Rules in Schools," *Wall Street Journal*, February 26, p. A4.

Gassy-Wright, Oxana V., 2005. "Commercial Speech in the United States and Europe," *LLM Theses and Essays*, Paper 13, http://digitalcommons.law.uga.edu/stu_llm/13

Gentile, Sal, 2010. "As White House Tackles Obesity, Lawmakers Eye Soda as Culprit," Need to Know, PBS, May 11. www.pbs.org/wnet/need-to-know/health/as-white-house-tackles-obesity-lawmakers-eye-soda-as-culprit/566/

Giddens, Anthony, 2011. *The Politics of Climate Change*. 2nd ed. Cambridge, UK: Polity Press.

Gillis, Justin, 2013. "White House Will Focus on Climate Shifts While Trying to Cut Greenhouse Gases," *New York Times,* November 1, p. A15.

Gingrich, Newt, 2011. *A Nation Like No Other: Why American Exceptionalism Matters*. New York: Regnery Publishing.

Glendon, Mary Ann, 1992. "Rights in Twentieth Century Constitutions," pp. 519–537 in Geoffrey R. Stone, Richard A. Epstein, and Cass R. Sunstein, eds., *The Bill of Rights in the Modern State*. Chicago: University of Chicago Press.

Globespan Poll, 2011. "Sharp Drop in American Enthusiasm for Free Market, Poll Shows." April 6, http://globescan.com/news-and-analysis/press-releases/press-releases-2011/150-sharp-drop-in-american-enthusiasm-for-free-market-poll-shows.html

Gold, Matea, and Kathleen Hennessey, 2013. "Michelle Obama's Nutrition Campaign Comes with Political Pitfalls," *Los Angeles*

Times, July 20, http://articles.latimes.com/2013/jul/20/nation/
la-na-michelle-food-20130712

Gollust, S. E., et al., 2014. "Americans' Opinions about Policies to
Reduce Consumption of Sugar-Sweetened Beverages," *Preventive Medicine*, March 11, 63C: 52–57.

Graham, D., and S. Glaister, 2002. "The Demand for Automobile Fuel: A
Survey of Elasticities," *Journal of Transport Economics ad Policy* 36: 1–26.

Grainger, Corbett, and Charles Kolstad, 2009. "Who Pays a Price on
Carbon?" NBER Working Paper No. 15239, August, http://www.
nber.org/papers/w15239

Grynbaum, Michael M., 2013. "In N.A.A.C.P., Industry Gets Ally
Against Soda Ban," *New York Times*, January 23, www.nytimes.
com/2013/01/24

Gundersen, Craig, 2013. "SNAP and Obesity," University of Kentucky
Center for Poverty Research Discussion Paper Series, DP 2013–2002,
http://www.ukcpr.org/Publications/DP2013-2002.pdf

Guthrie, Amy, David Luhnow, and Jose de Cordoba, 2013. "Companies
Brace for Mexican Food Fight," *Wall Street Journal*, October 19–20, p. A10.

Guzman, Andrew, 2013. The Human Cost of Climate Change. New
York: Oxford University Press.

Gye, Hugo, 2012. "British Whites Are the Minority in London for the
First Time as Census Shows Number of UK Immigrants Has Jumped
by 3 Million in 10 Years," *Mail Online*, December 11, www.dailymail.
co.uk/news/article-2246288

Hagstrom, Jerry, 2014. "First Lady Has Food Industry in a Frenzy," *National Journal,* March 16, http://www.nationaljournal.com/outside-
influences/first-lady-has-food-industry-in-a-frenzy-20140316

Hampden-Turner, Charles, and Fons Trompenaars, 1997. *Riding the Waves of
Culture: Understanding Diversity in Global Business*. New York: McGraw-Hill.

Hannan, Daniel, 2013. *Inventing Freedom: How the English-Speaking Peoples
Made the Modern World*. New York: Harper Collins.

Harper, Matthew, 2011. "Why There Will Never Be Another Drug Like
Lipitor," *Forbes*, November 30, http://www.forbes.com/sites/
matthewherper/2011/11/30/why-there-will-never-be-another-drug-
like-lipitor/

Hartocollis, Anemona, 2010. "Failure of State Soda Tax Plan Reflects
Power of an Antitax Message," July 2, *New York Times*, www.nytimes.
com/2010/07/03

Harvard School of Public Health (HSPH), 2012. "The Obesity Prevention Source: Economic Costs," Harvard School of Public Health,
http://www.hsph.harvard.edu/obesity-prevention-source/obesity-
consequences/economic/

Harvard School of Public Health (HSPH), 2013. "Television Watching and 'Sit Time,'" HSPH Obesity Prevention Source, accessed September 16, 2013, http://www.hsph.harvard.edu/obesity-prevention-source/obesity-causes/television-and-sedentary-behavior-and-obesity/

Hatch, Michael T., 1995. "The Politics of Global Warming in Germany," *Environmental Politics* 4(3): 415–440.

Hatch, Michael T., 2007. "The Europeanization of German Climate Change Policy." Prepared for the EUSA Tenth Biennial International Conference, Montreal, Canada. May 17–19.

Hawkes, Corinna, 2006. "Uneven Dietary Development," *Globalization and Health* 2(4), http://www.globalizationandhealth.com/content/2/1/4

Health Central, 2013. "Obesity Treatments and the Affordable Care Act," *My Bariatric Life, Health Guide*, October 3, http://www.healthcentral.com/obesity/c/276918/163239/treatments-affordable-care/

Healy, Melissa, 2011. "A Sleeve for the Intestine: As Effective as Bariatric Surgery, Without the Surgery Part?" *Los Angeles Times*, April 5, http://articles.latimes.com/2011/apr/05/news/la-heb-diabetes-bariatric-sleeve-20110401

Henderson, Nia-Malika, 2010. "After Delays, Final Vote Set for Child Nutrition Bill," *Washington Post*, December 2, http://www.washingtonpost.com/wp-dyn/content/article/2010/12/02/AR2010120201407.html

Hilzenrath, David, and Eric Pianin, 1993. "Senator Boren Targets Clinton Energy Tax; Lawmaker Seeks Deeper Budget Cuts," *Washington Post*, May 21, p. A1.

Hofstede, Geert, 2001. *Culture's Consequences: Comparing Values, Behaviors, Institutions and Organizations Across Nations*, 2nd ed. London: Sage Publications.

Hoover, Herbert. 1928. "Rugged Individualism," Speech at New York's Madison Square Garden, October 23, http://livefromthetrail.com/about-the-book/speeches/chapter-5/herbert-hoover

Hosler, Karen, 1993. "Clinton Abandons Btu Tax; Energy Industry Lobbyists Cited by Bentsen," *Baltimore Sun*, June 9, http://articles.baltimoresun.com/1993-1906-09/news

House of Representatives, 2013. H.R. 152: Disaster Relief Appropriations Act, 2013. https://www.govtrack.us/congress/bills/113/hr152/text

Hovi, Jon, Detlef Sprinz, and Guri Bang, 2010. "Why the United States Did Not Become a Party to the Kyoto Protocol: German, Norwegian, and US perspectives," *European Journal of International Relations* 18(1): 129–150.

Hufbauer, Gary Clyde, and Jeffrey J. Schott, 2005. *NAFTA Revisited: Achievements and Challenges*. Washington, DC: Institute for International Economics.

Huffman, Fatma, Sankarabharan Kanikireddy, and Manthan Patel, 2010. "Parenthood: A Contributing Factor to Childhood Obesity," *International Journal of Environmental Research and Public Health* 7(7): 2800–2810.

Huntington, Samuel P., 2004. *Who Are We? America's Great Debate.* New York: Simon & Schuster.

Immergut, Ellen M., 1990. "Veto Points, and Policy Results: A Comparative Analysis of Health Care," *Journal of Public Policy* 10(4): 391–416.

Institute of Medicine (IOM), 2013. "U.S. Health in International Perspective," IOM of the National Academies, Report Brief, January, http://www.iom.edu/~/media/Files/Report%20Files/2013/US-Health-International-Perspective/USHealth_Intl_PerspectiveRB.pdf

Intergovernmental Panel on Climate Change (IPCC), 2001. "Summary for Policy Makers," A Report of Working Group III, https://www.ipcc.ch/ipccreports/tar/wg3/pdf/WG3_SPM.pdf

Intergovernmental Panel on Climate Change (IPCC), 2007. IPCC Fourth Assessment Report: Climate Change 2007. Working Group III: Mitigation of Climate Change. Box13.7. www.ipcc.ch/publications_and_data/ar4/wg3/en/ch13-ens13-13-3-3.html

Intergovernmental Panel on Climate Change (IPCC), 2013. "Working Group 1 Contribution to the IPCC Fifth Assessment Report. Climate Change 2013: The Physical Science Basis." First Draft Underlying Scientific-Technical Assessment, June 7, http://www.climatechange2013.org/images/uploads/WGIAR5_WGI-12Doc2b_FinalDraft_Chapter13.pdf

Intergovernmental Panel on Climate Change (IPCC), 2014. "Summary for Policy Makers," Final Draft, Working Group III, AR5. http://www.ipcc.ch/index.htm

Intergovernmental Panel on Climate Change (IPCC), 2014b. "Climate Change 2014: Impacts, Adaptation, and Vulnerability. Summary for Policymakers," IPCC WGII AR5. http://ipcc-wg2.gov/AR5/images/uploads/IPCC_WG2AR5_SPM_Approved.pdf

International Energy Agency (IEA), 2010. *Global Gaps in Clean Energy RD&D Update and Recommendations for International Collaboration*, IEA Report for the Clean energy Ministerial OECD/IEA, Paris, http://www.iea.org/publications/freepublications/publication/global_gaps.pdf

International Social Survey Program (ISSP), 1991. B.I. and Lucile Cohen Institute for Public Opinion Research, http://www.gesis.org/en/issp/issp-home/

IQWiG, 2006. *Benefit Assessment of Non-Drug Treatment Strategies in Patients with Hypertension: Weight Reduction. Final Report A05–21A. Version 1.0.* Cologne: German Institute for Quality and Efficiency in Health Care, August.

Jacobson, Michael F., 2009. "Health Care Reform: *Prevention* Is Essential." Center for Science in the Public Interest. Statement prepared for Roundtable Discussion on Financing Comprehensive Health Care Reform, Senate Finance Committee, May 12.

Jaffe, Daniel L., 2009. Comments of Daniel L. Jaffe, Executive Vice President, Association of National Advertisers, Panel on "Advertising to Children and the First Amendment," FTC Public Forum on Sizing Up Food Marketing and Childhood Obesity, December 15.

Jalonick, Mary Clare, 2014. "USDA Adds Foods to Moms and Kids Food Program," February 28, *BloombergBusinessWeek*, http://www.businessweek.com/ap/2014-2002-28/usda-adds-foods-to-moms-and-kids-food-program

Jaumotte, Florence, 2003. *Female Labor Force Participation: Past Trends and Main Determinants in OECD Countries*. OECD Economics Department Working Papers, No. 376.

Jefferson, Thomas, 1801. "First Inaugural Address, in Washington, D.C.," March 4, http://www.bartleby.com/124/pres16.html

Johnson, Carolyn Y., 2011. "Ingenuity vs. Obesity," *Boston Globe,* March 7, p. B5.

Kagan, Robert A., 2001. *Adversarial Legalism: The American Way of Law.* Cambridge, MA: Harvard University Press.

Kapstein, Ethan, 1990. *The Insecure Alliance: Energy Crises and Western Politics Since 1944.* New York: Oxford University Press

Kartch, John, 2009. "Obama Floats Soda Tax," The Spectacle Blog, September 8, www.spectator.org./blog/2009/09/08/

Kasperowicz, Pete, 2014. "West Virginia Threatens to Sue over EPA's 'Blatantly' Illegal Carbon Emissions Rule," *The Blaze,* June 9, http://www.theblaze.com/stories/2014/06/09/west-virginia-threatens-to-sue-over-epas-blatantly-illegal-carbon-emissions-rule/

Katzenstein, Peter J., 1985. *Small States in World Markets: Industrial Policy in Europe*. Ithaca, NY: Cornell University Press.

Keith, David, 2013. *A Case for Climate Engineering*. Cambridge, MA: MIT Press.

Kempton, Willett, James S. Boster, and Jennifer A. Hartley, 1995. *Environmental Values in American Culture*. Cambridge, MA: MIT Press.

Kerr, Jennifer, and Jennifer Agiesta, 2013. "Poll: Obesity's a Crisis But We Want Our Junk Food," Associated Press, January 4, http://www.apnorc.org/news-media/Pages/News+Media/poll-obesity-a-crisis-but-we-want-our-junk-food.aspx

Kim, K. H., J. Sobal, and E. Wethington, 2003. "Religion and Body Weight," *International Journal of Obesity Related Metabolic Disorders* 27(4): 469–477.

Kolata, Gina, 2011. "Catching Obesity from Friends May Not Be So Easy," *New York Times,* August 8, http://www.nytimes.com/2011/08/09/health/09network.html?_r=0

Kolata, Gina, 2014. "Rare Mutation Kills Off Gene Responsible for Diabetes," *New York Times*, March 3, p. A12.

Kolmes, Steven A., 2011. "Climate Change: A Disinformation Campaign," *Environment*, July/August, pp. 33–37.

Kotz, K., and M. Story, 1994. "Food Advertisements during Children's Saturday Morning Television Programming: Are They Consistent with Dietary Recommendations?" *Journal of the American Dietetic Association* 94(11): 1296–1300.

Kroger, Gregory, 2010. *Filibustering: A Political History of Obstruction in the House and Senate*. Chicago: University of Chicago Press.

Kuchler, Fred, and Hayden Stewart, 2008. "Price Trends Are Similar for Fruits, Vegetables, and Snack Foods," USDA, Economic Research Report No. (ERR-55), March, http://www.ers.usda.gov/publications/err-economic-research-report/err55.aspx#.U4DYWsfSdgM

Kuhnhenn, Jim, and Ken Thomas, 2012. "Not Heard or Seen in Charlotte: TARP, Stimulus, Cap and Trade," National Politics, United Press, September 6.

Kumanyika, S., 1987. "Obesity in Black Women," *Epidemiologic Reviews* 9: 31–50.

Kummer, Corby, 2012. "Can Technology Save Breakfast?" *Smithsonian*, June, http://www.smithsonianmag.com/science-nature/can-technology-save-breakfast-88382438/?no-ist

Kunzig, Robert, 2014. "Clean Coal Test: Power Plants Prepare to Capture Carbon," National Geographic, March 31, http://news.nationalgeographic.com/news/energy/2014/03/140331-carbon-capture-kemper-coal-climate/

Kwan, Samantha, and Jennifer Graves, 2013. *Framing Fat: Competing Constructions in Contemporary Culture*. New Brunswick, NJ: Rutgers University Press.

Lakdawalla, D., and T.J. Philipson, 2002. "The Growth of Obesity and Technological Change: A Theoretical and Empirical Examination," NBER Working Paper No. W8946, National Bureau for Economic Research, Cambridge, MA.

Lancaster, Thomas D., and W. David Patterson, 1981. "Comparative Pork Barrel Politics: Perceptions from the West German Bundestag," *American Journal of Political Science* 25(1), https://www.google.com/#q=Comparative+Pork+Barrel+Politics%3A+Perceptions+from+the+West+German+Bundestag

LaReau, Jamie, 2011. "Are Too Many Americans Too Fat to Fit into Compact Cars?" *Automotive News*, June 1, 2011, www.autonews.com

Larsen, John, Alexia Kelly, and Robert Heilmayr, 2009. "Brief Summary of the Waxman-Markey Discussion Draft," Washington, DC, World Resources Institute, April 20, www.wro.org/stories/2009/04/brief-summary-waxman-markey-discussion-draft

Larson, Reed W., 2001. "How U.S. Children and Adolescents Spend Time: What It Does (and Doesn't) Tell Us about Their Development," *Current Directions in Psychological Science* 10(5): 160–164.

Lawrence Livermore National Laboratories (LLNL), 2013. "Energy Flow," https://flowcharts.llnl.gov/

Lee W. J., M. T. Huang, W. Wang, et al., 2004. "Effects of Obesity Surgery on the Metabolic Syndrome." *Archives of Surgery* 139(10): 1088–1092.

Leiserowitz, A., Maibach, E., and Roser-Renouf, C., 2009. *Saving Energy at Home and on the Road: A Survey of Americans' Energy Saving Behaviors, Intentions, Motivations, and Barriers.* Yale University and George Mason University. New Haven, CT: Yale Project on Climate Change.

Lempert, David, 2007. "Women's Increasing Wage Penalties from Being Overweight and Obese," US Bureau of Labor Statistics, Working Paper 414, December, http://www.bls.gov/ore/pdf/ec070130.pdf

Leonhardt, David, 2009. "Soda as a Tempting Tax Target." *New York Times,* Economic Scene, May 19, NYTimes.com

Let's Move, 2013. Healthier US Schools Challenge, http://www.letsmove.gov/join-healthierus-schools-challenge

Lieberman, Daniel E., 2013. *The Story of the Human Body: Evolution, Health, and Disease.* New York: Pantheon Books.

Lindberg, Nangel M, Stevens, and Halperin. 2013. "Weight-Loss Interventions for Hispanic Populations: The Role of Culture." *Journal of Obesity* 2013, http://dx.doi.org/10.1155/2013/542736

Lipset, Seymour Martin, 1996. *American Exceptionalism: A Double-Edged Sword.* New York: W.W. Norton & Company.

Luers, Amy, Carl Pope, and David Kroodsma, 2013. "Climate Risks: Linking Narratives to Action," *Stanford Social Innovation Review*, August 19, http://www.ssireview.org/blog/entry/climate_risks_linking_narratives_to_action

Ma, Yunsheng, et al. 2003. "Association between Eating Patterns and Obesity in a Free-living US Adult Population," *American Journal of Epidemiology* 158(1): 85–92.

Macauley, Molly K., 2011. "Investing in Information to Respond to a Changing Climate," *Resources for the Future* 178 (Summer): 27–31.

Macauley, Molly K., and Daniel F. Morris, 2011. "Climate Change in the United States: Expected Environmental Impacts and Necessary Federal Action." *Resources for the Future* 178 (Summer): 20–26.

MacVean, Mary, 2012. "Studies Show Promise for Obesity Surgeries," *Los Angeles Times*, September 12, http://articles.latimes.com/2012/sep/18/news/la-heb-studies-show-promise-for-obesity-surgeries-20120918

Maddison, Angus, 2006. *The World Economy,* Vol. 2: Historical Statistics, Tables 1c and 2c. Paris: OECD.

Madsen, Deborah L, 1998. *American Exceptionalism.* Jackson: University Press of Mississippi.

Malkin, Elisabeth, 2013. "Mexico Takes a Bloomberg-Like Swing at Soaring Obesity," *New York Times,* October 16, p. A4.

Mann, Traci, 2007. "Medicare's Search for Effective Obesity Treatments: Diets Are Not the Answer". *American Psychologist* 62: 220–233.

Marchione, Marilynn, 2014. "Surgery Gives Long-Term Help for Obese Diabetics," Associated Press, March 31, http://www.abc27. com/story/25116859/surgery-gives-long-term-help-for-obese-diabetics

Mather, Mark, 2010. "US Children in Single-Mother Families," Population Reference Bureau, Data Brief, May, http://www.prb.org/ Publications/Reports/2010/singlemotherfamilies.aspx

Matthews, Alan, 2012. "OECD Reports EU Farm Transfers at Lowest Level Ever," CAP Reform.eu, September 21, http://capreform.eu

Matthews, Merrill, 2013. "About Those Tax Breaks for Big Oil . . ." *Wall Street Journal,* April 2, 2013, http://online.wsj.com/article/SB100014241 27887324789504578380684292877300.html

Mayer, Jane, 2010. "Covert Operations: The Billionaire Brothers Who Are Waging a War Against Obama," *The New Yorker,* Reporter at Large, August 30.

Mayo Clinic, 2013. "Metabolic Syndrome," April 5, http://www. mayoclinic.org/diseases-conditions/metabolic-syndrome/basics/ definition/con-20027243

McCormick, Ty, 2013. "Anthropology of an Idea: Geoengineering," *Foreign Policy,* September/October, pp. 28–29.

McCright, Aaron M., and Riley E. Dunlap, 2011. "Cool Dudes: The Denial of Climate Change among Conservative White Males in the United States," *Global Environmental Change* 21(4): 1163–1172.

McCully, Clinton P., 2011. "Trends in Consumer Spending and Personal Saving, 1959–2009," *Survey of Current Business,* June, http://www.bea. gov/scb/pdf/2011/06%20June/0611_pce.pdf

McDermott, Andrew J., et al., 2010. "Cost of Eating: Whole Foods Versus Convenience Foods in a Low-Income Model," *Family Medicine* 42(4): 280–284.

McDonald, N. C., 2007. "Active Transportation to School: Trends among U.S. Schoolchildren, 1969–2001," *American Journal of Preventive Medicine* 32: 509–516.

McKay, Betsy, 2012. "The ABCs of Beating Obesity," *Wall Street Journal,* May 9, 2012, p. A3.

McKay, Betsy, 2014. "Obesity in Young Children Falls Sharply," *Wall Street Journal*, February 26, p. A4.

McKibben, Bill, 2011. "Resisting Climate Reality (A review of *Smart Solutions to Climate Change*, edited by Bjorn Lomborg, Cambridge University Press)," *New York Review of Books*, April 7, http://www.nybooks.com/articles/archives/2011/apr/07/resisting-climate-reality/?pagination=false

McKibben, Bill, and Mike Tidwell, 2014. "A Big Fracking Lie," *Politico*, January 21, http://www.politico.com/magazine/story/2014/01/fracking-natural-gas-exports-climate-change-102452.html#.Uu_JfI2E660

Medina, Jennifer, 2014. "California Seeing Brown Where Green Used to Be," February 14, http://www.nytimes.com/2014/02/14/us/california-seeing-brown-where-green-used-to-be.html

Milne, Janet, 2008. "Carbon Taxes in the United States: The Context for the Future," pp. 1–30, in *The Reality of Carbon Taxes in the 21st Century*, A Joint Project of the Environmental Tax Policy Institute and the Vermont Journal of Environmental Law, Vermont Law School, South Royalton, Vermont.

Ministry of General Affairs, Japan, 1999. *Price Comparison of Japan and Other Countries*. Tokyo.

Mission: Readiness, 2010. "Too Fat to Fight: Retired Military Leaders Want Junk Food Out of America's Schools," http://cdn.missionreadiness.org/MR_Too_Fat_to_Fight-1.pdf

Moravcsik, Andrew, 2005. "The Paradox of U.S. Human Rights Policy," pp. 147–197, in Michael Ignatieff, ed., *American Exceptionalism and Human Rights*. Princeton, NJ: Princeton University Press.

Morgan, Edmund S., 1967. *Roger Williams: The Church and the State*. New York: W. W. Norton.

Morrissey, Taryn, Rachel E. Duniform, and Ariel Kalil, 2011. "Maternal Employment, Work Schedules, and Children's Body Mass Index," *Child Development* 82(1): 66–81, http://onlinelibrary.wiley.com/doi/10.1111/j.1467-8624.2010.01541.x/abstract

Mozaffarian, M. D., et al., 2011. "Changes in Diet and Lifestyle and Long-Term Weight Gain in Women and Men," *New England Journal of Medicine* 364: 2392–2404, June 23, http://www.nejm.org/doi/full/10.1056/NEJMoa1014296

Munroe, Tony, 2014. "Indian State Bars Foreign Supermarkets in Latest Blow for Chains," Reuters, March 6, http://www.reuters.com/article/2014/02/02/us-india-retail-idUSBREA1006Q20140202

Murray, Charles, 2013. *American Exceptionalism: An Experiment in History*. Washington, DC: AEI Press.

Myers, Matthew L., 2009. "Congress, President Deliver Historic Victory for Children's Health by Increasing Tobacco Taxes to Fund SCHIP Program," Tobacco-Free Kids, February 4, https://www. tobaccofreekids.org/press_releases/post/id_1128

Nandi, Alita, and Lucinda Platt, 2011. "Effect of Interview Modes on Measurement of Identity," Understanding Society Working Paper Series, 2011–2002, March 31, University of Essex.

Nassauer, Sarah, 2011. "The Salad Is in the Bag," *Wall Street Journal*, July 27, p. D1.

Nassauer, Sarah, 2012. "What Tastes Like Chicken But Dips Like Chips?" *Wall Street Journal*, June 12, http://online.wsj.com/news/articles/SB 10001424052702303768104577462473394465122?mod=WSJ_hps_ editorsPicks_3&mg=reno64-wsj&url=http%3A%2F%2Fonline.wsj.co m%2Farticle%2FSB10001424052702303768104577462473394465122. html%3Fmod%3DWSJ_hps_editorsPicks_3

National Academies of Science (NAS), 2002. Board on Energy and Environmental Systems. *Effectiveness and Impact of Corporate Average Fuel Economy (CAFE) Standards (2002)*. Washington, DC: The National Academies.

National Institutes of Health (NIH), 2013. *Prescription Medications for the Treatment of Obesity*. NIH Publication No. 07–4191, April, http://win. niddk.nih.gov/publications/prescription.htm

National Institutes of Health (NIH), 2014. *How Are Overweight and Obesity Treated?* Sourced February 5, http://www.nhlbi.nih.gov/health/health-topics/topics/obe/treatment.html

National Park Service (NPS), 2014. "Lightscape/Nightsky," Great Basin National Park, accessed March 1, http://www.nps.gov/grba/ naturescience/lightscape.htm

National Science Foundation (NSF) 2012. *Science and Engineering Indicators: 2012,* http://www.nsf.gov/statistics/seind12/?CFID=9399677 &CFTOKEN=99950003&jsessionid=f030497a8be86fb788f33f3165 43e7043214, Table 7–13.

Navarro, Mireya, 2013. "New Building Codes Passed after Lessons From Hurricane Sandy," *New York Times*, November 14, http://www. nytimes.com/2013/11/15/nyregion/new-building-codes-passed-after-lessons-from-hurricane-sandy.html

Nelson, Colleen McCain, and Alicia Mundy, 2014. "President Steps Up His Focus on Climate," *Wall Street Journal*, May 6. http://online.wsj. com/news/articles/SB20001424052702303417104579544301704247142

Nelson, Colleen McCain, and Carol E. Lee, 2014. "Crafting the Use of Executive Power," *Wall Street Journal*, June 4, p. A5.

Nelson, Gerald, et al., 2009. *Climate Change: Impact on Agriculture and Costs of Adaptation*. International Food Policy Research Institute, Food Policy

Report, October, http://www.ifpri.org/sites/default/files/publications/pr21.pdf

Neporent, Liz, 2013. "Hospitals, Chairs, Buses, Toilets, Caskets Redesigned to Accommodate Obese People," June 23, http://abcnews.go.com/Health/hospitals-chairs-buses-toilets-redesigned-obese/story?id=18287750

Nestle, Marion, 2006. "Food Marketing and Childhood Obesity—A Matter of Policy," *New England Journal of Medicine* 354 (June 15): 2527–2529. http://www.nejm.org/doi/full/10.1056/NEJMp068014

Nestle, Marion, 2011. "Congress Caves in Again. Delays IWG Recommendations." *Food Politics*, December 17, http://www.foodpolitics.com/2011/12/

Nestle, Marion, 2012. "The Defeat of California's Soda Tax Initiatives: Lessons Learned," *Food Politics*, December 2, www.foodpolitics.com/2012/12/

Neuman, William, 2009. "Proposed Tax on Sugary Beverages Debated." *New York Times*, September 16.

New America Foundation, 2013. "Federal School Nutrition Programs: Background & Analysis," July 1, http://febp.newamerica.net/background-analysis/federal-school-nutrition-programs

Nhan, Doris, 2012. "Census: Minorities Constitute 37 Percent of U.S. Population," *National Journal*, May 17, http://www.nationaljournal.com/thenextamerica

Nixon, Ron, 2014. "Nutrition Group Lobbies Against Healthier School Meals It Sought, Citing Cost," *New York Times*, July 2, p. A18.

Nordhaus, William D. 2009. "Economic Issues in Designing a Global Agreement on Global Warming," Keynote address for *Climate Change: Global Risks, Challenges, and Decisions*, March 10–12. http://www.econ.yale.edu/~nordhaus/homepage/documents/Copenhagen_052909.pdf

Nordhaus, William 2013. *The Climate Casino: Risk, Uncertainty and Economics in a Warming World*. New Haven, CT: Yale University Press.

Norton, Amy, 2012. "Severe Obesity Still Rising Fast in America," Reuters, October 18, http://www.reuters.com/article/2012/10/18/us-severe-obesity-idUSBRE89H14D20121018

Norton, Amy, 2013. "Most Americans Oppose Soda, Candy Taxes," April 25, *U.S. News and World Report Health Day*, http://health.usnews.com/health-news/news/articles/2013/04/25/most-americans-oppose-soda-candy-taxes

Novak, William J., 2008. "The Myth of the 'Weak' American State," *American Historical Review* (June): 752–772.

Obama, Barack, 2014. "Remarks by the President," The White House, February 14, http://www.whitehouse.gov/the-press-office/2014/02/14/remarks-president-california-drought

OECD, 2008. *The Environmental Performance of Agriculture since 1990.* OECD. http://www.oecd-ilibrary.org/agriculture-and-food/environmental-performance-of-agriculture-in-oecd-countries-since-1990_9789264040854-en

OECD, 2010. *Taxation, Innovation, and the Environment.* OECD Publishing. http://www.oecd.org/env/tools-evaluation/taxationinnovationand theenvironment.htm

OECD, 2010a. *Obesity and the Economics of Prevention: Fit, Not Fat,* http://www.oecd.org/els/health-systems/obesityandtheeconomicsofpreventio nfitnotfat.htm

OECD, 2011. *Environmental Outlook to 2050: Climate Change Chapter.* Pre-Release Version, November 2011. Paris: OECD.

OECD, 2011a. *Doing Better for Families,* http://www.oecd.org/els/soc/47701118.pdf

OECD, 2012. "Obesity Update 2012," http://www.oecd.org/health/49716427.pdf

OECD, 2012a. *Inventory of Estimated Budgetary Support and Tax Expenditures for Fossil Fuels, 2013.* Paris: OECD.

OECD, 2012b. *Agricultural Policy Monitoring and Evaluation 2012: OECD Countries.* Paris: OECD. http://dx.doi.org/10.1787/agr_pol-2012-en

OECD, 2013. *Taxing Energy Use: A Graphical Analysis.* Paris: OECD.

OECD, 2013a. *World Family Map,* http://worldfamilymap.org/2013/articles/world-family-indicators/family-processes

OECD, 2013b. *OECD Factbook 2013. Economic, Environmental and Social Statistics,* http://www.oecd-ilibrary.org/sites/factbook-2013-en/12/02/03/obesity_g1.html?itemId=/content/chapter/factbook-2013-2100-en

OECD, 2013c. *Health at a Glance 2013,* http://www.oecd.org/els/health-systems/Health-at-a-Glance-2013.pdf

Oil & Gas Journal, 1993. "U.S. Industry Girding for Battle Against Clinton Energy Tax Plan," 91(9), March 1, www.ogj.com/articles/print

Oliver, J. Eric, 2006. *Fat Politics: The Real Story Behind America's Obesity Epidemic.* New York: Oxford University Press.

On the Issues (OTI), 2009. Ontheissues.org.

Oommen, V. G., and P. J. Anderson, 2008. "Policies on Restriction of Food Advertising during Children's Viewing Times: An International Perspective," Proceedings Australian College of Health Service Executives, 2008 Conference: Going for Gold in Health—Motivation, Effort, Performance, Gold Goast, Australia.

Orciari, Megan, 2013. "Fast Food Companies Still Target Kids with Marketing for Unhealthy Products," *Yale News,* November 4, http://news.yale.edu/2013/11/04/fast-food-companies-still-target-kids-marketing-unhealthy-products

Oudhof, Ko, 2007. "Ethnic Minorities, Discrimination and Well-being in the ESS," 33rd CEIES Seminar Documents, June 7–8, http://epp. eurostat.ec.europa.eu/portal/page/portal/conferences/documents/ 33rd_ceies_seminar_documents/3.2%20OUDHOF%20EN.PDF

Palin, Sarah, 2010. *America by Heart: Reflections on Family, Faith, and the Flag.* New York: Harper Collins.

Parker-Pope, Tara, 2011. "Less Active at Work, Americans Have Packed on Pounds," *New York Times*, May 25, http://well.blogs. nytimes.com/2011/05/25/less-active-at-work-americans-have-packed-on-pounds/

Paul, Marla, 2011. "Religious Young Adults Become Obese by Middle Age," March 23, Northwestern University, http://www.northwestern. edu/newscenter/stories/2011/03/religious-young-adults-obese.html

Pear, Robert, 2011. "Senate Saves the Potato on School Lunch Menus," *New York Times*, October 18, http://www.nytimes.com/2011/10/19/ us/politics/potatoes-get-senate-protection-on-school-lunch-menus. html?_r=0

Pelham, Brett, 2009. "Awareness, Opinions about Global Warming Vary Worldwide," April 2, http:///www.gallup.com/poll/117772/Awareness-Opinions-Global-Warming-Vary-Worldwide.aspx).

Peters, Joey, 2010. "Soda Taxes Fizzle in Wake of Industry Lobbying," *Post Business,* July 13, http://www.washingtonpost.com/wp-dyn/ content/article/2010/07/13/AR2010071303494.html

Pew Research Center, 2009. "Fewer Americans See Solid Evidence of Global Warming," October 22, http://www.pewtrusts.org/our_work_ report_detail.aspx?id=55583

Pew Research Center, 2013. "Climate Change: Key Data Points from Pew Research," June 24, www.pewresearch.org/key-data-points

Pew Research Center, 2013b. "Climate Change and Financial Instability Seen as Top Global Threats," June 24, http://www.pewglobal.org/2013/06/24/ climate-change-and-financial-instability-seen-as-top-global-threats/

Pew Research Global Attitudes Project, 2007. "America More Religious Than Other Wealthy Nations," October 4. http://www.pewglobal. org/2007/10/04/chapter-4-values-and-american-exceptionalism/

Pew Research Global Attitudes Project, 2011. "The American-Western European Values Gap," November 17 (updated February 29, 2012). http://www.pewglobal.org/2011/11/17/the-american-western-european-values-gap/

Plumer, Brad, 2013. "Europe's Cap-and-Trade Program Is in Trouble. Can It Be Fixed?" www.washingtonpost.com/blogs/wonkblog/ wp/2013/04/20, April 20.

Plumer, Brad, 2013a. "Wealthy Nations Pledged Billions to Help the Poor Adapt to Climate Change. Where Did It All Go?" *Washington*

Post, November 18. http://www.washingtonpost.com/blogs/ wonkblog/wp/2013/11/18/wealthy-nations-promised-billions-to-help- the-poor-adapt-to-climate-change-where-did-it-go/

Political Calculations, 2010. "Battle of the Titans: U.S. vs. E.U. GDP per capita, 2008," January 19, 2010, http://politicalcalculations.blogspot.com

Pollack, Andrew, 2011. "FDA Fails to Approve Diet Drug," *New York Times*, February 2, p. B1.

Pollack, Andrew, 2013. "Few Signs of a Taste for Diet Pills," *New York Times*, July 1. http://www.nytimes.com/2013/07/02/business/few- signs-of-a-taste-for-diet-pills.html

Poti, J. M., M. M. Slining, and B. M. Popkin, 2013. "Where Are Kids Getting Their Empty Calories? Stores, Schools, and Fast-Food Restaurants Each Played an Important Role in Empty Calorie Intake among US Children During 2009–2010." *Journal of the Academy of Nutrition and Dietetics* 114(6): 908–917.

Rabin, Roni Caryn, 2009. "Bad Habits Asserting Themselves," *New York Times*, June 9, p. D5.

Rasmussen Reports, 2012. "63% Oppose 'Sin Taxes' on Junk Food and Soda," May 6, Rasmussen Reports, Lifestyle, www.rasmussenreports.com

Rasmussen Reports, 2013. "Just 23% Think Feds Should Regulate What School Kids Eat," March 8, Lifestyle, http://www.rasmussenreports. com/public_content/lifestyle/general_lifestyle/march_2013/just_23_ think_feds_should_regulate_what_school_kids_eat

Rasmussen, Mette, et al., 2006. "Determinants of Fruit and Vegetable Consumption among Children And Adolescents: A Review of the Literature. Part I: Quantitative Studies," *International Journal of Behavioral Nutrition and Physical Activity* 3: 22, http://www.ijbnpa.org/content/ 3/1/22

Reagan, Ronald, 1992. "Speech to the Republican National Convention," Houston, August 17, http://reagan2020.us/speeches/RNC_ Convention.asp

Rector, Robert, 2007. "How Poor Are America's Poor?" *Backgrounder*, No. 2064, August 27, published by the Domestic Policy Studies Department, the Heritage Foundation.

Redish, Martin H., 2011. "Childhood Obesity, Advertising, and the First Amendment: A White Paper," Northwestern University School of Law, June 8, http://www.gmaonline.org/file-manager/Health_Nutrition/ childhood_advertising__firstamendment.pdf

Richardson, Robert D., Jr., 1995. *Emerson: The Mind on Fire*. Berkeley: University of California Press.

Rickard, Bradley, Abigail Okrent, and Julian Alston, 2012. "How Have Agricultural Policies Influenced Caloric Consumption in the United States?" *Health Economics*, DOI: 10.1002/hec.2799.

Rickerson, Wilson, and Richard C. Grace, 2007. "The Debate over Fixed Price Incentives for Renewable Electricity in Europe and the United States," White Paper, Heinrich Boll Foundation, http://www.futurepolicy.org/fileadmin/user_upload/PACT/Learn_more/Rickerson_Grace__2007_.pdf

Ridaura, V. K., et al., 2013. "Gut Microbiota from Twins Discordant for Obesity Modulate Metabolism in Mice," *Science*, Vol. 341, No. 6150. DOI: 10.1126/Science.1241214.

Ritter, Tara, 2014. "Climate Change in the 2015 Federal Budget and Farm Bill," Institute for Agriculture and Trade Policy, 15 April, http://www.iatp.org/blog/201404/climate-change-in-the-2015-federal-budget-and-farm-bill

Robert Wood Johnson Foundation (RWJF), 2013a. "New Report: Adult Obesity Rates Hold Steady But Remain High," August 15, http://www.rwjf.org/en/about-rwjf/newsroom/newsroom-content/2013/08/new-report--adult-obesity-rates-hold-steady-but-remain-high.html

Robert Wood Johnson Foundation (RWJF), 2013b. "Fit as in Fat," http://www.fasinfat.org/

Robert Wood Johnson Foundation (RWJF), 2014. *The State of Obesity 2014*, September, http://stateofobesity.org/files/stateofobesity2014.pdf

Robertson, Campbell, 2011. "Preaching a Healthy Diet in the Deep-Fried Delta," *New York Times*, August 21, http://www.nytimes.com/2011/08/22/us/22delta.html?pagewanted=all&_r=0

Rokita, Todd, 2013. "Rokita Statement: Hearing on School Meal Regulations: Discussing the Costs and Consequences for Schools and Students," June 27, Committee Statements, Education & the Workforce Committee, US House of Representatives. http://edworkforce.house.gov/news/documentsingle.aspx?DocumentID=340704

Romney, Mitt, 2010. *No Apology: The Case for America's Greatness*. New York: St. Martin's Press.

Roosevelt, Franklin D., 1932. "Campaign Address on Progressive Government at the Commonwealth Club in San Francisco, California," Speech in San Francisco, California, September 23, http://www.heritage.org/initiatives/first-principles/primary-sources/fdrs-commonwealth-club-address

Rosenberg, Tina, 2013. "To Fight Obesity, a Carrot, and a Stick," *New York Times*, November 16, http://opinionator.blogs.nytimes.com/2013/11/16/to-fight-obesity-a-carrot-and-a-stick/?_r=0

Rueter, Gero, 2013. "Carbon Capture Technology Loses Out in Germany," *DW: Climate*, July 8, http://www.dw.de/carbon-capture-technology-loses-out-in-germany/a-16999567

Rugy, Veronique de, 2012. "Solyndra Not the Only Questionable Obama Loan to 'Green' Energy," *U.S. News and World Report*, Economic

Intelligence, June 12, http://www.usnews.com/opinion/blogs/
economic-intelligence/2012/06/19/solyndra-not-the-only-
questionable-obama-loan-to-green-energy

Saltonstal, David, 2009. "President Obama Says 'Sin Tax' on Sodas Is
Food for Thought, Despite Gov. Paterson's Failed Proposal." *New York
Daily News*, September 9, http://www.nydailynews.com/news/politics/
president-obama-sin-tax-sodas-food-thought-gov-paterson-failed-
proposal-article-1.384437#ixzz2yEdKBr5e

Sarewitz, Daniel, and Roger Pielke, Jr., 2013. "Learning to Live with
Fossil Fuels," *The Atlantic*, May, p. 59.

Sargent, John F., 2013. "Federal Research and Development Funding:
FY2013," Congressional Research Service, 7–5700, R42410, December
5, www.crs.gov.

Saul, Michael Howard, 2012. "Obesity Debate over Where to Serve
School Breakfasts," *Wall Street Journal*, August 21, http://online.wsj.
com/news/articles/SB10000872396390443989204577603751277244414

Schmeiser, M., 2012. "The Impact of Long-Term Participation in the
Supplemental Nutrition Assistance Program on Child Obesity," *Health
Economics* 21: 386–404.

Schor, Juliet B., 1998. *The Overspent American: Why We Want What We
Don't Need*. New York: Harper.

Schwartz, John, 2013. "Young Americans Lead Trend to Less Driving,"
May 13, http://www.nytimes.com/2013/05/14/us/report-finds-
americans-are-driving-less-led-by-youth.html

Schweitzer, April, 2011. "Soda Taxes: A Missed Opportunity or an Un-
tested Tactic?" *Annals of Health Law* 20 (Spring): 112–123.

Senauer, Benjamin, and Masahiko Gemma, 2006. "Reducing Obesity:
What Americans Can Learn from the Japanese," *Choices* 21(4), http://
www.choicesmagazine.org/2006-2004/grabbag/2006-2004-12.htm

Shah, Neil, 2014. "Suburbs Regain Their Appeal," *Wall Street Journal*,
May 22, p. A3.

Sharpe, Lindsey, 2013. "U.S. Obesity Rate Climbing in 2013," Gallup,
November 1, http://www.gallup.com/poll/165671/obesity-rate-
climbing-2013.aspx

Shear, Michael, 2011. "Obama Used Speech to Address America's
Greatness—and His Critics," January 27, *New York Times*, http://
thecaucus.blogs.nytimes.com/2011/01/27/obama-used-speech-to-
address-americas-greatness-and-his-critics/?_r=0

Shepsle, Kenneth, and Barry Weingast, 1981. "Political Preferences for
the Pork Barrel: A Generalization," *American Journal of Political Science* 25(1), http://www.jstor.org/discover/10.2307/2110914?uid=3739
696&uid=2134&uid=2129&uid=2&uid=70&uid=4&uid=3739256&
sid=21103362547037

Shorr, David, 2014. "Think Again: Climate Treaties," *Foreign Policy* (March/April): 38–43.

Singer, S. Fred, 2013. "SCOTUS Revisits EPA Regulation of CO2," *American Thinker,* November 5, http://www.americanthinker. com/2013/11/scotus_revisits_epa_regulation_of_co2.html

Sjostrom, L., A. K. Lindroos, M. Peltonen, et al., 2004. "Lifestyle, Diabetes, and Cardiovascular Risk Factors 10 Years after Bariatric Surgery." *New England Journal of Medicine* 351(26): 2683–2693.

Skocpol, Theda, 2013. "Naming the Problem: What It Will Take to Counter Extremism and Engage Americans in the Fight Against Global Warming," Prepared for the Symposium on the Politics of America's Fight Against Global Warming, co-sponsored by the Columbia School of Journalism and the Scholars Strategy Network, Harvard University, February 14.

Smil, Vaclav, 2011. "Gluttony," *Foreign Policy* (November): 67.

Smil, Vaclav, and Kazuhiko Kobayashi, 2012. *Japan's Dietary Transition and Its Impacts.* Cambridge, MA: MIT Press.

Smith, Lindsey P., Shu Wen Ng, and Barry M. Popkin, 2013. *Nutrition Journal* 12: 45, http://www.ncbi.nlm.nih.gov/pubmed/23577692

Soon, Grace, Yang Huang Koh, Mun Loke Wong, and Pin Woon Lam, 2008. *Obesity Prevention and Control Efforts in Singapore*, National Bureau of Asian Research, Seattle, http://pacifichealthsummit.org/downloads/ Obesity%20Prevention%20and%20Control%20Efforts%20in%20 Singapore%20-%202008%20Case%20Study.pdf

Speer, Albert, 1981. *Infiltration: How Heinrich Himmler Schemed to Build an SS Industrial Empire.* New York: Macmillan.

Speth, James Gustave, 2012. *America the Possible: Manifesto for a New Economy.* New Haven, CT: Yale University Press.

Stein, Rob, 2006. "Medicare Backs Obesity Surgery," *Washington Post*, February 22, http://www.washingtonpost.com/wp-dyn/content/ article/2006/02/21/AR2006022101664.html

Steinmo, Steven, 2010. *The Evolution of Modern States: Sweden, Japan, and the United States.* New York: Cambridge University Press.

Stern, Joanna, 2014. "Fork Says One Bite (Wait for It), Now Two," *Wall Street Journal*, January 2, p. D2.

Sterner, Thomas, 2011. "How Regressive Are Fuel Taxes? A Comparison of Countries Around the World," Resources for the Future, RFF Policy Commentary Series, May 2, http://www.rff.org/Publications/ WPC/Pages/How-Regressive-Are-Fuel-Taxes-A-Comparison-of- Countries-from-Around-the-World.aspx

Stewart, Katherine, 2012. "How the Religious Right Is Fueling Climate Change Denial." *The Guardian*, November 5, http://progressivevalues. org.s150046.gridserver.com/how-the-religious-right-is-fueling- climate-change-denial/

Strom, Stephanie, 2012. "Fat Tax in Denmark Is Repealed after Criticism," *New York Times*, November 12.

Suskind, Ron, 2011. *Confidence Men: Wall Street, Washington, and the Education of a President.* New York: Harper.

Tau, Byron, and Helena Bottemiller Evich, 2013. "Michelle Obama Policy Initiatives Are a Big Deal for Big Business," *Politico*, October 30, http://www.politico.com/story/2013/10/michelle-obama-policy-initiatives-big-business-99069.html

Tavernise, Sabrina, 2012. "Obesity in Young Seen as Falling in Several Cities," *New York Times*, December 10, http://www.nytimes.com/2012/12/11/health/childhood-obesity-drops-in-new-york-and-philadelphia.html?pagewanted=all&_r=0

Tavernise, Sabrina, 2013. "Children in U.S. Are Eating Fewer Calories, Study Finds," *New York Times*, February 21, http://www.nytimes.com/2013/02/21/us/children-in-us-are-eating-fewer-calories-study-finds.html

Tavernise, Sabrina, and Denise Grady, 2014. "For Diabetics, Healthy Risks Fall Sharply," *New York Times*, April 17, p. A1

Tepper, Beverly J., and Kathleen L. Keller, 2011. "Sensing Fat," *The Scientist,* December 1, http://www.the-scientist.com/?articles.view/articleNo/31439/title/Sensing-Fat/

The Obesity Society (TOS), 2013. "Obesity Community Supports the Treat and Reduce Obesity Act of 2013," June 25, http://www.obesity.org/news-center/obesity-community-supports-the-treat-and-reduce-obesity-act-of-2013.htm

Thorndike, Joseph J., 1996. "The Tax That Wasn't: Mid-Century Proposals for a National Sales Tax," Tax History Museum, March 19, www.taxhistory.org/thp/readings.nsf

Tocqueville, Alexis, 2003. *Democracy in America.* New York: Penguin Classics.

Todd, Jessica E., 2014. *Changes in Eating Patterns and Diet Quality among Working-Age Adults, 2005–10.* Economic Research Service, USDA. Economic Research Report No. 161, January.

Turner, Frederick Jackson, 1920. *The Frontier in American History.* Ann Arbor: University of Michigan Library.

United Health Care, 2014. "Bariatric Surgery." Medical Policy, Policy Number 2014T0362S, January 1. https://www.unitedhealthcareonline.com/ccmcontent/ProviderII/UHC/en-US/Assets/ProviderStaticFiles/ProviderStaticFilesPdf/Tools%20and%20Resources/Policies%20and%20Protocols/Medical%20Policies/Medical%20Policies/Bariatric_Surgery.pdf

US Census Bureau, 2012. *Characteristics of New Housing*, http://www.census.gov/construction/chars/completed.html

US Chamber of Commerce, 2014. "Energy Institute Report Finds That Potential New EPA Carbon Regulations Will Damage U.S. Economy," May 28, https://www.uschamber.com/press-release/energy-institute-report-finds-potential-new-epa-carbon-regulations-will-damage-us

US Department of Agriculture (USDA), 2013a. "Food Availability and Dietary Trends," Economic Research Service, http://www.ers.usda.gov/data-products

US Department of Agriculture (USDA), 2013b. "Food Dollar Series," http://www.ers.usda.gov/data-products/food-dollar-series/food-dollar-application.aspx#.U1-vQsfSdgM

US Department of Agriculture (USDA), 2013c. "FY 2013 Budget Summary and Annual Performance Plan," USDA, http://www.obpa.usda.gov/budsum/FY13budsum.pdf

US Department of Agriculture (USDA), 2013d. "Healthy, Hunger-Free Kids Act of 2010, Section 204: Local School Wellness Policies," Food and Nutrition Service, July, http://www.fns.usda.gov/tn/healthy/lwp5yrplan.pdf

US Department of Health and Human Services (HHS), 2012. "Obesity Data/Statistics," Office of Minority Health, September 6, http://minorityhealth.hhs.gov/templates

US Global Change Research Program (USGCRP), 2014. "National Climate Assessment," May, http://nca2014.globalchange.gov/

Van Hook, Jennifer, and Claire E. Altman, 2012. "Competitive Food Sales in Schools and Childhood Obesity," *Sociology of Education* 85(1): 23–39.

Vartanian, L. F., M. B. Schwartz, K. D. Brownell, 2007. "Effects of Soft Drink Consumption on Nutrition and Health: A Systematic Review and Meta-Analysis," *American Journal of Public Health* 97(4): 667–675.

Veblen, Thorstein (1994) [1899]. *The Theory of the Leisure Class: An Economic Study of Institutions.* Penguin twentieth-century classics. Introduction by Robert Lekachman. New York: Penguin Books.

Ver Ploeg, Michele, Katherine Ralston, 2008. "Food Stamps and Obesity: What Do We Know?" Economic Research Service, USDA, March, www.ers.usda.gov/publications/eib34

Viard, Alan, 2009. "Cap and Trade Giveaway," *The American*, June 26, http://www.american.com/archive/2009/june/the-cap-and-trade-giveaway

Victor, David G. 2011. *Global Warming Gridlock: Creating More Effective Strategies for Protecting the Planet.* Cambridge: Cambridge University Press.

Victor, David G. 2009. *The Politics of Fossil Fuel Subsidies.* Global Subsidies Initiative, International Institute for Sustainable Development, Geneva, Switzerland, www.globalsubsidies.org.

Victor, David G. 2014. "Why Do Smart People Disagree about Facts?"
Presentation to Scripps Institution of Oceanography, January 29,
http://www.slideshare.net/Revkin/victor-on-climate-denialism-
29-jan-2014

Virginia State Board of Pharmacy, 1975. *Virginia Consumers Council, Inc. v.
Virginia State Board of Pharmacy et al.*, 373F.Supp 683 (1975).

Wade, Nicholas, 2011. "Longer Lives for Obese Mice, With Hope for
Humans of All Sizes," *New York Times*, August 18. http://www.
nytimes.com/2011/08/19/science/19fat.html?_r=0

Wang, Y. C., S. N. Bleich, and S. L. Gortmaker, 2012. Pediatrics 2008;
121:e1604–1614. March 23. http://www.cityofboston.gov/news/default.
aspx?id=5051.

Washington Post, 1978. "The FTC as National Nanny," Editorial, March 1,
p. A22.

Weidner, Helmut, and Burkard Eberlein, 2009. "Still Walking the Talk?
German Climate Change Policy and Performance," pp. 314–343 in
Burkard Eberlein and G. Bruce Doern, eds., *Governing the Energy Chal-
lenge: Canada and Germany in a Multi-Level Regional and Global Context*,
Toronto: University of Toronto Press.

Wheeler, D., 2011. *Quantifying Vulnerability to Climate Change: Implications
for Adaptation Assistance*. Washington, DC: Center for Global Development. http://www.cgdev.org/content/publications/detail/1424759

White House Report, 2010. *Solving the Problem of Childhood Obesity Within a
Generation*, White House Task Force on Childhood Obesity Report to
the President, May.

White House, 2012. "Executive Order—Establishing the Hurricane
Sandy Rebuilding Task Force," December 7, http://www.whitehouse.
gov/the-press-office/2012/12/07/
executive-order-establishing-hurricane-sandy-rebuilding

White House, 2013. "Remarks by the President on Climate Change,"
Georgetown University, June 25, http://www.whitehouse.gov/
the-press-office/2013/06/25/remarks-president-climate-change

Whiteman, Honor, 2013. "Weight Loss Surgery 'More Effective Than
Diet and Exercise,'" *Medical News Today*, October 23, http://www.
medicalnewstoday.com/articles/267722.php

Whitman, Glen, and Raymond Raad, 2009. "Bending the Productivity
Curve: Why America Leads the World in Medical Innovation," *Policy
Analysis*, No. 654, November 18, http://object.cato.org/sites/cato.org/
files/pubs/pdf/pa654.pdf

Wilde, Parke, Joseph Llobrera, and Michele Ver Ploeg, 2014. "Population
Density, Poverty, and Food Retail Access in the United States: An Empirical Approach," *International Food and Agribusiness Management Review*
17 (Special Issue): 171–186.

Winship, Scott, 2013. "The Affluent Economy: Our Misleading Obsession with Growth Rates," *Breakthrough Journal*, Winter 2013, Brook-
ings Institution, http://www.brookings.edu/research/articles/2013/02/
affluent-economy-winships

Wolfe, Alexandra, 2014. "Pastor Rick Warren: Fighting Obesity with
Faith," January 17, *Wall Street Journal*, http://online.wsj.com/news/
articles/SB10001424052702304549504579320892682765178

Wootan, Margo, 2012. "Little Improvement Seen in Food Marketing to
Children," Center for Science and the Public Interest, December 21,
http://www.cspinet.org/new/201212212.html

World Bank, 2011. "Representative GHG Baselines for Cities and Their
Respective Countries," http://siteresources.worldbank.org/INTUWM/
Resources/GHG_Index_Mar_9_2011.pdf

World Bank, 2013. *Mapping Carbon Pricing Initiatives: 2013*. Washington,
DC: Ecofys, by order of the World Bank.

Xu, Rena, 2012. "Is Bariatric Surgery the Solution to America's Obesity
Problem?" *The Atlantic*, April 4, http://www.theatlantic.com/health/
archive/2012/04/is-bariatric-surgery-the-solution-to-americas-
obesity-problem/253500/

Yang Su, Eleanor, 2013. "School Meals Face Rules on Fat, Meat, Veggies—But No Limits on Sugar," Center for Investigative Reporting,
October 3, http://cironline.org/reports/school-meals-face-rules-fat-
meat-veggies-%E2%80%93-no-limits-sugar-5323

Young, Rob, 2013. "A Year after Sandy, The Wrong Policy on Rebuilding the Coast," Yale University, Environment 360, http://e360.yale.
edu/feature/a_year_after_sandy_the_

Yujoongjae, 2013. "Penalty for the Long Waist: Japan, Going Against
Obesity?" Social and Behavioral Foundation of Primary Health Care,
SBFPHC Policy Advocacy, March 9, http://sbfphc.wordpress.com/2013/
03/09/japan-going-against-obesity-the-metabo-law/

Zhang, Qingyuan, 2004. "Residential Energy Consumption in China
and Its Comparison with Japan, Canada, and USA," *Energy and Buildings* 36: 1217–1225.

Zhao, Yong, and Kara Maria Kockelman, 2002. "Household Vehicle
Ownership by Vehicle Type: Application of Multivariate Negative Bi-
nomial Model," paper presented at the Transportation Research Board's
81st Annual Meeting, January.

Zielinska, Edyta, 2012. "Obesity Vaccine Success," *The Scientist*, July 9,
http://www.the-scientist.com/?articles.view/articleNo/32308/title/
Obesity-Vaccine-Success/

Index